What
Confi

"There are books ... inspire us, then there are books that empower us. Every so often we are blessed to have one that does both. This new book by Kimberly "Brownie" Vaughn is enlightening and a continuation of her work in helping women navigate the rugged terrain of relationships. She masterfully articulates the challenges and the trappings of dysfunction women face while giving them strategies to move forward in healthy personal and interpersonal relationships. I am so proud of the work Kimberly is doing, and this book is a necessary read. Every parent should give it their daughter, and every friend should share it with another friend. If you are serious about being who are called you to be and attracting what God desires you to attract, this book is for you. I highly recommend it."

—Bishop Joseph W. Walker III, Senior Pastor of Mount Zion BC Nashville & International Presiding Bishop, Full Gospel Baptist Church Fellowship

"As a single woman, this is a must-read. *Confidence B4 Commitment* will be my go-to guide to share with friends, colleagues, and in my line of work. Brownie takes behaviors we so often hide and excuse and turns them into a compelling read that will have you crying, laughing, and shouting . . . but overall you'll be motivated to be your best."

—Coach Livi Anderson, founder of A Queen's Worth, life & relationship coach

"In regards to relationships, the weight of the *wait* is one of the most frustrating aspects of life for a single woman. We think it is the most fundamental mistake most people (women

and men) make in relationships: moving too fast. Brownie's candid ability to 'keep it real' is absolutely energizing! This book will definitely help women see that rushing romance leads to regret, yet being solid in your standards during the wait leads to success."
—Pastor Clarence & First Lady Hope Moore, New Era Church, Indianapolis, Indiana

"*Confidence B4 Commitment* is a must-have for anyone who is looking to start their journey of love, because it teaches you how to love yourself prior to loving someone else. Brownie's ability to deliver practical advice in a genuine way creates a powerful book that is joyfully engaging and life-changing."
—Dr. Corey Guyton, speaker, author, & relationship coach

"What a fabulous read! Brownie will have you hanging on every word in *Confidence B4 Commitment*. Her wittiness and real-life stories make this book a fun and easy read. You will be empowered and encouraged after reading the tips and points on how to move forward in confidence. Brownie is amazing on and off stage. She has spoken at two of my events and was a crowd favorite. I am so excited to see all the lives changed from this amazing work!"
—Amanda Roberts, founder of The Ball in the Fall

"It's rare to find a book that fearlessly shows just how God's truth (or lack of it) plays out in real-life romance, lust, and heartache. This is a must-read for any Christian woman in the dating world!"
—Ginny Priz, author of *Ditch the Drama*, speaker, and professional life coach

"*Confidence B4 Commitment* offers practical tools to help women discover their confidence in Christ, while preparing them for a successful relationship in the future. Brownie's transparency and approach is real, relatable, and transformative!"
—Brittany Morton, founder & executive director of Saved in the City

"This book contains a variety of relatable issues that single women are faced with every day. We love its relevant and practical approach that will no doubt inspire the reader to take action."
—Adonis & Heather Lenzy, authors, speakers, relationship coaches

CONFIDENCE

B4

COMMITMENT

Also by Kimberly "Brownie" Vaughn

Sane in a Sex Filled World
(Amazon)

10 of the Biggest Mistakes Single Women Make & How to Avoid Them
(Amazon & iTunes)

CONFIDENCE

COMMITMENT

Release the baggage.
Embrace your power.
Attract Mr. Right.

KIMBERLY "BROWNIE" VAUGHN

Y.A.S.O. Books
Confidence B4 Commitment

This title is also available on Amazon.com as an eBook.

Editing & interior layout: Mike Towle of Win-Win Words, LLC.
Cover design: Eric Jackson of Jackson & Watson
Back cover photography: Nora Canfield of Ms. Dig Photography
Printed in the United States.

Vaughn, Kimberly R.
Confidence B4 Commitment: release the baggage, embrace your power, & attract Mr. Right / Kimberly R. Vaughn
p. cm. ISBN: 978-0-692-82354-5
1. Dating (Social customs). 2. Dating (Social customs) – Religious aspects – Christianity.

To all the ladies who've turned from love
and have been burned by love,
To those who yearn for love,
yet wish to learn from love,
this book is dedicated to you.

CONTENTS

ACKNOWLEDGMENTS

MY LIFE WOULDN'T BE THE SAME WITHOUT THESE INDIVIDUALS. Each of you have sown incredible amounts of love, faithfulness, and unmistakable beauty into me . . . for which I'll be forever grateful.

A wholehearted thank you to my magnificent parents, Lynn and Douglas Vaughn. I'm grateful to be born your daughter, but blessed to be prayed for, lifted up, and cheered on by you as a woman. You've undoubtedly helped me to soar further by providing for me. You've taught me what it means to selflessly and relentlessly serve others. I'll always love you for your merciful patience and heartwarming generosity with me. I pray this project makes you proud. There's no *me* without our "*we*."

To my lovely sister, Christina, who radiates with a powerful mind, compassionate spirit, and amazing beauty, I love you for always listening with your heart and loving me with care. Our sisterhood is absolutely unbreakable and means the world to me! For every early-morning catch-up, midday venting session, and late-night call to share the latest to the greatest, I thank you. To my amazing brother, Doricles, you're a special part of my life. You exemplify steadfast dependability. Thank you for stepping up and covering bases whenever called upon.

To my sissy and ray of sunshine, Reisha Kidd, thank you for your sincerity and encouragement in my personal life and all throughout this book-writing process. We've experienced a lot together, and I appreciate you always motivating me to reach higher through the highs, mids, and lows—our bond won't ever be broken. To my loving godparents, Chuck and Sharon Kidd, thank you for opening the doors of your heart. I'm a stronger, better, and wiser woman because of your ample example of love. I've learned so much just being in your presence. You are a dream team that I'll always adore, and I'm honored to be a part of your family.

To Pastor Clarence and First Lady Hope Moore (Uncle Clarence and Aunt Hope) and family, I treasure the countless yet priceless moments we've shared for years. I admire you not only as kingdom builders, but you've been rock steady light-bearers that triumph over darkness. You shine brighter than ever—I love you and praise God for you all!

To my gifted sister and beautiful confidant, Tia Mitchell, thank you for always welcoming me to let my hair down (literally) and be myself. You heard about Y.A.S.O. first and genuinely celebrate me. You're a rare jewel and I treasure all of our secrets, aspirations, and testimonies that will keep inspiring me for life.

To Bishop Joseph Walker III, thank you for being a man of vision, faith, and giving principles to help me reach my destiny. Through your messages I see the immense power of how *spirituality and practicality* is God's actuality . . . and how the combination has changed my reality. Without your water-walking lifestyle and perseverance as my pastor, I wouldn't see where I was or be where I am today.

To my phenomenal Y.A.S.O. teammates, I wholeheartedly appreciate you! Michelle Richardson, you've been right by my side since the public debut of Y.A.S.O., and your care and trustworthiness is an absolute gift from heaven. TJ Ojehomon, you have been such an innovative thinker, always willing to push me to greater, and I cherish your friendship, motivation, and being an amazing business strategist. To Alexander Raspberry, Shontrell Hartsfield, and Keena Turley, thank you for each ounce of love, sacrifice, patience, skills, creativity, and contributions to not only Y.A.S.O., but to me as a woman on a mission to uplift others. I'm in awe of you teammates! Let's keep rising and reaching further!

Special thanks to Charelle Lans for motivating and helping me map out and measure vision so my dreams become reality, and therefore the reality for many women will change for the better. To Tamora Young, I simply cherish your smile that has the power to defrost the world, your spirit to see me succeed, and always being willing to take me to the airport. To Kellie Morgan, thank you for being a safe haven to vent, to share laughter while being big kids for a day, and finding victory in the unexpected chapters of our life stories. Thank you Jocelyn McCoy, Natalie Lynn Martin, and Amanda Stratton for being magnificent women to look up to and glean from. You've blessed me with your transparency, kindness, and energetic displays of generosity.

To Dr. Janet Walsh, you are absolutely a friend and fellow businesswoman of fortitude, compassion, and determination. Thank you for hearing my heart's cry and helping me push past doubts—plus your editing eye and blend of teas are nutrients to my soul. To Dr. Corey Guyton, thank you for being an answered prayer when I was mentally confused and exhausted. Your priceless business insight, given with a calm, cool disposition, helped me to see a brighter horizon. To Michael Hyatt, I greatly appreciate meeting and learning from you—you selflessly and wisely walk in integrity. Your sharing has increased my caring for those who are in need of my transparency so they can get to a triumph. To Michelle Cushatt, thank you for your perceptivity you gave at the SCORRE conference regarding this book. The changes were a lifesaver. I had to start all over, but stayed the course, and it's better because of your resourceful direction.

A very special thanks to Mike Towle of Win-Win Words, LLC. This project wouldn't have manifested without your extraordinary source of knowledge, willpower, and your YES. Your professionalism and honesty is truly admirable, and you are literally enlightening generations to come with every page, chapter, and book you work on. To Eric Jackson and Daemon Watson of Jackson & Watson, thank you for being exceptional trailblazers within graphic design and overall branding. Your eye for detail, expression, and creativity has made an indelible impact on this project.

To God, I had to save the greatest for last. As I've searched and cried over Mr. Right, you've been Mr. Always by My Side. I wanted you to take away thorns in my life. But you refused, amazed me with your grace, and instead allowed me to blossom as a confident rose. You've used the thorns to be a part of my calling. Jesus, you've also blessed me to soar like a butterfly and learn from each stage of metamorphosis. You give me thoughts to think and words to write. You're my strength to speak. My wheel of wisdom. My illumination for innovation. My hand to hold. My matchmaker for marriage. My family planner for the future. Thank you for your peace and patience. Your grace and guidance. Your vision and victory. Your protection and provision. You've shown me that GREATER is up ahead. So I'll keep walking with you in confidence. With all my heart I love you. Always . . . *always*.

INTRODUCTION

IN THE WORLD WE LIVE IN, BEING A PRETENDER IS EASY. Wearing a mask is fashionable. Continuously celebrating your unique journey is a foreign way of living. Being happily authentic is unmistakably hard.

I haven't always been as confident as many perceive. I haven't always been as strong as I look. I played cover-up for a long time. Really years, when I think about it. Covering up struggles, pain, and emptiness can be so engrained in your system until it becomes a second layer of skin. Literally a covering in which you start believing you were born with and will rock until the day you die.

I've pushed the feeling of inadequacy over breakups, dashed hopes, and mental anxiety about Mr. Right far from sight. Kind of like how you would stuff a pair of sweaty old gym socks in a duffle bag after hitting the gym. (Far from being fab n' fierce to being stink-a-licious!) But deep inside, I'd pray my "air of confidence" would distract people from smelling the stench of self-doubt. After disappointing dates and difficult decisions to move on, I would try to shrug off the frustration like an "official undercover agent of downplaying hurt." (So far from James Bond being 007 in a movie where everything magically works out and ends with dismantling the enemy, being adorned with praise for your achievements, getting the lover you want, sex on the beach, and a happily ever after in the end.)

Yeah, I admit I've attracted some guys who were Mr. Right-for-someone-else, Mr. He'll-do-for-now, and some Mr. Wrongs. I've definitely run across some Mr. Right's along the way. Perhaps I was just too blind and too immature to see stature of his merit n' manhood at the time. After all when it comes to men, what you drool over when you're twenty, is not necessarily what you'll adore when you're thirty-plus.

But skepticism about romantic attraction use to haunt me with an array of *whys*. Like why a guy broke my heart without a goodbye. Why three other guys didn't ask for my hand in marriage but chose another woman instead. Why I was dateless for fifty-two Fridays straight (no need to calculate, it's a year). I used to think it was my hair. Possibly my skin tone. Maybe my sweaty hands (hyperhidrosis is no joke). Or could it have been because I didn't measure up to the BMI chart numbers at my doctor's office? I'm a far cry from the girls in *Vogue*. Rather I'm a petite in height, yet classified curvy, plus-size woman. Maybe it was my ambition for more and being more than average.

I acted like these questions and wonderings didn't faze me. But the front only lasted until I would lock myself in the bathroom or schedule a cry under the covers when my side of the world was fast asleep. Hidden tears would appear when a train's whistling or the siren of an ambulance could be heard in the distance.

It didn't mean my pain wasn't there. I just was a master of disguising it. A true go-to gal, as Debi Pearl states in *Preparing to be a Help Meet*. You know the kind of girl who's perceived as the "she's always the resourceful and responsible *She-ro*." I admit there's a sense of fulfillment when you are able to be a solution-finder and pom-pom girl for others. But on the other end of the spectrum lies an elusive mindset. Fully indulging myself to save others, made me vacate personal issues I didn't want to face. Yet all the while, I was drowning in a sea of hating my body, suppressing my voice, searching for purpose, and dating out of desperation. Longing for a man to swoop in and save me. To validate me. To awaken me and ignite me to live.

All of these issues brutally marred my definition of confidence. My lips may have quoted *Webster's*, but my actions portrayed confidence as: "snuggly wearing the persona of looking *good* and saying what's *good* while disguising the *bad* and the *ugly*." God forbid someone seeing my heart stark naked with vices and vulnerabilities hanging up like fine works of art.

Perhaps you have been here, too.

Maybe you can relate to these issues now.

However, a shift took place in my life. Beyond relocating from the Midwest. Beyond enjoying hot chicken dipped in batter and spicy blends in Nashville. Beyond laying to rest the dreams of having a successful music career with my live band. I had to travel through my past to propel toward the future. I learned that confidence isn't a look, it's a state of being that takes intentionality every day. It exudes from the inner. Confidence impacts how you *care for yourself and how you carry yourself*. Now through this book, I have the honor of sharing vivid experiences I've survived. The pain I've pushed through. The mistakes I've made. The wonders I've seen. The regrets I've dodged. The confidence I've gained.

Confidence B4 Commitment is absolutely living proof that no matter how many years you've sealed boxes, zipped up bags, and locked up safes full of personal baggage, you can't deny their existence. As you continue to read, you'll see how willfully facing your trials will increase your triumphs. And increase the probability of connecting with Mr. Right vs. holding your breath for Mr. Yesterday.

I wrote this book to sincerely help you to transition into the confident woman you are destined to be. Honestly, you don't have to be a pretender. A full-time worker at covering up. A pro at being clueless about your power. Looking like a she-ro on the outer, yet feeling like a zero on the inner. A closed jar of greatness. An isolator of wholeness. A daydreamer of Mr. Right vs. being Miss Ready for his companionship coming into reality. There IS more to life!

I dare you to quit trying to make chaos fit and realize you were created to rock a crown that's lit with confidence. Now is the time for you to release what's holding you back. Now is the time to be free from the past! To rise up with power in the present! To get ready for an incredible future! The "B4" is symbolic because it represents four key areas of life where you need confidence: *with God, in yourself, among others, and with Mr. Right*. So get ready for intriguing stories to learn from, to answer questions to gain more self-awareness, and to repost the Brownie Points all across social media. Each chapter concludes with practical tips you can use today and reference for years to come. I sincerely hope your mind will be challenged, your heart will be changed, and your future love story will be championed.

But most of all, may your path of destiny be forever paved with *confidence*.

– Brownie

CHAPTER 1

GOD SPECIALIZES IN GUIDANCE, NOT GUYDANCE

THERE WAS NOTHING LIKE BEING HELD ON THE DANCE FLOOR BY TERRANCE. The strong grip of his arm around my waist and his hand in mine made me feel: Wanted. Safe. Nervous. Even worth bragging about. I remember taking in a lungful of his intoxicating cologne that lingered on his five o'clock shadow. His sense of brave coolness seemed, dare I say, *hypnotically sexy.* As the bass of the music pulsated throughout the club, I somehow managed to feel the race of his heartbeat. Perhaps subconsciously, I really wanted to be in his heart, not just dancing on the outside perimeters of it. We laughed. We exchanged unspoken syllables. He spun my body around effortlessly. I made mental notes of his caramel sun-kissed skin and strikingly cute dimples. (I admit a weakness of mine.) Another song floated through the air. Awakened wallflowers and alerted lovers hit the dance floor. It didn't matter. The more they came, the more they disappeared from my sight. I was focused on one among the crowd. And yet my heart was torn between relaxing in the rhythm and thinking of ways for us to connect beyond the DJ's final groove of the night. I wanted this magnetism to last forever.

Fast forward several months. Terrance and I repeatedly came back to the dance floor. But away from clubs and crowds, spending time together was limited to his apartment or mine. No wining and dining me. No going out of his way to get to know me. Sure, we would lie in each other's beds. But upon awakening, I was left pulling back sheets from the truth. Sure, we would spend nights in each other's arms. But when I really needed a shoulder to cry on beyond the weekend or occasional call, I was alone. Yet I knew I was much more than a dance partner. More than a great kisser. More than a movie-cuddle-then-spend-the-night buddy. I wanted to prove it; however, he just didn't see it.

Christmas rolled around and a lot more than colorful strings around a present broke loose. Terrance stood me up for a Christmas date. (And believe me, he had plenty of my heart strings pulled in his direction.) I had cleared my schedule, bought gifts, and was totally psyched up for quality time with him. He never showed up and didn't call until days later. I was in pretty deep but officially had enough. I had to cut him loose.

Unfortunately, Terrance wasn't the first or last time I was in a state of working OT for commitment. Or going through cycles of begging God to "*Please make this work.*" Yes, the more I danced in and out of relationships with other men, the more my feet kept getting bruised. And no product from Dr. Scholl's innovations or cute shoes from Shoe Dazzle could come close to relieving the pain.

Why? Because I kept dismissing the guards around my heart from duty. I was dependent upon a false sense of security. I had a love I could fathom but just couldn't convert to reality. Sooner or later, the dance ended. The music faded. And with a broken heart, I learned that if I wanted to be entranced by a masculine aroma while dancing, I could simply buy my own bottle of Armani Code and crank up my favorite playlist on my iPod. This, my friend, has certainly proven to be a lot less costly than guydancing.

But let's be honest. One of the highest-rated desires of most single women is to have a man be her dance partner for life, her soul mate. Don't count me out! I wholeheartedly desire this, too. Indeed. And there is nothing wrong with admitting this aspiration. You're justified in wanting commitment. However, many single women become *dancing dames of desperation* in their quest for companionship.

When you constantly hope and hop from one guy to the next, what happens to your sense of self-worth and confidence? How do these decisions impact your future Mr. Right? What can a single woman do to combat these temptations when loneliness lingers longer than a line at the DMV? Lean in a little closer and let me share the dangers you can face when choosing the slippery slope of guydancing.

The Definition

Guy•dance—[*guy-dans*]—verb

1. The willful act of a woman floating in and out of vicarious relationships without being mindful of internal and external implications.
2. Similar to trying on clothes in a dressing room, a woman tries various men on while seeking fulfillment and commitment. Finding neither, she moves on to the next man with the same expectations.
3. In a guydance, the man (or dance partner) changes. The dance partner might exemplify the same tendencies and behavior as the previous dance partner. However, the

connection results in the reality of "different face, but same dance."

5 Dangers of Guydancing

Danger #1: Dependence on a Man's Validation

You have to admit it. The strength, humor, romance, and ambitious "guts n' glory" are often magnetic forces that easily pull a woman to a man. But that attraction can easily go into overdrive due to excessive dependency. What takes place when you suffer from the "*I need a man to complete me*" syndrome? Your life becomes very unstable and insecure when your self-worth is solely based on a man's perception.

Take for instance Sabrina. Her confidence was only as strong as the relationships she welcomed. She hung onto Eric's words as if he was the last man on earth able to form a sentence about her or compliment her. All of Andre's requests were sugar-coated with a hidden agenda, because he could sense her desperation and shallowness . . . even through their exchanges from online dating. Kevin's smooth words seemed to melt away the embarrassment she secretly harbored about being single (after all, she could at least say, "I'm seeing someone.") But then there was Marcus. He pressured her to physically prove how much she loved him. Honestly, the sex only made her feel like Wednesday night's garbage. Cold. Trampled on. Forgotten and left on the curb for someone else to deal with. With each relationship, her mind became more discombobulated.

After a breakup, Sabrina eagerly jumped into another man's arms because her sense of self-value was, well, undervalued. Adapting the "lay and leave him, before he leaves me" lifestyle only poured salt on her wounded heart. The lonely aftermath only deepened the wounds. This continued until one morning, when Sabrina gazed at her reflection in the mirror. She didn't recognize herself. She hated what she saw . . . the buried brokenness had finally surfaced. There in the quietness, Sabrina heard God give her the answer to questions she couldn't even verbalize. She—not the guys—was the common denominator in every chaotic relationship. But she no longer had to fall for the blame games. The sexcapades. The empty-hearted chases. A life-changing revelation came to show her the issues within herself.

Syrupy Syllables

Some relationships will literally have you reflecting, "Wow, he started speaking, and I started listening. The more his words entered in my ear, the more my mind believed that what he desired of me was worth giving him. He continually campaigned for his agenda. *My guards wore down. Until I finally nominated him as the president of my mind and emotions. He said whatever was necessary to be voted into my life, but he had no intention of being devoted to my heart.* Although he's out of my ear, he's not out of my system. I'm still suffering from his broken promises. I really thought he was campaigning to commit."

Ever experienced being in this state before? Ever wonder why? Well, God wired you, as a woman, to be deeply sensitive to what you hear. And men are hypersensitive to what they see. (Think about it. In the Garden of Eden, Eve was tempted to disobey by ear, before Adam was lured by looks.) Whether shared verbally or visually, words can severely impact a woman's perception. Ultimately, they can alter the course of her life. Just think about how you've blinked back tears while reading a Hallmark card. Remember the lyrics to that special song, which reminds you of your first love? Recall the way you felt after being called "ugly," "skinny," "fat," "slut," "b****h," or "stupid." Hearing these words even one time can leave mental scars for years. You can often trace the root of a single woman being lured into lying, cheating with someone else's boyfriend/husband, having sex, living with guilt, contracting STDs, birthing illegitimate babies, and years of bitterness . . . back to words. And not just any words. Typically syrupy syllables that sounded good, felt nice, and aroused romantic attraction at the time, but eventually led to reckless reactions.

Brownie Point:
Everything that sounds good to you, doesn't mean it's good and sound for you. #CB4C

Worshipping words that drip from a man's mouth is absolutely dangerous! There's nothing wrong with accepting compliments and motivational convo from a man. But many single women have a never-ending hunger for validation from a man. Their lifestyle pleads: "Affirm me!" "Rescue me with your applause!" "Justify me!" "Put your stamp of approval on me!" When a man can't pacify those screams (nor is he created to), you are more likely to pick up your bags of emptiness and camp out with the next man. Guydancing will have you seeking everywhere for the next man, much like a drug addict who is rummaging for another hit. As you keep guydancing, you rob yourself of the confidence in knowing you're already a validated woman. Whether you are with Mr. Right or not.

Finding & Rewinding the Reasons

Let's take a pause for the cause and see why you might be constantly seeking validation from a man in the first place. You might be suffering from one or a mixture of these three validation issues.

1. Poor Self-Image

Perhaps it began during childhood, when you were repeatedly criticized, berated, or beaten. As you've gotten older, you might have become driven by a man's approval because you still view yourself as the same little girl who is doing anything possible to earn acceptance. Maybe you've moved away to college and have been trying to live up to the "status quo of companionship" on campus. But somehow the confidence you had in high school has dwindled to zilch. Now you're uber-depressed and strategizing galore over meeting "the one" before you graduate. Perhaps, you haven't dated in a while and recently went to a speed-dating event or decided to give online dating a shot. Your constant craving for attention and quick replies are literally dictating your mood swings moment by moment. Some of your co-workers are having to tip-toe around you in the office lately because your temperament is officially high-strung because you're holding out for a complete stranger's validation of you. Really? Yeah, really.

2. Selfishness

Guydancing for validation can cause you to be selfish and inconsiderate of a man's time, efforts, and feelings. Yes, men might have the upper hand in the realm of physical strength and authority, but our influence as women is undeniable. There have been many women throughout history who exploited the weaknesses of men by using manipulative tricks while guydancing. Delilah teased and tantalized Samson. Cleopatra seduced Julius Caesar, Marc Antony, and many other Roman generals. Catherine the Great was known for playing with men as toys and then hiring them to interview her next lover. Wow. Talk about being bold with two snaps!

Brownie Point:
Your influence can make a man's knees buckle without throwing a jab. So be wise and be kind.
#CB4C

John Piper, the founder of *Desiring God* ministry, pastor, and author once wrote:

"She [a woman] can very often run circles around him with her words and where her words fail she knows the weakness of his lust. If you have any doubts about the power of a sinful woman to control a sinful man, just reflect for a moment on the number-one marketing force in the world—*the female body*. She can sell anything because she knows the universal weakness of man and how to control him with it. The exploitation of women by sinful men is conspicuous because it is often harsh and violent. But a moment's reflection will show you that the exploitation of men by sinful women is just as pervasive in our society."

Selfishly deceiving men through sex, flirtatious luring, or entrapment while guydancing is repulsive to say the least. A "shegotistic" (egotistical) woman is self-centered and doesn't care about hurting others. Men are not to be treated as boy toys you pick up and throw down. They have hearts and sensitivities. And they have destinies to fulfill, too. So be considerate. (I think I just heard all the men in the universe applaud.)

3. Role Exchange

Ladies, many of us have a tendency to misconstrue how we view God and man. They are oh so different. Quit trying to make them switch roles in your life! A man is not designed to completely define you or give you unadulterated fulfillment in life (and neither is he capable). When you are increasingly dependent on a man's validation to make you feel like life is worth living, watch out! You are falling into the trap of worshipping him as if he's God Almighty. Believe me, it will be a lost cause for both of you.

Recently a friend of mine, Nathan, was telling me about a discussion he had with one of his boys. They had been meeting various women who are good-looking, stylish, and intelligent. However, the initial attraction went downhill once they got a closer look. Or shall I say, a *closer listen*. They vividly sensed how these ladies heavily relied on men to fill their void of self-worth. He admitted, "That's too much for us as men to take on and too big of a job for us to do! At first, it's surprising, because you believe she's a complete package. But it winds up being a complete turn-off in the end. If the expectations of a man are beyond the universe, a man is going to do an about-face and look elsewhere." Wow, it really takes a *superman* to admit even he can't save every dame from despair. A man may rock a cape, but it doesn't mean he can cope or contend with doing God's job. So salute honest men and wise up, ladies!

On the flipside, there are men who quickly move in for the kill when a woman is not secure in her identity. They try to act as if they're God. Some will judge and aim painful words to fly through your ear canal only to pierce the bull's eye of your heart. In response, you start believing that you're incompetent, undeserving, and even unlovable. Unfortunately, numerous women are swept up in a rollercoaster ride of emotional and verbal abuse because they depend on how men define their mind, body, beliefs, and future.

The scary side of validation dependency is forgetting Men. Are. Human. In no way, shape, or form do I condone or concur with male bashing. I can't imagine life, much less a day without men (insert a few bars of the *Hallelujah Chorus* here). But honestly, men have mood swings too, and their opinions of you will inevitably change. One minute you can be appealing; the next minute you can be aggravating. Every day, women around the world get cosmetic surgeries done to their breasts, butt, face, lips, hips, and all in between. Many are done in hopes of being validated as beautiful by men. Sadly, countless women are addicted to these procedures and hopelessly vacillate between which product to buy and which procedure to purchase. They wind up being a victim instead of a victor who celebrates their unique design.

Whatever you do in life, please remember this: *a man might compliment you, but he can't complete you.* You were a completely gift-wrapped package when you arrived on earth. Real talk: God had the very first dibs on affirming you as an amazing woman.

Brownie Point:
Charming words can be very nice getting, but knowing your worth is a gem worth keeping.
#CB4C

No Longer a Victim, Now Validated

Having confidence before commitment means having wholeness while being single. "So you also are complete through your union with Christ, who is the head over every ruler and authority" (Col. 2:10). And this includes every man on earth; no one is higher than God. Every day you wake up, you're invited to look into his eyes. Believe me, they light up brighter than any high-end vanity mirror or spotlight on a Broadway stage. You are unquestionably adored. His eyes reflect the image you long for . . . the truest, most authentic you. The woman you crave to be and the woman you are destined to become.

So even when no one applauds, even when no one showers you with compliments, or asks you for your number, you can walk with your head held high. Why? Because you have access to a fascinating line of communication. God is always there to remind you of his irrevocable stamp of approval. Listen closely and be amazed. Post this heartfelt love note where you'll be reminded: *"You are beautiful. You are intelligent. You are creative. You are wise. You are mighty. You are loved. You are mine. Love, God.*" There isn't any person, app, quick fix, plastic surgery, TV show, pop-up ad, date, hookup, relationship, or social media post that can outshine this love. Claim your confidence by knowing you are validated.

Mirror Moment

Are you depending on a relationship to make you feel important or like "you've arrived" in life?

Has someone's opinion ever changed from positive to negative about you? How did you feel?

Danger #2: Neglecting to Listen

"I know where I'm going. If I cross over the bridge, veer left at the tropical deli store, take a right turn at the drugstore, and pass those two gas stations, I will be right on my way," Amanda stated out loud, although she was riding by herself. As a child, she would persuade her classmates to play by her rules and even appoint her as student council president for five consecutive years. Needless to say, Amanda heavily relied on her own instincts and persuasiveness to get her way.

Speeding down the freeway, she grew increasingly upset at the GPS interrupting her playlist and phone conversations. The nerve-tapping voice of the GPS just couldn't contend with her memory. After all, it had been only two years since her last visit to the beach. Some of the local landmarks hazily came back to mind. Her heart pounded anxiously, thinking about the orange and lavender sunsets that seemed to personally bid her adieu each night. The delicate night breeze brought the savory aroma of jerk chicken and pineapples while playfully tickling her scalp. Her stomach growled. "Who knows, this time I might meet a gorgeous guy and strike up a hot summer romance." She secretly hungered for love. A break from her weekly routine. With every passing mile, her mind moved further away from the 4:30 P.M. paperwork Bob always brought on Fridays. The nauseating smell of car fumes during the after-work commute. The bland taste of another microwaved chicken pot pie dinner. Her life would transition to "Easygoing Avenue" once her feet dove into a freshly sunbaked pile of sand.

Nearing the city, Amanda rolled down the windows. She wanted nothing more than to inhale the smell of the crystal blue water and experience the kiss of sunshine on her sleeveless arms. She smiled as she saw couples enjoying bike rides. The palm trees seemed to salute her arrival. Intoxicated by the scenery, Amanda tuned out the repeated instructions from the GPS to make U-turns and to take an alternate route. She flew by the fluorescent detour signs, believing they didn't pertain to her destination. Amanda had no idea the intersection she easily passed through on her previous trip was now under massive construction.

To her dismay, Amanda ended up sitting for three hours in bumper-to-bumper traffic. She had to inhale nauseating car exhaust from the old truck in front of her and nearly ran out of gas before she finally made it to the beach. Feeling heavier than her two suitcases combined, Amanda didn't have an ounce of strength to enjoy the beauty of her room, much less the cool island breeze that night.

Dating with Closed Ears & An Open Heart

Amanda's trip symbolizes how many single women get deterred from guidance in relationships. Yes, guydancing can look fabulous and smell divine. But some guys are strictly eye candy, or a pleasure to view only. The connection you make might taste sweet. But remember you have to *walk by faith and not guydance by sight.* And faith comes by letting God reveal and confirm who Mr. Right is.

I remember diving head over heels with Chris. Physically, he absolutely fit my ideal guy profile. Strong, chocolate skinned, handsome, beautiful smile, and a lot taller than me! (I believe a nice six-foot-three) A few of his friends introduced us after leaving a night spot. Uh oh, here comes the usual cascade of butterflies. The jitters. The wonderings: *Will he really call? When will I see him again? Is he the one?* I prayed, asking for spiritual guidance. But as Chris and I spent more time together, my desire to be more than just friends was intensified.

In the whirlwind of my emotions, I ignored the *still, small voice.* I disregarded the *gut checker* telling me neither of us was ready for a relationship. In the morning, I would toss and turn in bed. I would try so hard to drown out the same voice telling me to really reconsider meeting him for dinner. Often when you're in this predicament, you keep telling yourself no one is perfect and neither is he. You keep sweeping all of his humongous neon red flags under your secret rug of hope.

While driving to work, I would crank up my favorite love songs to drown out the uneasy feeling in my spirit. All the while I'd be thinking *I earned my stripes, waited enough, and deserve this.* I've stood in line. Now I'm buckled in for the ride. And just like inching up the first hill of a rollercoaster, the reality

I committed to hit me smack dab in the face. I was in too deep to turn back.

I fought with God over Chris. I wrestled with wisdom. But one day something snapped me out of the whirlwind. We had made plans to go to an outdoor concert. I anticipated spreading out a blanket on the freshly cut summer grass and cuddling. Kissing. Laughing. Dancing alongside each other in the golden sunset. Enjoying freedom underneath the stars. Holding hands and making sweet memories all in the key of love. *Errrr. Pshhh. Ughhh.* Stop. The day of the concert, he was nowhere to be found. No texts. No returned calls. No dreamy moonlight date to tell my grandkids about.

The closest I got to the concert was playing some of the headliner's album at home while sitting in a pile of frustration and tears. Our relationship dissipated without an argument or an official goodbye. I felt slighted but had to confess that I betrayed God's guidance in the first place. I learned that ignoring his direction causes either detours not worth taking or your heart breaking.

Out of Step, Out of Line

Neglecting to listen can cause serious repercussions. You can easily be lured into these three dangerous moves on the guy-dance floor.

1. Dance of pride

Amanda believed she knew more than her GPS. I thought I knew more than God and tried to convince him to flow with my love agenda. Do you have more faith in your dance steps (decision making) than God's infinite wisdom of the entire dance floor (the earth) and every eligible dance partner (potential mates)? Thinking you know it all just prohibits you from arriving safely to your destination of commitment. Possessing a spirit of humility will be respected and keep you from being an object of hilarity that winds up broken.

2. Dance of ignorance

While searching for the beach, Amanda forgot the GPS was connected to a satellite far from her sight. I told my internal GPS (God's voice) to ride in the backseat. However, listening to the GPS would have prompted me to take an alternate route based on unforeseen delays/heartbreak ahead. Did you know God has the highest aerial view of your life today and every fraction of your future? Personally, my belief in Jesus equips me with the Holy Spirit who reveals truth. I get discernment about dating, relationships, and even crushes I entertain. You were not created to nonchalantly disregard divine warnings. Yes at times, the truth hurts. But believe me, the truth doesn't hurt nearly as much as believing and living a lie based on ignorance.

3. Dance of depletion

Amanda's pride and ignorance pushed her to the end of her rope. I ended up being emotionally exhausted after falling for Chris. Do you want to be in a state of absolute fatigue and distress the day you meet Mr. Right?

Each time you guydance, there is a bond created that often requires you to give a piece of yourself away. Sometimes these bonds come with a high cost such as: sexual soul ties, mental strongholds (the Ex vs. the Next comparisons), emotional distrust, financial debt, and abandoning your relationship with God. Years ago Frank Sinatra was famous for singing a song in which he repeated the phrase, "I did it my way." Well, when you guydance "your way," you might momentarily feel light on your feet. But the aftermath feels like you're trudging through life with cement blocks on for shoes with gravity working against you.

His Motion	Her Interpretation
Lies	"He's just shielding me from hurt."
Fighting	"He's needing me to help restore his dignity as a man."
Possessiveness	"He's just protective and cares about who I'm with and where I go."
Criticizing	"He's just wants me to evolve into a better person."
Isolation	"He just wants my absolute undivided attention."
Sex	"He shows physical interest which must mean commitment."

Song in the Key of Pain

"Real love, I'm searching for a real love, someone to set my heart free . . . " When this song hit the airwaves in 1992, people all over the world were bobbing their heads to the infectious beat and singing the words. Including me. Not until years later were many able to see how the "Queen of Hip-Hop Soul," Mary J. Blige, was actually living out the lyrics. She entered the music industry talented yet haunted by the lack of knowing her worth. Her father was MIA. She suffered from drug and alcohol issues. In VH1's *Behind the Music* she stated, "I didn't have any self-confidence. I didn't have any self-love. So how could I have any expectations for someone to love anything I did?" She also was abused in a volatile relationship with her then-boyfriend, K-Ci from the music group Jodeci. "The song, 'I Don't Want to Do Anything Else' says—it explains exactly how I felt. If I couldn't love you, I didn't want to love anyone else. And I really did think I was in love."

However, the fighting and jealousy resulted in Mary masking her pain through drugs and depression. After reaching a boiling point, Mary made a shift. She dropped the guydancing and reconnected with God's unbeatable love. With his guidance, she learned to forgive others and herself. And above all realized she was worth being accepted for simply being Mary.

Danger #3: Misunderstanding Love

What is love? A noun. A verb. A word overused, yet underserved. Downplayed and diluted. A facet of life you might fail to notice even when it's flashing brighter than a neon diner sign in an old horror movie. For centuries love has been highly regarded by kings and beggars. Fought for in street battles. Sought after by the lost. Pronounced differently in native tongues. But miscomprehending true love is a crime many single women commit. This only leads to having your *aspirations arrested, heart handcuffed, and integrity imprisoned.*

Today many imitations are purchased and paraded as the real thing. And there's no difference in the love department. Not knowing how to decipher between what love is and isn't can lead to dangerous repercussions.

Picture yourself at a fashion expo in New York City or Atlanta. Options to shop till you drop are too many to count. You are really in the mood to buy a new designer handbag. Literally, the kind you can pack half your life in and still have serious swag around town. You enter and your focus zooms in like a superhero quickly spotting things you adore. Shoes. Jewelry. Food. Clothes. An enticing blend of vendors try to make eye contact with you for an impulse buy. But you're on a mission. You see a booth two hundred feet away with a sign that reads "Purse Paradise." Perfect. Thank God you made the last-minute stop at the ATM! Your excitement builds as you see Louis Vuitton, Gucci, Michael Kors, and Coach bags.

You weave in and out of baby strollers. Dodge screaming toddlers. Hurriedly say "Excuse me" and try not to bum-rush to an elderly couple. And practically defy gravity upon arriving at the makeshift storefront. The bags are outfitted with a protective cloth covering. *These must be real*, you convince yourself. But not until you open the bag do you notice there isn't an authenticity tag . . . inside.

As if equipped with X-ray vision, the seller sees your heart drop. He reassures you he'll give a good price for whatever you desire. His offer is unbelievable. Plus the color would look so cute with the outfit you bought last week. The purse looks genuine, but there's no denying the facts. It's just not the real deal.

What He Says, What She Sees

Failing to identify fake love can no longer be overlooked like an insignificant topic printed on the back pages of *Cosmopolitan*. Like a designer bag impostor, you have to take time to look closely at a guy before being swept away by first impressions, good looks, and alluring words. A relationship can look real. Feel real. Have public appeal. But as time passes, you will come to realize whether it's more fabricated than authentic. The true quality of a relationship often shows with some wear and tear.

Manipulative games are played in guydancing. And each one results in a big stinking *L*. A loss for you and a loss for the world being able to see you genuinely sharing love in a healthy relationship. Believe me someone, somewhere, somehow is taking notes on how you portray love.

Loaded Guns to Her Head

There once was a woman named Leslie. When she was twenty-two, she graduated from Harvard and moved to New York City for her first job as a writer and editor at *Seventeen* magazine. She got a new apartment and had a job that was related to her degree, so she was doing well for being fresh out of college. However, shortly after moving she became the possessor of a humongous secret. The person she loved more than anybody on Earth, was the same man who held a loaded gun to her head and threatened to kill her more times than you and I would wish on our worst enemy.

During the onset of their relationship, Leslie didn't see these three primary red flags Connor was waving:

1. ***Rapid fire interest*** (He showered her with adoration and attention to make her feel like she was in control).
2. ***Restraint from familiarity*** (He distanced her from friends, family, co-workers, and neighbors).
3. ***Reversal of control*** (He introduced violence to see her reaction. As she remained, he would ramp up the abuse).

They eventually decided to get married, and just five days before their wedding, Leslie was put in a chokehold so tight she couldn't scream or breathe. The bruises faded, but the beatings continued. And for the next two and a half years, she endured all sorts of abuse. Connor would punch her in the head, push her down stairs, pour coffee grounds on her head as she dressed for a job interview, and threatened to kill their dog. He even would pull the keys out of the ignition while she was driving down the highway and point loaded guns to her head over and over and over.

Finally Leslie got amplified, she broke free. In regards to letting her voice be heard, this is what Leslie says, "I was able to leave, because of one final, sadistic beating that broke through my denial. *I realized that the man who I loved so much was going to kill me if I let him.* So I broke the silence. I told everyone: the police, my neighbors, my friends and family, and total strangers. What I will never have again, ever, is a loaded gun held to my head by someone who says that he loves me."

Getting Amplified about Abuse

Right now, you may be shocked to silence. You may be thinking this could never happen to you. But did you know:

- There's *43 percent* of dating college women who report experiencing violent and abusive dating behaviors including physical, sexual, tech, verbal or controlling abuse.
- Each year, there are *18.5 million* mental health care visits as a result of intimate partner violence.
- Every minute, about *20 people* are physically abused by an intimate partner in the United States.
- Every day, *3 women* are murdered by a current or former male partner in the United States.

Abuse and domestic violence is real, but it doesn't have to be your reality. Keeping quiet about this form of chaos is not cool. Abusive and disrespectful relationships survive when you stay, but they thrive in silence. I often say, "Stitched lips can result in stitches all over!" Get amplified! Speak up when you are being mistreated and violated.

I recently spoke at a singles conference and afterwards a woman came up to me with tears spilling out of her eyes. She just wanted to hug and thank me after speaking on domestic violence. She had flashbacks and saw fragments of her former life. Yet she could celebrate because of finally being free from an abusive relationship. Now she is working to emotionally heal while her victimizer is in a state prison. She got amplified and so can you! If you need immediate help, call the national hotline: 1(800) 799-SAFE. Your life is priceless and there are ways of escape and places of refuge. No matter what you've done or where you come from, there's just no excuse for abuse! Don't allow this despicable behavior trick you into thinking: this is love.

What Love Is & What Love Ain't

How would you respond if I asked you to define love? You may or may not have a clue. You see in the chase of *designer dates, collector crushes,* and *name-brand boyfriends*, it's easy to overlook the tag inside to see if it's real love. At the core of its glory, 1 Corinthians 13:4-8a truly defines love as this:

> *"Love is patient and kind; love does not envy or boast; it is not arrogant or rude. It does not insist on its own way; it is not irritable or resentful; it does not rejoice at wrongdoing, but rejoices with the truth. Love bears all things, believes all things, hopes all things, endures all things. Love never ends."*

Notice how charming lies are excluded. Getting slapped, strangled, and serving as a human punching bag is left out. Suppressing your identity as a woman is not in the picture. Being made to feel stupid or unworthy of respect is not included. Snatching you away from the wisdom of your support system (friends and family) is nowhere to be found. Sacrificing your body for sex and hoping to win his heart is not even mentioned. All of these are purposely omitted, because none of these are evidence of true love.

Brownie Point:
Stop cashing in on impostors of love whose interest rate is high but leave your heart in debt and doubt. #CB4C

Guydancing often results in a counterfeit's stranglehold. God leads you to a "He'll love you like a queen" kind of love. Why settle for the weight of Mr. Wrong, when getting real love is well worth the right man. The right treatment. The right dance.

Danger #4: Comparing Your Love Life

"Well, if she has a man, there just has to be something wrong with me." "It seems like love is passing me by, I got to catch up." "All my friends either are married, have children, or at least boyfriends. I feel like I'm missing out." How many times have these words traveled from your mind and out of your mouth? Let's be honest. Battling comparisons are like trying to slap a little monkey who keeps dodging your attempts yet constantly stays on your back. You gaze at pics on social media, commercials, reality TV shows, and peek at push notifications on your phone feeding you the latest updates about celebrities. And bam! Comparisons will sneak up on you with a grip that's hard to shake. As the grip gets tighter, you become brainwashed into believing you're the ONE & ONLY woman traveling down Loneliness Lane, Passionless Parkway, or Broken Heart Boulevard.

The Brink of Death, the Breath of Life

As a child, Sherry mimicked bedtime fairytales while playing with her Barbie and Ken dolls. In high school, she happily immersed herself into reality shows that highlighted the drama and sizzle of relationships. On rainy days she would read explicitly juicy romance novels. Sherry dreamed of a love saga, with her playing the leading lady and her undeniably gorgeous Prince Charming being right by her side.

As time went on, Sherry became addicted to comparing her love life. Desperation crept in as an unwanted guest for Friday night slumber parties. She meticulously watched female vixens and sex symbols of the Hollywood glam era like Mae West and Marilyn Monroe. Sherry studied their alluring tricks and ploys used on men. After all, they always seemed to know how to *rack up and reel in* the guys they wanted.

Just like being in a dressing room with fifty different outfits, she became lost in the shuffle of trying on different Prince Charmings. The more she tried fitting various men into her life, the more her confidence tanked. Her identity got lost worse than a three-year-old at the mall on Black Friday.

But nevertheless, Sherry wanted to score a man. She memorized articles on *How to Attract a Man in Seven Days or Less.* She made repeated changes to her social media and online dating profiles for more traction. Plus her BF Katie had a "go get yours, girl" attitude toward her frantic quests for love. But little did Sherry know that Katie had a secret motive—she felt empowered whenever Sherry acted out her insecurity of never being good enough.

Going into work one day, Sherry's boss called her in and registered her to attend an out-of-state business conference. Upon checking into the hotel, Sherry was completely distressed and despondent. For the last two years, she had been reflecting on all the time she had spent comparing herself to others. Trying to keep up with guydancing had led to so much emptiness. Never in a million years could she imagine being so low that her mind couldn't even process still being solo.

The night before the conference, she unpacked the pink and blue flowery stationery her grandmother had bought her before she passed away. She missed the warmth of her embrace and the gentleness of her wrinkled smile. Her grandmother always knew what to say.

Sherry's hands shook nervously as she took a pen from the hotel desk. The room fell silent. But in her head a thousand voices chanted, "Write. Write. Write." With every ounce of strength she could muster, she wrote. She wrote to say goodbye. Although it was the middle of October in Boston, her temperature rose faster than the sunrise in June. Her heartbeat was deafening as it pounded in her ears. It was hard to hear herself think. She wiped the sweat from her forehead and turned to open her purse. There they were . . . the bottle of pain pills. All of a sudden they were a road never traveled but seemed like a pathway to an eternal escape. She wanted to be through with the agony. The chase. The regret. The endless comparisons.

Sherry gasped for air, convincing herself this decision was justified. She moved to the bathroom counter to fill up a glass of water. Feeling a bit lightheaded, she grabbed the walls for support. She ordered her legs to move toward the nightstand and sit on the bed. The bottle became emptied as the pills cascaded into her sweaty palm. Her throat was parched. She took a sip of water first. With pills in hand and the will to end her life, suddenly an interruption came.

The phone rang. The voices to write her final goodbyes trailed off. Like an instant reflex, her hands opened. The glass tumbled to the floor, spilling the water over the carpet. Instead of racing down her throat, the pills now raced against each other to the tan and navy blue bedspread. *Who is calling me? Who is trying to reach me especially at this moment?*

Her mother had been rushed to the hospital after having a near-fatal heart attack and insisted that her only daughter be by her side. Sherry's life was saved. After hanging up the phone, she opened the nightstand's top drawer in hopes of finding tissues. Instead, she stumbled across something greater, a Bible. Hungry for direction and utterly startled by the phone call, she opened it and right before her eyes read: "The Lord is my Shepherd, I shall not want." Tears wouldn't allow her to read another sentence. But those nine words leaped from the page and painted a picture of much-needed hope.

No longer would she take life for granted. No longer would she settle for comparing herself or her relationship status by the merit of other people. By saying farewell to guydancing, Sherry said hello to living. And opened her heart to God's life-saving guidance. At one point in time, Sherry believed comparisons would yield a version of her BEST self. She felt it was her destiny to collect fractions of other people and create an identity worthy of commitment. She believed those *pieces* would ultimately bring her *peace*. They didn't for Sherry. And they never will for you, either.

In her book *The Art of Being Different: Why You Shouldn't Compare and Compete, but Seek to Change the Game*, author Justine Musk writes:

"When you compare/compete, you are buying into a specific set of criteria. Am I as young and blonde and skinny and busty as she is? You are accepting that criteria as desirable and valid. I need to be young and blonde and skinny and busty. You're allowing that criteria—those rules—to define the category, set the agenda, and dictate your experience. Problem is, those rules were created to serve someone else. Someone who is decidedly not you. Which means it's someone else's game. Sooner or later, you lose."

Brownie Point:
Love is not about a dash to the finish, keeping score, or who gets a ring first.
Love makes everyone a winner in the ever-changing seasons of life. #CB4C

God is such a genius at making masterful love stories. He wants yours to be entirely different from anyone else's in the universe. I believe the unveiling of your never-seen-before journey to love will have a reverberating impact on generations to come. During this season, hold your head up with confidence and stop devaluing the uniqueness of your journey.

Mirror Moment

Who are you giving permission to make you feel second-rate or inadequate?

How often do you compare yourself to celebs, colleagues, complete strangers, or others on social media per day?

When was the last time you were grateful for having that "one thing" you've always longed to change about yourself?

Danger #5: Post Breakup Revenge

The desire to retaliate is a very common reaction after a painful breakup. You might want to publicly humiliate him at work. (Kind of like Janet Jackson's character did in the movie *Why Did I Get Married?* Wowzers. Dignity smashed. I actually felt sorry for Gavin.) You might want to flat-line cuss him out in front of his friends. You might want to take your anger out on his possessions (bank account, cars, electronics, jewelry, or house). You might even start scheming on how to deliver a TKO to his manhood. I'm talking about striking the *intangibles*, but oh so unforgettables. Like his pride, integrity, and respectability among mutual friends. Or venting embarrassing secrets about him across every social media platform within reach. I believe one of William Congreve's famous quotes from *The Mourning Bride* says it best: "Heaven has no rage like love to hatred turned, Nor hell a fury like a woman scorned."

Bitterness Gone Wild

Ashley was introduced to Michael at a cocktail party. He possessed such an adorable-ness, broad shoulders, chiseled abs, and a smile that was from another planet. Over the first few months, the ease of conversation during lunch dates, NBA games, or over the phone until the wee hours of the morning was incredible. Her no-nonsense side was melted away by his witty, fall-out-of-your-chair humor. He relished how her intellect made him focus on events and decisions that were constantly shaping the world. They painted the perfect picture of the yin and the yang coming together as one.

Time moved on and Ashley had no doubt Michael was her soul mate. Their bond was unshakable. Their affection was growing by the minute. If *Webster's* had an entry for "so in love", Ashley and Michael would have been the walking embodiment of the definition. Well . . . so it seemed.

After two years, five months, and three weeks of loving Michael like no one else in the world, everything came to a halt. Ashley's world was devastated when she caught Michael cheating with two other women. To add fuel to the flame, Michael denied the accusations . . . despite photographic proof. Undisclosed streams of sexting. Secret online profiles. And feeding her lies about "business trips." Ashley fell into a pit of depression for eight months. Eventually her depressive state wore off and she became livid. She wanted revenge. ASAP.

They had officially called it quits, but she wasn't through with Michael. The last goodbye just didn't do her heart justice. Michael made her heart bleed, and now she had to even the score. But instead of making Michael the target of her rage, she unapologetically threw herself into guydancing. Ashley became a man-eater by chewing and spitting out men for laughs, money, sex, and especially psychological damage. All in the bittersweet name of revenge.

Time passed and Ashley got to a boiling point. No matter how many men she played or misused, no one could erase the painful memories Michael created. No one could fill the enormous void resulting from Michael's apathy toward breaking her heart.

One night a friend insisted she attend a small discussion group for women. Surprisingly, the main topic for the night was about avoiding revenge and forgiveness. Ashley later stated, "It felt as if someone had poured anti-freeze all over me, from the top of my head to the bottom of my feet. The bitterness melted away. The heaviness vanished. I learned how revenge kept me in a prison fighting for my life, instead of living in freedom. I forgave Michael. I forgave myself for hurting other men, thinking that would undo the pain. When I opened my heart, I knew I would never be the same. I had the confidence to rise above the pain. To release the rage. And embrace God's love." Ashley came to Christ that night. Several months later she met Rick, and they've been happily married for five years!

Yes, you might be raging madder than a fuming bull behind a gate before a fight in Barcelona. Your stress levels might have you tossing back and forth, spiraling down, and twisting sideways. And it seems like the rollercoaster ride from hell is never going to end. But seeking revenge is too risky and flat-out dangerous. You have to consider how others (even people you love) will receive backlash because of your revenge. Consider the lifelong consequences you'll face beyond the brief pleasure of payback. Shattered dreams. Irreversible choices. Public humiliation. Lawsuits. Prison. C'mon now. Is the pain worth risking your life as you now know it?

Revenge does nothing but boomerang back to attack your character. It holds you hostage in the *present* and sabotages your *pending*. And you're too amazing of a woman to be stamped and stuck with a dirty, muddied rep. I know you were done wrong. But you got to believe God will defend your honor. Nobody on earth can punish or payback those who've hurt you like he can. Leave the revenge to him. Place every fragment of your brokenness and rage in God's hands. Engaging in random relationships out of revenge will not bring you to a state of peace and power. So clip the guydancing. You won't regret dropping the chaotic lifestyle of revenge.

Freedom

Make no mistake, freedom from guydancing is not imaginary. It's real and available today, just as sure as the sun shines and water is wet. The next step is simply letting go. Quit trying to figure everything out. Just ask God to guide you and follow through. Now don't get me wrong, I have to relentlessly squeeze the hand of hope every day. My desires for companionship haven't magically vanished or diminished. But ditching the desire for guydancing was one of the most rewarding decisions I could ever make. The confidence I now possess is wonderful to see when I look in the mirror and when others see *who I mirror*.

Today it's possible to start enjoying total freedom. Freedom from depending on others to define your sense of self. Freedom from racing against the clock (whether on the wall or in the womb). Freedom from ignoring wisdom. Freedom from the expectations of how others want you to live. Freedom from foolishly falling for love impostors. Freedom from comparisons. Freedom from denying your hurt. Freedom from revenge. Freedom from guydancing.

Chaos to Confidence

5 Steps to Avoid Guydancing with Confidence

1. **D**eclare your intentions. Make sure you have multiple conversations with a man regarding your desires, aspirations, and life direction. Stay alert and listen to the unspoken (actions) and pay attention to God's voice regarding warnings and advice.
2. **A**pply your limitations. Have healthy spiritual, physical, emotional, and mental boundaries. List them and stick with them. (i.e. no late-night house visits, no sexting, meeting in public, building trust, having an accountability partner.)
3. **N**urture your mind. Don't feed fantasies which will motivate you to make irrational and dishonorable decisions. Don't rush and allow your mind to lead your feet into harm's way. Watch what is engulfing your mind.
4. **C**onsider your future husband. The less baggage and drama you can carry, the better your marriage will be. What you pursue and attain now can impact the inner and outer health of your future husband, home, and children.
5. **E**liminate unhealthy relationships. Ask those who love you and have a discerning eye for their view before committing. Take note of his personality traits, consistencies, dependencies, and what he is involved in. If he's a wolf in sheep's clothing, clip the ties. And run, run quickly away.

CHAPTER 2

DEALING WITH THE SILENT TREATMENT

I'M KNOCKING. KNOCKING ON THE DOOR TO A HEART THAT ONCE seemed reachable or at least warm and caring. Now it seems like I'm sentenced to a life with splinters instead of enjoying the solace from a smooth piece of finished wood. My heart is bleeding and my brokenness continues, but I knock with hopeful intention. After all, I knew with every fiber of my being I deserved a rock-steady companion by my side. At least by now. Instead, only an empty void loomed over my head as a gray cloud, without a sunny forecast or suitor in sight. I was moving past college crushes and the romantic teases of my twenties. And along comes, (drum roll please), the big 3-0.

The night of my thirtieth birthday party started with the moon chasing the golden sunset off so the sun could rise on another side of the world. I chose to wear my heart on my dress since I was sleeveless. It was covered with a print of palm trees and seashores. My dress was the framing of a romantic getaway, to say the least. I admit to being a planner and a penny-pincher, but on this night my worrying about expenses went out the door. I hired a makeup artist and had a new hairstyle. I even bought a scrumptious cherry and almond cake from one of Nashville's historic bakeries, custom designed for the occasion with butterflies adorning the top layer.

The guests and gifts came pouring in. Games, comedy, and great food induced the laughter that permeated the air. Even my friends were invited to strike up a freestyle jam session in my music studio. The candles were lit on the cake. I made a birthday wish while eyes around the room waited with anticipation. I secretly knocked on the door of hope again with all my might, wanting Mr. Right to be right around the corner. Hoping he would be within my zip code ASAP, and a "till death do us part" plainly in view.

My guests left one by one with their stomachs filled, offering hugs and well wishes on their way out the door. Each goodbye peeled back a layer of uninvited loneliness. I sat in silence as the gray cloud resurfaced as if cued in a theatric production. Bracing myself for the emotional shift, I am alone. *God, I never thought I'd be here, especially at this age.* Never mind the pile of gifts patiently waiting to be opened. Never mind the party pics waiting to be shared and laughed over.

I can't swallow. The lump in my throat grows. I feel like Niagara Falls is about to gush out of me. At this very moment, I don't want to be strong. Tears mixed with mascara and eyeliner stain my face, running down onto my new dress and soaking into the fabric. My lips tremble. My brain sends a million messages, ordering my mouth to speak. Only liquid syllables fall. I'm so sick of crying. I want to scream. I don't want to pretend like everything is OK. I'm tired of asking. *If life will be like this, maybe I don't want to live anymore. Why should I care?* Not even 911 can respond to this call. God, I'm about to break. I need an answer. NOW.

I wipe back a few tears and look down at my hands. Even more so, I look into the spirit of my hands. The brown-coated knuckles are smooth, but internally they are calloused, a witness to all my secluded battle wounds only God's eyes had seen. Like years of:

Being left.
Being lied to.
Being looked over.
Being misunderstood.
Being cheated on.
Being fooled by guys who were "quick teases" and "extended stays."
Being the listening ear for another friend's relationship.
Being there to celebrate someone else's wedding, not mine.

And winding up with what?

A humongous slice of waiting.

I wanted to know: *Why in the whole wide world am I still single?*

Silence . . . for Real?

Have you ever quietly received an unwanted response so loud, it's almost deafening? Your world is rocked so hard, it's dizzying? The discomfort makes you nauseous? You want to resist it because it feels like rejection and being flat out disrespected. When we ask a question, especially about our love life, we want an answer! The sooner, the better.

Sometimes, you can be so focused on the *answer*, it's nerve-racking just forming a *question* to God. As if asking just the right question will unlock an immediate end to your struggles with romance and reveal the exact reply your heart beats for.

Common Questions Asked about Mr. Right

- How are we going to meet?
- Will I be physically attracted to him?
- When will we fall in love?
- How will I know if he is "the one"?
- When will we get married?
- Will our marriage last?
- Will we be better, stronger, and happy together?

Waiting for an answer is like fighting on a battlefield. By day, you dodge arrows of inadequacy, confusion, and impatience. By night, terror lurks and laughs at the mere fact another day has passed without your receiving a romantic forecast. Or even a hint of confirmation that it will happen. Many days it feels like World War III is breaking out inside of you! The fear of the unknown can make even the strongest woman want to hide under the covers and despise waking up the next morning. If only there was a Purple Heart for the wounds to our wombs and catastrophes from commitment casualties endured during singlehood.

You say "Amen" after praying, but your mind wonders: Why can't I get a date or even be approached? Maybe I need to step to that guy. Or download a new dating app or totally change up my profile on Match or eHarmony. Maybe I should change my look. How can I speed up the process? Eventually you wonder: God, do you even care? Will you ever respond to me?

But in spite of all of these contemplations, I dare to ask: Has God truly given you the silent treatment? *Or have you denied a reply because you don't agree with the answer . . .* and mistake this for silence?

Think about it for a moment. Even when questions fill our minds quicker than sidewalks around Times Square on New Year's Eve, God answers. Now I'm not talking about a YES.

Getting the green light about a guy, a job promotion, an upgraded apartment, a new Coach bag, or a vacation is thrilling. The side effects of a YES impact everything don't they? You're suddenly extra kind to strangers. You laugh at someone cutting you off in traffic. You are overcome with uncontrollable giddiness. You bust out in your "happy dance" like you're a pro on *America's Got Talent.*

But there are answers that aren't so inviting. Single women often ignore them because they evoke disappointment and anxiety. The strength of your confidence is tested whenever these replies appear. But in due time, you'll learn how they come to your rescue greater than an immediate YES . . . and prep you for Mr. Right.

3 Answers Single Women Often Reject

Answer #1: No

No, don't touch the stove. No, you can't stay up past nine. No, you won't leave home in that outfit. No, you can't go to that party. Remember when you were young and heard those words that made you feel nervous, upset, and dejected, all at the same time?

As soon as we hear no, a spark of curiosity jumps off a shelf in our mind and says, "Well . . . what if I do this, does that still mean NO? Maybe, that NO really doesn't apply to me. Perhaps if I tried one more time, it won't hurt, and I'll turn that NO into a yes." Yeah, right girl. And maybe you could be the first woman to defy gravity. Accepting and comprehending no is a hard pill to swallow. Face it. As women, we scheme, cry, daydream, and try to finagle a way to make it work. It can be an internship. A crush you want to date. A career path. A friendship. A relationship. We literally lay every fiber of our being out on the line.

Until we're sick of trying to persuade reality to work in our favor. Sometimes we've already got a YES colorfully tattooed on our hearts and encrypted in our plans prior to asking God about the situation. And yep, even a few friends on speed dial who are ready to co-sign why you deserve an absolute yes.

Mirror Moment:

How have you handled rejection in the past? Are you bitter or better now?

Is there something/someone you really want now, but keep hitting a blockade?

Do you handle a no today the same way you did five years ago?

3 Times Ain't Always a Charm

Many believe "third time's a charm." But to me, it's more like three times, sound the alarm. I recall getting a no handed to me three times in a row. I was living comfortably in my two-bedroom, two-bathroom apartment. I was working in sales and marketing by day, and hustling on my music career by night. I just knew this would be my address until a mini-orchestra was playing the wedding march while I glided down the aisle. After all, I wanted to share my first house with my husband. But in a short span of time, life changed.

I drifted off to sleep like I had the previous five years—without a care. Early the next morning, there was a knock on the door, and it turned out to be my neighbor. She led me downstairs to my truck, which had been broken into. It was not a total shock: I had sensed two days before the break-in that either I or my business partner would come under attack after starting a community initiative to empower women.

Less than two weeks later, my neighbor came knocking again. This time, neither the newly installed alarm system nor having my windows re-tinted stopped another thief from breaking into my truck. As I went down the stairs, my knees went weak and a nauseous feeling filled my stomach. *I hope they didn't take the only backup for my computer; it just crashed.* Sure enough, it was gone. Priceless information, memories, and music recording sessions on that hard drive were forever gone. Now don't get me wrong; the hard drive wasn't lying in the open. It was securely disguised in an undetectable cardboard box on the floor of the backseat. But my security was threatened. I was a target and no longer safe. I had to leave.

Over the next several months, I went through the rigorous task of looking for a house. But, how was that possible? Especially since this wasn't according to my life plans and wishes. My soul mate wasn't in view. The paperwork, credit checks, review of house listings, and a load of fine print papers to review were so overwhelming. Decisions. Decisions. And more decisions.

Finally, I found a house that was worthy of my family traveling from out of state and approving before placing an offer on it. I loved the neighborhood, the vaulted ceilings, and the amazing bonus room. I prayed earnestly for God to say yes. I made an offer and was given a *no*. I felt awful, but found enough strength to go back to the drawing board with my realtor.

The second house was absolutely gorgeous! The coziness of the living room was like walking into a ginormous bear hug. The upstairs loft was perfect for my grandmother's piano. The entire house was pre-wired for surround sound. Absolutely a music lover's dream. I prayed again for a yes. The days of waiting seemed endless. And as I wiped back tears after another no, I looked up at the scoreboard in the game of house hunting.

God was no doubt winning, up by two to my nada.

Now this ain't right. God, if you would just go along with the plans I was praying for . . . this painful process would be over. Besides, in my dreams, house hunting was a couple's outing, not a solo act. Why are you rejecting everything I select? With all due respect, you know I didn't sign up to be in this predicament . . . right?

So, it's off to the third house and into a different neighborhood. This house was vacant with wooden floors and a spacious, fenced-in backyard. I just knew this was my house. I submitted my offer. It literally seemed like two minutes passed before I could dream of where to place my furniture and décor. Rejection knocked louder this time. It felt as if someone had triple-slapped me in the face. The shock sent me into believing God was unequivocally mad at me. I felt like a two-year-old who was about to fall out and roll around on aisle nine at the grocery store.

Later I found out the previous owners of that third house were pretty wacked out. They had creepy rituals which disturbed the entire neighborhood, had an unhappy home, and ended up getting divorced. All things considered, those were pretty good reasons why God said *no* three times in a row.

Given a No, Guided to a Yes

Today I live in a wonderful house which God *singled out* just for me. I could have chosen to ignore his answers. Or misconstrued his no for silence. Wasted time with counter offers. Stayed in a place of rising crime. Stopped asking for direction. But I would have missed out on a lot of blessings.

I would have missed out on seeing my house being built before my very eyes. There were days when I would just go by and pray over the pile of dirt in the unpaved driveway. Or sit in an unfinished room and visualize the décor. Initially, I only looked at resells. Since I wasn't a house expert, I wanted the house to be "tried and true." But God wanted me to have "brand new."

But if I had been stubborn to the tenth power, beautiful connections and experiences would have been subtracted from my life. I would have missed out on living close to Tamora, a faithful friend who gives me rides to the airport. I would have missed out on my landscaper and interior painter's special neighbor discounts. I would have missed out on producing amazing music projects with Matt, my incredibly gifted next-door neighbor. And I would have missed out on the state park down the street, along with the stunning sunset crossing over the lake. Plus, being several miles away from a brand-new, mega-shopping area that's growing by the day. Wowzers. All of this was made possible, because GOD. SAID. NO.

Brownie Point:
God blocks and blesses. But when he blocks, it is a blessing. #CB4C

Inner strengths I didn't know I possessed surfaced only when I was in an "unlikable, uncomfortable circumstance." With every no, God was unapologetically steering me in the right direction. What's really crazy is the three houses I was rejected for are located to the right of an interstate exit. The house that got a YES is located off the same exit, except you take a left turn! *Sometimes the right way really comes by way of a left*. So even though rejection might hurt like an infection, understand it's given for your direction.

Victim for His Yes

I remember once meeting a group of fraternity brothers with two close friends at a football game in Atlanta. Later on we instinctively coupled up with the guy we liked the most. Numbers were exchanged before the night was a wrap. Juicy gossip and reporting what the guys said in private carried us all the way back during the four-hour drive home to Nashville. Several months went by and feelings for my guy crush were growing faster than imagined.

Looking back, it's kind of crazy why I was feeling Darien. It wasn't that he said all the right things, or promised to hop on a plane to visit me from Detroit. But he broke the monotony. We didn't discuss business contracts, tradeshows, and sales margins. He splashed some color to ordinary nights and made me laugh throughout the day. I started banking a lot of hope on him and wanted to find out if those feelings were mutual.

Talking on the phone just didn't suffice after a while. You know as women, we need that "I want to see you, be near you, because it tells me more about you" time. So one weekend, my friends and I decided to go to Detroit. But after traveling well over five hundred miles, did Darien come to see me? No, ma'am. He wouldn't even drive across town. Adding injury to insult, he told me he wouldn't be coming to the party his frat brothers were throwing that night. I wound up being the victim while my hopes for his YES were on the line.

Is this for real? I traveled eight hours for a guy who I thought at least cared a little about me. Why is he treating me like a Grade A jerk? Instead of Darien explaining, God responded. "I know you want him to like you. But remember, Darien never begged you to visit in the first place. You can't force him into commitment. Look at his actions. He's telling you exactly how he feels. Look, listen, and let go." God wasn't silent. Yet it was still another *no*. Ughhh.

I arrived at the party later that night. I tried to wear my "I'm ready to have a good time, even though I'm extremely disgusted" face. I moved past the entry door and boom! Another guy, Hassan, singles me out and immediately asks his frat brother about me.

Somehow Hassan finds me on the dance floor. After dancing, he pulls me to the side to chat. His charm was magnetic. His gorgeous hazel green eyes gazed into mine. We were surrounded by others, yet on our own secluded island. I was smitten to the third degree. I was sharing so much info in the span of minutes, it freaked me the heck out later. We talked about jobs. Dreams. Backgrounds. Parents. Faith. Past relationships. I even told him my weight and that the hair I was wearing was bought, not grown (never front-page news, but he asked). To top it off, he kissed me. Whoa, pump the brakes! After all, my rule had always been "My kisses ain't free; they come with a cost called trust . . . and even that takes time." But Hassan became the exception. And Darien instantly became a blurred figure in my rearview mirror.

Hassan and I went out later that night with promises of hooking up the next day. But did that happen? Did he keep his word? Nope. Instead, I found myself breaking another one of my rules by blowing up his phone like crazy. I wanted to track him down and relive the magical night we shared. Well, it never happened.

Hassan's refusing to return my dump loads of calls only infuriated me more. Fighting against the no (twice served) made me fuss and cuss like nobody's business. Perhaps, I needed a Snickers to snap me back into being myself again. But even the delicious taste of chocolate couldn't coat the heartache and knots in my stomach on the long ride back to Nashville.

Brownie Point:
Don't be a victim over a NO because you are vulnerable for a YES. #CB4C

The No	The Know
That relationship won't work.	Your heart will take years to mend.
That job is not for you.	It's too emotionally and mentally demanding.
You won't go to that college/university.	A connection elsewhere will enhance your life.
That married man is not "the one" for you.	He's lying with no intent on divorcing his wife.
That business meeting is not going to take place.	You'll be enticed to make an unwise life decision.
You won't go on that date tonight.	He's on the rebound and just playing the field.
You won't hang out at that party.	You'll regret having sex and battle with soul ties.
You won't see him anymore.	He's manipulative and will rob you of joy.

The No vs. The Know

Ever wonder if a denied request is really working for your good, even though it doesn't feel good? God (The Know) sees a lot more than you. Now I'm not saying the reasons listed in the chart are exactly why you receive a no. However, they can help you see how a no can actually come to your rescue.

A refusal doesn't mean God is rejecting you as his child. *He's just addressing the request.* So don't clam up. Keep the communication lines open and the bond close!

Additionally, when you confidently trust God's will, you won't attempt bribing him into saying yes. *Maybe if I do this, he'll let me have this.* Good deeds done with ill intent (or a "God owes me" mentality) are nothing but bad seeds sown. Plus it's an uphill battle that you won't win. Unlike many people we know, God doesn't loosely throw out words. His every no is sincere and from the heart. Just like his every *yes.*

So recognize when you are receiving a no. Heed the numerous red flags laced with warnings in bold white letters: No! Wrong Direction! Pain straight ahead! He doesn't love you! Different man, same drama! Accept that rejection is for direction, because you are the *exception*. You're an exceptional woman who God would never go out of his way to hurt, harm, or hinder from moving in the right direction.

Case Closed, Eyes Opened

On the way home my friends and I were void of giddiness and good stories to swap unlike our return from Atlanta. Weeks later, Hassan called me, informing me about how he had lost his phone. His insincere reply was said in an "I'm just explaining not apologizing, cause it wasn't really my fault" tone. Little did he know, the NO regarding him arrived way before his phone call.

The case was closed for both Darien and Hassan. But my eyes opened up to a trail of evidence left behind. I realized a few key things. First off, and technically speaking, Darien could have easily gotten in touch with his friend who had my number (if he really wanted to). Secondly, any guy who violates my heart with lies doesn't deserve my attention or commitment. Thirdly, I learned a man really doesn't care about you if he's not willing to meet you halfway (or even a fourth of the way) to see you. Especially after traveling hundreds of miles to visit.

Now I'm not saying Darien or Hassan aren't good guys. But they weren't great matches for me. And there's a huge difference between what is *good and great*! You see my emotional state was rooted in neediness, impatience, and determination to get a yes. (And when you're like this, you'll believe any guy that glitters is truly gold.) However, in the end, the double-whammy rejection turned in my favor. Both pushed me toward embracing my power as woman. And evolving with greater confidence as woman who wants Mr. Right.

The road to confidence requires you to look deep within and courageously decide who you should live without. Your dignity is worth defending. Like me, your journey toward Mr. Right might not be dreamy and always smooth sailing. But look on the brighter side. You can live knowing that settling for disrespect and dishonesty is an option worth dropping. So push your will for a yes out of the way, so you can see the greater good in the *no*.

Brownie Point:
In the simplicity of no, there's a multiplicity of things to know. #CB4C

Accepting No & Mr. Right

Surrendering your wishes is never easy. After all, you're a strong woman equipped with beauty, determination, skills, and plans. You have the whole Mr. Right shebang planned out too, right? Who he should be. His looks. His career. The way you'll meet. The wedding bouquets. The dream house. The number of kids. Family vacations. College choices. Maybe even grand-babies.

One primary reason why a no is hard to accept is because we're so headstrong. Pride is nestled in the heart of a lot of our wishes. Fighting in tug-of-war mode for your way and getting dragged to the other side is humbling. Someone else's will wins over yours. You think your yes is best. But often you wind up with tension higher than Mount Everest, and a bruised heart crying out for healing. Plus, if you got a yes to your every wish, you would be spoiled rotten and become flat out manipulative. Attracting Mr. Right involves knowing that you can't treat a man like a vending machine (i.e. putting a demand in, and instantly getting what you requested).

You will face no repeatedly while dating and in marriage. Will you be humble enough to accept decisions that don't swing in your favor every time? A no now might be preparing you for companionship. *Some say a no hurts like hell*. But oftentimes a no is really help from heaven.

Mirror Moment:

Do the majority of the people in your life say "yes" to you a lot? If so, why?

Would you want a man who was spoiled rotten and couldn't ever accept no for an answer?

Do you want a relationship in which you are constantly taking advantage of each other because neither of you are unable to say no?

Answer #2: I've Got Something Better

At times I admire my parents' beautifully lasting marriage and say, "Uh, hello God, what's up? When am I going to even get started?" But I digress.

Another man was in Mom's heart before my Dad started dating her. This other man and my mom eventually got engaged. She thought they were in love and destined to be soul mates. But after a year of engagement passed, both knew a heaven-sent marriage was not theirs to share.

My Mom prayed and believed God would send her a husband. In due time, a young, intelligent, business-minded, respectful man came knocking on the door of her heart. And in walks my incredible Dad. He honored God, respected my grandparents, and was head over heels in love with my Mom. They now celebrate more than forty years of shared commitment and covenant. Even the destinies of my brother, sister, and I were in the forefront when God responded to my mom's cry and said, *I've got someone better*.

There once a woman named Hannah. She wanted a child with every ounce of her soul. She and her husband kept coming up short after repeatedly trying to conceive. To make matters worse, her husband had another wife, and she was cranking out babies faster than a bagel in a toaster at 7 A.M. It seemed like God had given her the silent treatment with a side order of hopelessness. But instead of becoming bitter, she made a long trek to a temple and deeply cried out to God. The intensity of her cries even made a priest believe she was drunk. Her lips moved, but nothing came out, except the anguish in her spirit. God heard her weeping from heaven and changed an inner tomb to a fruitful womb.

Yes, Hannah wanted a baby. But God chose to bless her with *an extraordinary baby*. And he had to be born at a specific time. Her son, Samuel, was one of the most notable prophets in the Bible who eventually would anoint one of the most admired kings of Israel, David. Hannah kept trusting, and even today her legacy lingers, all because God said, *I've got something better*.

Getting my first car while in college (vs. high school) was certainly a course I didn't sign up for. However, I walked away with something more valuable than credits toward graduation. My brain was fixated on a new Pontiac Grand Am or Grand Prix. I could see myself in a sleek, black model rolling down the highway, bumpin' my music, and melting miles away. I pleaded with my dad to consider my wish. He took one look at the sticker price and swiftly delivered a resounding NO. My parents ended up getting me a Honda Civic. I was upset, but slightly cooled off when they had a new Alpine sound system installed.

Several years later I was driving to a business meeting, and boom! I was in an accident. My car was in the shop for a few days. When the rental car company informed me they only had mid-size cars to choose from, I quickly chose a Grand Prix. But by the time my Honda was ready, I nearly threw the car keys at the rental company rep and ran to my car like a mother reuniting with a child coming home from his first tour of duty. The Grand Prix guzzled so much gas compared to my fuel-efficient Civic! Although it took an accident to realize all this, God factored in my finances and car efficiency when he revealed to me, *I gave you what was better.*

Brownie Point:
When a WHY NOT comes to mind, you can either embrace what's better for tomorrow or be stuck in a YESTERDAZE. #CB4C

Sometimes what you wish for is inappropriate, inadequate, or less significant than what is intended for you. Imagine God hearing your request, and singing, *I've got something better* to the tune of "Ring Around the Rosies." Imagine him rubbing his hands together, smiling down on you, and thinking, "She has no idea what I'm about to do. What I have planned is going to totally blow her mind! Wait till she sees this!"

I know you want to unwrap a YES to your request. But God has a way of miraculously making his better become your best. You are limited to what you can see, but he has the best and eternal view of your life. Trust his genius so you can receive his better!

Control Freaks & Commitment

Marsha Burns once stated in her online devotional: "There will always be things that are beyond your scope and ability to perform—where only time and grace will bring you through."

The reply of *I've Got Something Better* is not always welcomed because of what I call the Control Freak Syndrome. It's crazy how we believe we're more secure by being totally in control. We want to control our love stories: when he'll come, how he should arrive, occupational preferences, financial status, and his all-around swag. As women, we can even get obsessed with trying to have a firm grip on every ordeal in our lives.

But c'mon! When everything is going as planned and you feel like concrete can't get any firmer, along comes an interruption to shake you up. It's the perfect time for God's better to arrive like a neon light to awaken you to his presence. This entails releasing the grip of control so you can receive what's better. Sometimes this takes being thrown for a loop, surprised, and taken off guard. It's the perfect antidote for being a control freak.

Flexibility is needed if you want a relationship to work. Release the baggage of being stubborn and always demanding the upper hand. Otherwise, holding on will only cause friction and frustration with Mr. Right! So leave space for grace and willingly accept the *better*. Even if it's not written in your lovely plans.

Mirror Moment:

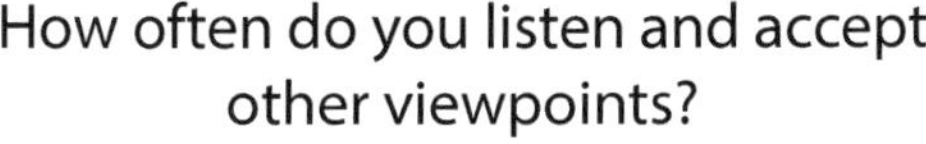

How often do you listen and accept other viewpoints?

Have you ever received something better than what you originally wanted? How did you react?

In a relationship, how could stubbornness stand in your way of what's better?

Answer #3: Not Yet

Not yet. These two words are easy to say but so hard to live with. I've experienced the emotional concoction of frustration, excitement, and anxiety all bundled together. There have been times when I would wake up singing or thinking about Michael Buble's hit "Haven't Met You Yet." I would stand in my closet with hands on hips and gaze over the colors from which to choose. Strategy was a priority as I thought about the outfit he would catch me wearing. Just in case we should meet. I would carefully pick out a perfume to wear. It had to be linger-proof. And not an aroma that was too flamboyant or an "I'll be ready for dinner around eight" scent.

I would imagine his favorites while fixing my breakfast. And if they might require me to wake up an hour earlier. Yes, I did all of this because God told me *not yet* . . . a while ago. Which I readily interpreted as, I must be prepared at any moment, even that day. But by the time I reached I-440 for the drive home after meetings and beating Nashville's humidity-filled rush hour, my hope would tank.

I would try my best to drown out my fears of being lonely until eternity by blasting upbeat songs. But arriving home meant the music would fade. And I realized my *not yet* was also known as not today. *Well, it's okay. Maybe tomorrow. Maybe this weekend. Maybe by Valentine's Day. Or by the time snowflakes fall* (a long stretch in Nashville, but possible).

Oops, I Didn't Mean That!

As a morning person, I love sharing QT with God. Sometimes I wake up with a happy song on the tip of my tongue. Sometimes there's doubt. Sometimes I write my feelings. But I'm always praying and hoping for the day's best. Hey, until my "Joe" wakes up next to me, this is the cup of brew that comforts me. I've gradually learned to keep it 100 percent real with God. We converse back and forth, and I absolutely love it.

Several years ago, I started praying for strength with weight management (and I still do since I wasn't born with the kind of DNA to keep me at a perpetual size eight). That's along with my usual request to "please hook me up with my husband." Months went by, until one morning a still, small voice told me, "You know there're two ways to spell *weight*. And I've been purposely helping you out with the other." Nooooo! (echo inserted here). His response was nowhere near silent. I had requested help with weight management but God saw my need for *wait management*. Like many say, "Be careful of what you pray for and be specific."

We live in a world where wait management is as foreign as taking a vacation on Jupiter. Rocking patience is never the "new black" most women want to flaunt. Think about it. The microwave takes too long. On Demand won't allow us to fast-forward past TV commercials. Our phone's signal drops or stalls a text and we have a fit. Replies to our latest post take . . . forever. Our attention spans are measured in nanoseconds.

So what can you do after being handed a *not yet* note from God, especially regarding Mr. Right? I like Betsy St. Amant's declaration from *The Waiting Rooms of Life*: "I want to use my time in the waiting room wisely, rather than being an example of what not to do. I want to make God proud of me, so that when my name is finally called and it's my turn to move out of my uncomfortable situation, I'm not only ready to go, I've got nothing to be embarrassed or ashamed about when I do."

Mr. Right's Not in Sight . . . But I See a Light

Another primary reason why a *not yet* causes a lump in your throat and a knot in your stomach is the enemy of optimism. The hellion against hope. The challenger of faith. The attacker of confidence. Yes, it's the one and only . . . doubt. When your eyes don't see signs that companionship is around the corner, the voice of doubt seems more amplified than a fire truck's siren heading to a four-alarm fire.

I love looking at the stars, the moon, and clouds. Sometimes, I'll even take my binoculars out to feel closer to a canvas bigger than me, while realizing we're both underestimated works of art. Several years ago, I peered out of my bedroom window and saw a small glimmering light far away. It was one of those nights where I wished my Mr. Right was holding me close, whispering in my ear, and sharing the view.

I blinked my eyes and adjusted the blinds to make sure I wasn't dreaming. Immediately, the hook to "Open Your Eyes" (by Bobby Caldwell, and popularly remixed by Common) floated from my lips: "There are times, when you'll need someone. I will be by your side. There is a light, that shines, special for you and me." God, why am I seeing this light tonight? Are you trying to tell me something? You know I'm still holding on to this *not yet*.

My heart started beating faster, and my hands started sweating. It was like a new seed of hope being conceived. Similar to the first kiss of warm sunshine on your skin after being in a frigid building with no windows all day. Perhaps the light is connected to some kind of radar or network system. I haven't a clue. But that night the blinking light became a symbol of promise. A promise for future commitment while living in the *not yet* season.

There are mornings when I wake up and can't see a trace of it because it's foggy or too bright. I'm reminded, *you walk by faith, not by sight*. There are nights when so I'm frustrated because it seems like everyone else is happily coupled up and I'm still rollin' solo. At times, I peer out the window disappointed. It's hard to see the light because my eyes are filled with buckets of tears. Or better yet, liquid prayers that only God hears. However, he's right there to comfort me with: "But they who wait for the Lord shall renew their strength; they shall mount up with wings like eagles, they shall run and not be weary, they shall walk and not faint" (Isaiah 40:31).

One time I tried viewing the light from downstairs. Nope, not even a peek of the view by a long shot. Again, God rescues me with an answer: "When you're standing at eye level, you can only see what's before you. But when you remain elevated and confident in what I've promised, you can see what's beyond your reach for now." I'm left chuckling and cherishing the moment of clarity as I head back upstairs. Leaving doubt underneath me and returning to my elevated place of hope.

Brownie Point:
Delays develop determination. Faith focuses your fight to BELIEVE. #CB4C

Mirror Moment:

Why do you think it's easier to doubt than to trust?

Do you have a symbol or go-to place that renews your hope regarding a future with Mr. Right?

Why My Plan by Thirty Didn't Work

Remember me knocking at the beginning of this chapter? I was knocking on God's heart and asking (and at times demanding) for a reason for my singlehood. Eventually my inquiry shifted. I started asking God about "me" instead of the "we." *Why in the world am I here? Why did you create me?* What do you want me to do? I journeyed for a very long time within a cycle of praying, reading books, listening, journaling, battling with past failures, analyzing my insecurities, and waiting . . . for more than a year.

At times God would speak through dreams at night and visions during the day. There was a bold and vivacious version of me having fun while speaking and empowering masses of women. Away from the visions, I would freak out, lose my breath, and absolutely resist my calling. I felt as if God made a mistake, not only regarding my love life, but also my purpose in life. Some days I would blame it on my imagination and try to cajole God into agreeing that I was unqualified and unequipped. The vision of being confident and speaking with such passion and blunt honesty was just never in my plans. Until, I took an unforgettable trip to Cincinnati.

As a marketing VP, I typically go to an annual business event hosted by Toyota. However, this one particular time was different. After finishing appointments, I went to check into my hotel room to relax before having dinner with my dad. To my surprise, I was told there would be at least a two-hour delay on my room. Thankfully, I brought a book, *Walking in Your Own Shoes* by Robert Schuller. I get very agitated with idle waiting and was still relentlessly pursuing my purpose.

Inevitably, the vision for You Are Singled Out (Y.A.S.O.) was revealed to me while reading the last chapter. Amazingly, a still, small voice was heard even among the busyness of the crowded hotel lobby. My hands could hardly keep up with taking notes. *Wait a minute God, you mean me? This little chick from Kokomo, Indiana? You want me to help single women do what?* When I finally came up for air, I was thrilled, in awe, and terrified. This was a defining moment which revealed why I was still single. Afterwards God said: "You've got to live it before you launch it." Every high, mid, and low of my experiences as a single woman was meant to impact many more people than just me.

My ultimate life plan was to have a beautiful husband, two kids, and a flourishing music career, all by the age of thirty. If God hadn't said *not yet*, Y.A.S.O. wouldn't exist and neither would our connection through this book. I now realize a romantic relationship would have been too much for me while starting Y.A.S.O. And I really didn't understand the power of balance between work and dating. I didn't have enough wisdom to really consider how a man's character impacts commitment, and how important it was for me to fulfill my purpose as well.

Being in an ultra-single state (i.e. dateless days/nights, no hookups on the side, deceptive mind games, or putting life totally on hold for romance) was necessary for me to hear, write, grow, learn, and evolve into a woman who has a life mission. Now this doesn't mean I wasn't tempted, approached, or pursued. I bleed blood just like you. I have feelings. I wonder and try my best not to worry about the unknowns and the unseen adventure ahead. But honestly these last few years of singlehood have allowed me to see that a woman doesn't have to be clingy for commitment and or violated for validation. Neither does she have to be manipulated and jerked around in a toxic or half-steppin' relationship like a yo-yo. And she doesn't have to desperately make a connection on the "meet market" (and belittle herself like in a meat market) and then pray it will endure for a lifetime. Or get her closer to saying I do. No ma'm, not at all. I've met so many women who are miserably married or divorced. And as they tell me their story, they recall how God told them *not yet*, but they said, "Nope, now is the time. We're in love. He is the one. God it'll work, just wait and see." Months or years later they still remember not heeding the halt and now wonder what life may have been like if they did.

You see I had to say yes to God's *not yet* now . . . so I could be a better woman, a better wife, and a better mother in the future. You got to believe a stronger me will yield a stronger we. There is no relationship, wedding ring, or the finest of men that could substitute purpose, drive, and vision in my life so I can impact many lives. Yes we want commitment and covenant with Mr. Right. And yet that's only a fraction of what is in store and what we're here for. You can see life on a bigger scale and decrease the regret by being receptive of the *not yet*!

Brownie Point:
Find confidence in being Miss Contentment before becoming Mrs. Commitment. #CB4C

Mirror Moment:

Are you so locked into your plans, you're ignoring a not yet and believing a relationship is going to "rescue you"?

Rate your confidence: is it growing or diminishing while you're single?

The Not Yet Before Tying the Knot

One of the most detested words single women hear is *wait*. Just seeing someone fix their mouths to pronounce "Weyyy-t" makes your eyes roll, lips cringe, and blood pressure rise. Especially if you've been waiting for a long time. I totally understand. There are days when I've felt more married to a "Mr. Wait" than moving closer to Mr. Right. "I, Kimberly, take this wait. To have and to hold this wait. From this day forward with this wait. For better, for worse, for richer, for poorer with this wait. In sickness and in health, to love and to cherish . . . *oh, God please no! Not till death do us part!*"

You might feel as if you've run headfirst into a brick wall of rejection. But don't get a *not yet* mixed up with a *no*, when it's really a right-on-time delay. You might not receive confirmation every single day about your future love story. But you can't dive into distrust and wallow in worry. A famous quote by Erma Bombeck states: "Worry is like a rocking chair. It gives you something to do, but never gets you anywhere."

Accepting delays is a strength you'll definitely need in marriage. Your relationship with Mr. Right will involve you being patient (i.e. waiting to get to know each other, meeting his family, his return from a business trip, having sex, getting test results from the doctor, working on dreams together, etc.). Waiting builds you into a stronger woman for unexpected holds in the future. After all, God is not in the business of making wimps, but winners! A *not yet* may sting at first, but a woman with confidence knows how to find beauty in life, even when she doesn't always get her way . . . right away.

Today you might be battling with one of the answers that is easy to reject and hard to accept. You might think God has it totally wrong and you've already premeditated your next move. But remember these words from Amie Hollmann: "If we stop to listen, we might truly hear what God is trying to say. And maybe if we hear, we will understand. And maybe if we understand, we will love. And maybe if we love, we will keep listening." God is not giving you the silent treatment. Embrace the power to open your heart to hear and you'll get a message loud and clear.

Chaos to Confidence

6 Steps after Receiving a Not Yet

1. **L**ist the top three things you're waiting on in life. Journal and take notes of "Ah-ha!" moments that reveal reasons for the wait. Looking back on these will boost your hope

and remind you that you're not forgotten or ignored.

2. **I**nteract with others who are waiting for similar requests. Have a support system whether in the community, at work, at church, or with positive friends. When you're impatient or depressed, they can listen and help you keep a healthy perspective.

3. **S**pend time with your ears open and mouth shut. Get away from all electronic devices and distractions. Sit or lie still, breathe deeply, and dedicate a special time to listen. An anonymous quote states: "Silence, in a sense, starves the ego; the normal things the ego loves to feed on aren't there anymore, and now we're just me—a soul in God's presence."

4. **T**ake note of signs around you. It's important to stay sensitive to signs around you while you're anticipating the direction you need to take. A special confirmation to increase your hope might arrive from a billboard, a commercial, a song, hearing a conversation in the checkout line, or sharing an unexpected cup of coffee with a stranger. Don't slump into a stupor—stay in expectation mode!

5. **E**mbrace goals you need to accomplish. Waiting doesn't mean you get a break from working. Get involved with some community organizations, take a mission trip, work on dreams you've been procrastinating on, and flow in your purpose. Stay passionate and productive during the wait.

6. **N**ever become best friends with doubt. Your confidence is tested every day with oncoming weapons of worry. When doubts knock, confidently tell them, "Back up! You ain't welcomed to stay here." Immediately find something to steer your focus on being optimistic.

CHAPTER 3
DE-MASK US ROAD DIVA

THE ROAD TO IDENTIFYING WHO WE REALLY ARE IS FULL OF TWISTS and turns, red lights, yield signs, and unexpected road blocks. Some days we just want to drive forward without paying attention to the rear-view or side mirrors. Why? Because we catch a glimpse of what we truly look like. Up close and personal. The bumps, bruises, and blemishes do exist. I own some. And so do you.

Our world is filled with quick fixes, easy cash-ins, and makeshift muzzles to a variety of problems. "Be a beauty bombshell every day of your life!" "High drama for every single lash!" "Limited offer to being the best you!" "Millions have downloaded this app and have found love, what are you waiting for?" "Change this, do that, and you'll have him for keeps!"

They can easily be mistaken for cures, but they are simply suppressants that further disguise the heart of the matter, the root of the issue. They're rigged to make you feel outer attraction is the only attraction for a woman to possess. Or a relationship will be the remedy to unleash the best and most celebrated you. Or a really glammed up, blinged-out facade is better than kick-fakeness-in-the-butt, guilt-free authenticity.

Brownie Point:
Oh, mirror mirror on the wall, I want to see my greatness but the mask hides it all. #CB4C

Are We There Yet?

Onward to Lover's Lane! Our GPS is fixed with our destination being in a man's heart and snug in his arms. How we long to just get there already. We don't want to use windshield wipers or the defogger on the journey to love. We want a crystal clear view to fluffy clouds. Tender touches. Rose petals. Dreams interlocked. Hands intertwined. Cologne-filled hugs and passionate kisses. Mind-blowing sex. And having him there for every morning after. We want so much happiness that even the richest man on earth would be tempted to make a name-your-price offer for a tenth of our bliss. We want all of this with Mr. Right (in slow motion, please) just like the unforgettable arms outstretched, together we can conquer the world scene from the movie *Titanic*.

Mmm, mmm, mmm. If only these sweet dreams of commitment would manifest into honey-coated reality after descending from our la land thoughts. (You know what many say, "See it, believe it, achieve it.") Well, I've done this a zillion times over. I've named it, claimed it, proclaimed it, and even tried to explain it. I've danced and shouted for it. Fasted and prayed about it. Sowed a seed on it. And still he hasn't arrived.

Now I'm not saying if you do these, ALL will be in vain. However, one major oversight I made was concentrating so much on him, I was neglecting Kim (yes it's my legal name and used here for rhyming purposes). Among all the outer decisions I made regarding my hair, makeup, flats or heels, outfit, accessories, perfume, and handbag . . . I had to face the *dilemma inside:* To wear the mask or not wear the mask? That is the question.

Today you may be wearing a mask so fit and sturdy, it would take a prize-winning body builder with chiseled muscles to pry it off you. Or perhaps, an ultra-strength dissolvent might make it dissipate. But seriously, you've started believing it is your identity. Your mask is no longer a guard of protection, it's a fantasy which births false hope. Nathaniel Hawthorne stated in *The Scarlet Letter*, "No man, for any considerable period, can wear one face to himself and another to the multitude, without finally getting bewildered as to which may be the true." Instead of being able to breathe in the fresh air of freedom, bask in the sunshine of your worth, and adore the skin you're in, you conceal your identity and wear a mask. It's kind of like being silently suffocated by the fumes of an eighteen-wheeler. You try to roll your window up quickly, and the gray clouds of smoke disappear, but ever so sneakily they overtake your car. They creep into your vents and into lungs. Living as if life is a masquerade creeps into every crevice of your livelihood, your moods, your dreams, your peace, and your prayers. Constantly inhaling these fumes and foregoing treatment can be deadly. It would shock you to smithereens to know about the many people you see every day who blend in, in society, but are closer to citizens of the walking dead. Beating hearts, yet dead in spirit. Blood flowing, yet stagnant inside. Inhaling, yet the oxygen only flows to their mask. Each of them secretly praying for their cover to not be blown and their mask not to be shattered. Do you want a mask to become an idolized lifeline?

These next five masks you'll read about are just as toxic and dangerous. I know you want to zoom faster than Usain Bolt to Mr. Right. But right now I want you to veer to the right for a minute and take the exit for De-Mask Us Road. Now look in the side mirror. You'll read, *Objects in the mirror are closer than they appear*. The object you're looking at is your image (i.e. the mask, or what sticks close to you for appearance's sake.) Now look in your rearview mirror. Look closer. Do you see it? Your identity has been left several miles back on the side of the road. There it waits to be rescued, to be revived, and revered as one of the most masterful imprints that reveals your irreplaceable existence in the world today.

Will you go back and grab your identity? You can quit living with a DUI (driving under illusion) or a DWI (driving without identity) over your head. Take off the mask so you can drive forward with your identity intact before engaging in another relationship.

5 Masks Women Often Hide Behind

Mask #1: Miss Please-a-Lot

The Outer Look

- Over-commits her time and energy
- Suppresses her opinions, goes with the flow
- Indecisive, has issues with making concrete decisions
- Allows stress to boil up inside
- Overly apologetic in conversation (says "I'm sorry" incessantly)

- Verbally puts herself down a lot ("I'm so stupid/weird." "It's probably my fault.")
- Battles with depression and being overwhelmed

The Inner Fears

- Not being loved, disapproved of, being left out
- Believes she's a burden or lets friends and family down
- Insecure about standing up for herself
- Thinks she'll burn bridges if she disagrees
- Feels inadequate, undeserving of being served or honored
- Becomes undone due to personal pressures of perfectionism

Road Blocks for You

Wearing the Miss Please-A-Lot mask can max out worse than a broken down car on the side of the interstate. One which is totally in neglect of all its rightfully deserved TLC. Sure, going just a few extra miles was the original intent, yet somehow the car was overworked and underserved in the maintenance department.

Constantly going into overdrive to appease others will have you taking costly detours. Detours that lead to others living it up (i.e. accomplishing their dreams, bailing people out of bad decisions they made, letting people draw from you and never pouring back into you) while your joy steadily declines. Have you forgotten about you? Are you putting unnecessary stress on yourself? What about your ambitions, passions, and goals? Being a "pleasure pusher" only robs you of time needed to fulfill your dreams and pursuing things in life that bring happiness. It won't be pleasurable to wake up one day with a "could of, would of, should of" cloud hanging over your head and haunting your heart. You may even age into a very bitter woman because of deep remorse from not establishing boundaries for yourself.

Face it, you are nobody's doormat! You can't please everyone and still be sane at the end of the day. The world didn't start revolving with you. And it won't stop if you say no. Some people will understand. Others can't and won't. These people are dream-drainers, ankle-biters, and fashionable-irrationals you don't need very close in your life anyway. Don't make it your full-time job to conform into what others want you to be and do at all times.

Brownie Point:
Showcasing versatility is great.
Yet sacrificing from vulnerability that's grounded in guilt, never blossoms into confidence. #CB4C

According to *Psychology Today*, ". . . the key is a well-thought-out policy of temperance. Retain positive people-pleasing traits like friendliness and sensitivity, but clarify your own needs and assert them more. If someone asks you for something, ask yourself if it's feasible, and consider your own needs, too. You might say, 'I can help you later in the day, but first I need to meet my own deadlines. If it's urgent, maybe we can find someone else to help you right away.'"

Your voice wasn't carelessly given to you as if it were a forgotten vacuum attachment buried in a closet and hardly used. Quit holding back as if someone will clip your wings and stomp on your halo when you share your opinions. The world is actually dimmer when you hide your amazing insight, creativity, and personality. Seize your confidence and know your voice is valuable. You're worth being loved not for what people can get out of you, but simply for being who you are.

Mirror Moment:

What past pain or experience did you go through that still makes you feel inadequate or insecure in winning/keeping the approval of others?

Make a list of your involvements and duties. Now separate them by motivations. Analyze to see which ones A) bring pleasure to serve and B) bring pressure to please/losing out.

Miss Please-a-Lot's Road Blocks with Mr. Right

1. Being Taken Less Seriously

If you are prone to always saying yes, a man could very well cheapen your relationship by sticking around just to see how much he can get out of you. Less self-respect yields a heart he's less likely to protect. This mask leads to compromising your standards, deal breakers, and thresholds, which can inevitably turn into being abused in a variety of ways.

2. Being Last on Your List

Who wants a relationship where they're rated as the last priority? I don't know of any man readily jumping for that option. Real men want to be wanted. When you over-obligate yourself, you may devote so much time elsewhere, you create unintentional friction in the relationship. There's no excuse for cheating. However, you don't want to leave so many voids that he's tempted big time to look elsewhere for relationship voids to be filled.

3. Being Less Included

A man wants to know you can be trusted to protect and pour into the relationship (i.e. spending quality time, discussing decisions, listening to his struggles, taking notice of his strengths).

Constantly running to please others causes a distance. If he truly cares about you, he won't want to hear about your other obligations with a "oh by the way" attitude. Along with being wanted, a man wants to be included. After all, what you sign up for directly is like signing him up indirectly. Serious commitment and covenant is about inclusion and two becoming one, right? Right.

Declaration of Confidence for Miss Please-a-Lot

"I am a strong and loving woman. Yet I realize my time, efforts, and energy are not to be abused to win the affirmation of others, but to genuinely connect with others. My opinions deserve to be shared and respected. Therefore, I will speak out. Although I am created to serve, I wasn't created to please everyone. So when needed, I will say NO with grace. I will not overlook my physical, emotional, mental, or spiritual needs. Because I only have one life to live, I will establish healthy boundaries to fully embrace life, express my beliefs, and view myself as a priority. I can make these decisions without guilt or shame. I am confident to be balanced and be my absolute best!"

Mask #2: Miss Over-the-Top

The Outer Look

- Over-dramatizes minor incidents
- Flirts a lot, sexually provocative, attention hungry
- Resists change initiated by others
- Views people in extremes (i.e. supporters or haters, none in between)
- Exaggerates the status of relationships
- Wants to be heard vs. being a listener

The Inner Fears

- Losing attention, applause, and affection
- Feeling powerless
- Being ignored or left behind
- Receiving disapproval and criticism
- Not being taken seriously in life or love

Road Blocks for You

It takes a lot of energy to keep up with the role play of Miss Over-the-Top. Even when there's no theater in sight or reality TV show in the convo, you are seen or dubbed as the "drama queen." Your extreme reactions often prevent sincere friendships from being established. People may often tip-toe around you because at any given moment you may explode or break in pieces like Grandmother's finest piece of china. *"Don't say this around her." "Don't even go there. If you do this, she'll blow a fuse."* Your tendency to embellish friendships, romantic relationships, projects at work, and storytelling is extreme. You often turn up to 100 when everyone else is on 10. Many wonder if you can be trusted and if you are really telling the truth. So closeness and transparency from others may really be lacking in your connections.

No need to front. You are wired as a woman who needs to connect in a genuine way. Not everyone can be declared as a 24-7 YES person or an absolute "HATER," just because they go or don't along with your agenda. In life, you have to learn how to agree to disagree and move on. Without the trust of family, friends, and co-workers, your life will repeat in a cycle of shallow, one-dimensional relationships that are devoid of lasting power. Even right now you may be exhausted from chasing down a new crowd of approvers and high-profile people. Instead of jumping from various clubs, churches, hot hangout spots, and parties trying to be seen, stop for a moment.

Brownie Point:
Open your heart to give and receive love, then you'll be able to command vs. demand attention.
#CB4C

Can life really be enjoyed if you're always wondering: Do they really like me? Will they invite me again? Did I impress them enough? Believe me, it would benefit you to have some authentically rooted friendships instead of chasing after superficial associations that lead you to being in a rat race, vying for status in the spotlight. Clip the show. Close the curtain on excessively trying to prove you are worth being accepted. You are accepted. If you weren't God wouldn't have placed you on earth.

You have a choice. Be known as a walking billboard who is excessive in *entertaining* or a phenomenal woman known for *interacting*. You'll get more mileage in life when you're not crossing lanes and driving others off the road in a rage. Sharing is caring. While driving toward your destiny, there's plenty of space to share the interstate without thinking your inner state will be overshadowed or kicked to the curb.

Mirror Moment:

Honestly describe most relationships you have with people you call friends.

When was the last time you genuinely celebrated someone else being the center of attention without being jealous or feeling left out?

What are the primary reasons you feel the need to compete for attention?

Miss Over-the-Top's Road Blocks with Mr. Right

1. Making Love a Competition

Neglecting to give him space to "be the man" psychologically cripples a relationship. There has to be balance! You and Mr. Right bring beautifully different characteristics to the table. But you have to be each other's biggest cheerleader when transitioning into commitment. The title of "we" comes with more responsibilities than rolling with just the "me."

2. Making Change the Enemy of Relationship Identity

Seasons shift. And usually more unexpectedly when two people are involved. Changes that impact him will impact you and vice versa. But you won't always be the initiator (leader) of the change. But you can choose whether to grow up together or give up altogether. The more you resist change for the better, the more you put your relationship in jeopardy. Ultimately you'll shift into reverse on the road to destiny.

3. Making Him Distrust You with Other Men

When you're over the top, you may have the inclination to be flirty and provocative with other men. Your need to feed off of attention can be damaging to the intimacy between you and Mr. Right. You may not be a cheater or mean to lure a man into thinking you're feeling him, but your disposition can be interpreted as "she's coming on to me." Without trust, a relationship will not thrive, much less survive.

Declaration of Confidence for Miss Over-the-Top

> "Yes, I have personality. Yes, I have panache. Yet I will be a woman who conveys and portrays the truth. I can gain attention and respect without manipulating people. Influence is not contingent upon me winning approval, but winning connections so there's mutual enjoyment in the company of others. We all have a leading role on this stage called life. I have the power to share the spotlight and applaud others because we are all stars in God's galaxy. So I don't have to work overtime to be liked or loved. The value of my voice is not predicated upon me blowing things out of proportion. I can blow minds by dropping the drama and simply be a queen who wears a crown of confidence not commotion."

Mask #3: Miss Long Distance

The Outer Look

- Paranoid about changes in life
- Persistently complains
- Guarded, secretive
- Self-sufficient, controlling
- Has difficulty with teamwork, judgmental
- Holds grudges, unforgiving
- Suspiciously assumes people will harm or deceive her

The Inner Fears

- Being taken off guard
- Suffering from hurt or abuse
- Having disappointments in relationships
- Exposing sensitivities and being publicly criticized
- Being perceived as weak

Road Blocks for You

Wearing the mask of Miss Long Distance can persuade you to stay at least one hundred feet from anyone's embrace, perspective, or influence. However, no one was created to be completely self-reliable. Teamwork, friendships, and comraderies are necessary to emotionally and mentally keep you active. They can inspire you to keep striving for more out of life, instead of becoming stale and stoic before your earthly expiration date arrives.

As a woman, it's vital for you to share your pain, struggles, wins, and celebrations with others. Your health depends on these mutual exchanges and relatability. But you must be determined to quit taking exits along the De-Mask Us Road that reroute you to live in your past pain. I've never met anyone who didn't experience their trust being taken advantage of before. So quit believing you are the only victim.

The assumption everyone is out to hurt you is absolutely a lie. This paranoia-ridden lie creates a fear, and fear is never meant to protect you. Instead it prohibits you from developing into a woman who is unafraid of isolating her shell to seize an opportunity to reach her potential and enjoy a well-rounded life. You have no idea how many extraordinary people were created to help you. And they don't possess a scandalous, manipulative agenda up their sleeve.

Brownie Point:
You may feel distant from others and cry a tear, but life is not about being controlled by fear. #CB4C

Yes, people may have disappointed you before. There is a time to grieve these occurrences. But existing in a perpetual state of discouragement is a choice. Holding on to grudges and being unwilling to forgive and move forward is not "getting back" at the person who caused the pain. You are imprisoning yourself. Do you really want to have the sweetest revenge on the enemy who's holding you back? If so, I challenge you to step out of your shell and declare you won't allow fear, grudges, or mistakes to suppress your confidence from living in the now and reaching for your not yet!

Mirror Moment:

Have you faced a painful or humiliating experience which makes you cynical (suspicious) toward anyone you meet?

Is it quite challenging for you to let someone get close to you because of a hidden secret? If so, why?

When was the last time you stepped out on faith to do something that would enhance your life?

Miss Long Distance's Road Blocks with Mr. Right

1. Holding Grudges

No matter how adorable his smile is or how the touch of his hand makes your heart skip a beat, no one is perfect. This includes Mr. Right. There will be times when he'll make a mistake, or make a bad choice, and your forgiveness needs to be extended. Always tallying his wrongs and keeping score just encourages a man to hold back the truth from you. You can hold onto to a grudge so tight, eventually it is all you will be holding. And grudges don't keep your warmhearted, they keep you cold-blooded. *If the relationship is worth your faithfulness, it's worth your forgiveness.*

2. Holding Back

A man ready for commitment will want to express his innermost thoughts to you. And he wants you to trust him enough and admit when you need help or when something is bothering you. A man who truly cares will become very agitated when you refuse to let him seek help on your behalf. Your Mr. Right will want and need to come to your rescue at times. This will be a serious boost to his manhood (Superman ego, cape and all). Plus you will get the needed relief in the safe haven of your relationship.

3. Holding on to Baggage

Harboring piles of bitterness and hostility from past seasons won't blossom into a beautiful relationship. What man really wants to keep hearing complaints and comparisons of what a past boyfriend did or didn't do? Or see you carrying dead weight from former bosses, co-workers, friends, and family members? Holding onto baggage is like being behind the wheel with the car in drive and you steadily looking back. Pretty soon you'll be in a wreck, on the wrong side of the road, or stuck in a ditch. You can't look back and move forward at the same time. Fully committing to the present means respecting and admiring Mr. Right for the man he is and the season you're sharing today, not what used to hurt you and who you used to have.

Declaration of Confidence for Miss Long Distance

> "What happened to me won't hinder me. My journey won't be in debt as a result of someone else owing me an apology or a reason for their actions. I won't let my past beat me to the finish line of my destiny. The span of my life means more to me than one fall-out, one fault, or one flawed decision. I won't punish everyone in front of me because of what I went through behind me. I will see life through the eyes of hope. I will look for the good over the bad. I will triumph over my trial. There is victory in my vulnerability. And today I take back my power and confidence to love again, to open my heart again, to try again, and to trust again."

Mask #4: Miss All-About-Me

The Outer Look

- Thrives on social status, prestige, dominance, applause, recognition
- Exaggerates talents and achievements
- Easily jealous of others, sees them as inferior
- Expects others to go along with her plans
- Competitive in conversation (cutting others off)
- Emotionally inconsiderate of others

The Inner Fears

- Having a fragile self-esteem
- Not being validated, affirmed
- Lack of a high-status spouse
- Not staying in first place (losing)
- Not receiving praise and admiration

Road Blocks for You

The journey for Miss All-About-Me has a lot of potholes and barriers. Why? Many view your intentions as purely self-centered. It's difficult confiding in and collaborating with someone who is superficial. Truthfully, meeting up or sharing a meal is difficult because you usually turn the conversation into a Broadway or curbside production of *It's All About Me. Starring, me. Featuring, me. Directed and produced by, me.*

At times, you are so busy admiring your outer reflection.

Other times you are pre-occupied in force feeding your greatness down other people's throats. You want to be justified, revered, and be at the top of list. But in order to reach your destination, you can't keep running over people as if they're a forgotten speed bump. Actions bring about reactions. You reap what you sow, and more than you know.

Narcissistic behavior gravely dims your ability to have meaningful relationships. The brightness of your future depends on your ability to bond with others and be considerate of their feelings. They have achievements, gifts, and abilities worth admiring, too. You don't have to feel like they are a threat. God didn't use a Xerox machine to make any of us as duplicates. What makes a bouquet of flowers beautiful? None of the flowers look exactly alike. So embrace the fact not everyone is supposed to look, sound, think, progress, laugh, and even love like you do. Also, life is not about you salutin' n' tootin' your own horn everywhere you go. There's nothing like someone's integrity and work doing more broadcasting about their identity than their mouth. The sooner you understand this the more freedom you will experience.

Even now you may be fighting to show others you want to be a leader. You want to be successful and significant. You may even want to lead overnight. Well you can't do it alone or do it without serving first. Leaders help to bring out the best in others and collaborate with those who complement their own weaknesses (yes, leaders have them, too). Leaders know how to hear others and collectively seek the best option for the greater good. After all even the fastest and most capable driver in the Indy 500 needs a team.

An amazing awakening takes place when you're at peace with not having to constantly hog the attention. You become more of a force than an enforcer of selfish agendas. Therefore you are more apt to be welcomed, included, and one of the first on "the list." A shift in your attitude will amazingly shift you to elevate much further than you could ever dream. Remember the "we" is always greater than the "me."

Mirror Moment:

Do you often believe you're unstoppable and invincible?

Why is it challenging for you to be compassionate toward others even when something doesn't directly benefit you?

When was the last time you volunteered in your community, church, school, or on a project without wanting or expecting to receive credit?

Miss All-About-Me's Road Blocks with Mr. Right

1. Always Your Shadow

Most men do not want to be perceived as just a side show. There will be times when Mr. Right is being awarded, honored, and praised. Jealousy of his success will only hinder joint happiness. Speaking over him, for him, and down to him is never beneficial either. You can't be so full of yourself, you start playing both roles (man and woman) in the relationship. After a while he may say, "She wants to be both, then she can be both. I'll go where my identity is not hidden behind her massive ego."

2. Always Emotionally Unavailable

There are instances when a man just needs a listening ear and loving heart. But if you're so focused on how to gain other's attention, you'll lose his attention. When a man starts opening his heart to share sensitive matters, it's no time to snooze. It's an opportune time to listen and show that you genuinely care. I guarantee Mr. Right will always remember you being a safe haven where he can strip off his armor and show you his wounds. *Being Miss Right also means being Miss Available to love.*

3. Always Seeking More

Having an insatiable craving for attention that rivals your relationship spells out T-R-O-U-B-L-E. This hunger will make him feel like he's insufficient. Consequently, a man may very well throw up his hands and decide to quit trying or vying for your love. From my knowledge of men, most loathe feelings of inadequacy because it bruises their dignity as a man. Mr. Right will want to be recognized as being the man in your life that is always enough, even as he strives for more.

Declaration of Confidence for Miss All About Me

"Life is a gift I am blessed to not only have, but to share. I realize true prominence is based on me being selfless, not selfish. I am a leading lady because of my strength to love others as I love myself. Yes, I have goals, desires, and dreams. But I won't allow achieving these to hurt or destroy people who come and go in my life. I have the power to look for the good in people without making them feel inferior. I can be the best me the world has and *celebrate vs. cele-hate* the success of others. I will be genuine in my generosity, growth, and guidance knowing that I too depend on helping hands to develop into my best. I will not compete, for I am a woman who is complete. And I'm clothed in confidence inside and out."

Mask #5: Miss Reduce to Seduce

The Outer Look

- Believes her body wins a man's heart
- Uses feminine ploys to lure men
- Driven by trends in the media
- Believes self-esteem is an outer appearance
- Seems imaginative, magical/whimsical
- Revengeful, rebellious, likes living on the edge
- Views men as projects

The Inner Fears

- Scared of being alone or ignored
- Possessing no power beyond her body
- Questions if life is boring or even useless without sex
- Insecurity in her intellect
- Becoming emotionally attached/invested

Road Blocks for You

The mask of Miss Reduce to Seduce can often be tempting for single women to wear, especially when you feel you're not getting anywhere on Lover's Lane. However, this mask only leads to temporary teases and a tarnished reputation. At the end of the day, one of the most valuable things you have is your name and the rep that precedes it. Picture this: your reputation is a blank piece of paper. When you choose to entrap men for attention and sex, you inevitably rip that paper to shreds. Every tease, rip. Each affair, rip. Every one-night stand, rip. Every sext message, rip. Each dating app profile that displays a sex-laced or pornographic image of you, rip. Every bait used to reel a man in, rip. After all of this tearing, you will wind up going into "emergency rep repair mode," trying to superglue your honor. Trying to mend your fractured heart. Trying to use band-aids where a band of gold protecting your heart used to be. Girl, that's two inches away from impossible. So why even go there?

No matter your age, location, relationships status, or state of mind, you should always hold your character to a high standard. Who you are in public and behind closed doors matters. Especially when you're striving to be a trusted trailblazer in life. If you are always using flirty games to progress, what will you do when those ploys won't work? Sex appeal may sell and turn heads, but using your body doesn't win in every case! And you only have one beautiful body to protect as a priceless gem.

Now I understand there are double standards in our society. The reputation of a woman who uses seduction and sex tarnishes faster and stronger than a man who wears this mask. I wish I could change it, but that's the way life is. Whipping out the sex card all the time will cause a lot of friction and distance between personal friendships. Many won't want to be guilty by association. You can even experience embarrassment, name-calling, and rep-shaming within the work environment. In addition, you'll have a very hard time being respected as a leader. Who in their right mind wants to follow someone whose main agenda is always advancing via sexual manipulation? You won't be taken seriously. It's too risky, too shifty. You may even get all sorts of surgeries and procedures done to reduce. But there's no way to win when you live to seduce.

You deserve to be respected by the merit of how you carry yourself instead of where you lay or throw yourself. The result of throwing this mask out the window will amazingly bring you honor beyond compare.

Mirror Moment:

Beyond your body, what other inner aspects of yourself do you love?

How much time do you spend per day thinking about ways to "win" a man over?

Do you find yourself investing in more external accessories to enhance appearance more than investing in your mind and spirit to enhance your quality of life?

Miss Reduce to Seduce's Road Blocks with Mr. Right

1. Lack of Emotional Health & Mental Openness

When you have a promiscuous track record, your emotional health can end up in a massive wreck with pieces of your heart scattered all over the place. The way we are wired as women, it's just impossible to separate our emotions from sexual or seductive engagement. Plus, you'll be hindered from having an openness to ecstasy, compared to someone who doesn't have a "been there, done that" inventory of previous seductive pursuits. Although Mr. Right may be in love with you, constantly having to emotionally compete with the guys of your past will be a hurdle Mr. Right won't love.

2. Lack of Self-Control

Having the ability to restrain and not seek sexual gratification outside of the relationship is certainly a trait admired by men who are ready to commit. Self-control takes focus and consistency even when you don't feel like it. There will be times in a relationship where you may be sexually attracted to another man. You may be approached by another man where you know right off the bat what's on his mind. Even in a committed relationship, you may be prone to entertain invitations from men on the side. A woman who lacks self-control and boundaries leaves a relationship with Mr. Right in a very weak and vulnerable state of survival.

3. Lack of Honesty

Not holding honesty to a high esteem can be detrimental when dealing with Mr. Right. Without it, there really is no relationship. Wearing the mask of seduction leads you to hide secrets and dismantles openness. When you withhold secrets, several domino effects take place. Your closeness starts to drift further apart and suspicions increase about your every move! Subconsciously, you may start comparing Mr. Right to a "potential" relationship you could easily entertain. You can also make a man very envious and want to seek refuge elsewhere from the hurt he's receiving from your dishonesty.

Declaration of Confidence for Miss Reduce to Seduce

"I must respect myself first before receiving respect from others. I will not allow my past to define or dictate me. I forgive myself for all the times I didn't embrace my internal beauty. My body was never intended for me to willingly put it in the way of devastation. My body is a work of art that deserves to be protected. My heart is a canvas that only those who truly love me have the right to paint on. My emotions are to be treasured and highly regarded. My value is not just confined to my external looks, but my intellect. My dignity. My honor. My soul. My spirit. I will no longer endanger my destiny through sex and seduction. But I will embrace my journey by loving myself and preparing to receive a genuine love from a man who will commit to me from the inside out."

Living Beyond the Mask

Overall, looking at yourself beyond the mirror you see in the morning can be difficult. I know deep inside you want to be loved, committed to, and adored. You may be wearing a mask thinking it will bring Mr. Right faster than you can download an app or swipe your debit card for another black handbag or tube of slammin' red lipstick. Or maybe you're just trying to survive, believing the mask is your shield of salvation. Perhaps you've become so comfortable with it, taking it off would be like publicly stripping down to the nude in Times Square. Oooowweee. However, now is the time for you to experience a conversion where you are free to evolve, stretch, mature, and be an extraordinarily phenomenal woman. To be on a journey where crookedness and cover-up is no longer a comfort zone. Knowing that a converted heart leads to the chains of bondage being broken.

This could be the first time you've been challenged to demask. This chapter is just an initial invitation to look within. You may need to get professional help such as counseling or therapy to further investigate the reasons you wear the mask and how to eradicate painful choices. Don't be afraid to take the next step to healing! Disguising broken fragments doesn't have to be your end-all. By shattering the mask, you'll move from pieces to peace. From jealousy to joy beyond syllables. From shame to security in whose you are. From guilt to glory shining through you. You may face rejection while making the bold choice to de-mask. But be encouraged. You will get the much need protection, instead of living with deception, as you move toward your destiny and loving Mr. Right with shining confidence.

Chaos to Confidence

6 Steps to Avoid Hiding Behind a Mask

1. **D**ecide. Take a moment before you react or respond to situations. Are you going to re-mask or de-mask? Decide if you'll allow the real you to shine through.
2. **E**ducate. If you are wearing a mask, find more information about it. Learning should never stop, because life is a classroom. To see a better you, find more about the current you.
3. **M**irror check. Pull to the side of the road and check your emotional, mental, and spiritual state at least once a week. Be honest about your struggles. Don't coast past and cover up frustrations as if they don't exist.
4. **A**ccept. Recognize de-masking isn't an overnight process. Be patient with yourself and accept that in making progress, you must endure a process.
5. **S**hare. De-masking can make you feel exposed and uncomfortable. So share this transition with someone you trust. Don't hold it all in and start wearing a new mask.
6. **K**eep. Keep in mind your future. One day you will look back. Do you want to see a woman who wore masks for the majority of her life? Or a woman who kept pushing to be her best and most authentic self?

CHAPTER 4

INTRODUCING . . . THE REAL ME!

SNOWFLAKES AND ICICLES FELL SOFTLY FOR AN AUDIENCE OF ONE at the corner of Devonshire Drive. I gazed across the ice-covered street to see the neighbor's homes decorated for the holidays. Being tucked behind the long, split-pea-soup-colored curtains was one of my favorite places to hide. I admired the red lighted candles gracing the window pane my dad would repeatedly paint to cover the scars of weather-beaten wood. Even as a child when my mouth was quiet, my hand was busy writing syllables and often practicing my autograph (although at this time on a window frozen to the touch). The Christmas tree stood silently shimmering with garland and miniature musical instruments. And of course the collection of school-made ornaments. They were plastered with a fair amount of Elmer's glue and glitter. How my mom faithfully warned us not to play or even joke around them. After all, even those makeshift masterpieces memorialized the precious years of elementary school art classes and couldn't be duplicated or relived.

As my brother, sister, and I were in countdown mode to Christmas, my parents were counting up the costs for presents. Perhaps you may have been like me, with a firm belief in Santa Claus all along. But one year I was too anxious and curious to sleep. In spite of hearing the late-night news on TV murmuring in the distance (which meant it was officially time for me to be fast asleep), I decided to tiptoe into the dining room. I was shocked into silence as a lump began to grow in my throat. To my complete surprise, my parents had converted the dining room table into a toy wrapping factory. They were working harder than an elf on third shift on the 24th. It seemed as though their adrenaline rush had to have come from No Doz. After a couple of minutes, my cover was blown. I was swiftly ordered back to bed with my stomach in knots. Did my eleventh-hour discovery ruin my chances to get what I wanted? What if all of my good behavior was now tarnished by last-minute naughtiness? In spite of the worries, the clock kept ticking. My parents kept wrapping. And Christmas morning arrived right on time. One of the gifts I cherished most was a Snoopy Sno Cone Machine (Yes, I'm a big fan of Charlie Brown). All the freezing temperatures across the Midwest couldn't make me isolate this gift until springtime. I wanted to taste the delightful cherry flavor. As I kept opening the box, I realized there were not only enough cups and flavor packs for me. But extra supplies were included for me to share with others. It was a gift that would keep on giving.

Rip that Gift Open!

Finding your life purpose has similarities and differences from this story. Unlike Santa Claus, the real *you* actually exists. You don't have to hide in the darkness and pray to be unnoticed while others are in the know. Unlike me receiving that

Sno Cone machine, you don't have to wait until Christmas. You don't have to conquer all naughtiness before discovering your life mission. Others may not understand your curiosity and restlessness to know more about your reasons for being. After all this makes some feel more insecure as they're unsure of their purpose.

However, all the intricacies inside you long to be unveiled starting now. You were an extraordinarily wrapped gift long before you knew your name. Now is the time to rip off the wrapping paper with confidence and unleash what's in your package. Purpose was never intended to be an unknown, unnoticed, and unused present that stays buried inside of you. Simply, it's a gift with a unique flavor that you were created to share with the world.

Brownie Point:
Confidence is not an act, an image, or a look. It's a layer of your soul that shines brighter when you know who and why you are. #CB4C

More to Life Than This

Like a pair of double doors at a five-star hotel, the semester will slowly but surely come to a close. The degree will be attained. The business project will travel from conception to conclusion. The cameras will stop flashing (even selfies are momentary). The press conference will wrap up. The raves about the event you were featured at will fall to a mum. The paycheck will be delivered, deposited, and spent. The vacation will end. The responses on your social media feeds will be a faded memory. I'm sure you had at least one of these experiences. And somehow beyond your regular routine, you long for more. Deep within your spirit you think, *"What in the world do I do next?" "Isn't there more to live for and work towards?" "Will I ever feel fulfilled?"*

I've seen so many women go from day to day just existing. They settle for jobs. Feed off of dramatized reality TV. Trying their best to blend in and stay up on trends. But there's no fire in their eyes to see more. No pep in their step to do more. No curiosity to shake the apathy out of them. No hopes and aspirations to keep working towards. Sometimes, I literally want to go up to them and check their pulse to see if there's a heartbeat and yell, "WAKE UPPPPP!" T. D. Jakes once stated, "Too many people are busy acting and not being. You want to look like you're rich, look like you're smart . . . but [they] are not what they portray. We must get past *the look* and start seizing *the life*."

Brownie Point:
Commit to being who you are, before being his Miss Right. #CB4C

Knowing your purpose causes you to live in the most beautiful, unabashed, and unflinching way possible. To snap out of the lull. To quit running after someone else's dream. To spend less time on wishing and more on winning. Right now you have the right to really come ALIVE! In your own skin. In your own lane. In your own unduplicated identity. Purpose is a continuing force of power that weaves a thread between past chapters of life and new chapters yet to be discovered. No matter who you are and where you want to be in life, God knew your heart would need to be motivated far beyond the excitement over a date. The spotlight. The status. The GPA. The paycheck. The recognition. You need a supernatural push in order to reach beyond complacently doing the same ol' routine. After all, life is not meant to be lived on autopilot or in a robotic stupor.

Yes, hopefully you have experienced some incredible

accomplishments and feel good moments that brought tears of joy, laughter, fun, and happiness. But these don't last forever. *You can't build a permanent residence on a momentary experience.* Purpose yields a hunger inside that keeps motivating you to reach higher, stretch wider, and go harder until you've reached the next level. Rinse and repeat.

Don't you want more out of life? Do you want to break free from a limited mindset? Who says aspiring for more and dreaming big is only something children can do? In order to rock your confidence and live out your mission, you must be alert to the awakening taking place inside of you. Continuing to press snooze and being comfortable as a "leading spectator" will eventually have you waking up with overwhelming remorse. You and I both know tomorrow is not guaranteed. This is the moment for you to redeem the time and kick the "one of these days I'll get to it" mindset to the curb. There is more to life than slowly allowing yourself to deteriorate from the inside out. There is more to life than daydreaming and thumb twiddling. You are here on earth to be discovering and finger-pointing while declaring, "Onward to GREATER."

When Dreams & Desires Collide

Before your birth, there were imaginations, desires, intrigues, passions, and instincts carefully woven inside of you. These were placed for you to follow, express, and fulfill during your stay on earth. Right now your mind might be bombarded with thoughts of living with Mr. Right in a field of wild yellow flowers while running towards the golden sunset and holding his strong, secure hands. Along with a gentle breeze blowing through your hair ever so slightly, and everything being blissfully beautiful . . . Errr uh. And, cut. Pardon the interruption.

But the key to unlocking who you are does not exist in a daydream or in a cinematic fantasy. It's not contingent upon your relationship status. In fact, tapping into your purpose is one of the most fundamental steps toward being in the right position for commitment. There is absolutely nothing wrong with being secure in who you're called to be and what you're called to do before Mr. Right. You'll have sharper focus to weed out the Mr. Wrongs. And even more confidence to not entertain timewasters and life drainers. But make no mistake. Flowing in your purpose is about real work and real sacrifice which yields real rewards, my friend.

Honestly, the dreams you have yet to discover, unlock, and walk toward are already the result of God's genius. Erik Rees states in his book *Only You Can Be You*: "Whatever dream you hold dearest was most likely planted there by God, but it needs to be given back to him before you can actually know what it's supposed to look like. When seen through God's eyes, your dreams take on clarity and purpose. He'll show you which elements of your dream are from him and which part is from your own selfishness and needs to be discarded."

I understand the desires you currently possess may have you feeling tossed around like a load of laundry in the spin cycle. But you must trust. You have to believe your freedom to flourish won't be suddenly zapped by an unloving, trap-you-in-a-box, kind of God. There's a beautiful masterpiece which evolves when your dreams and desires coincide with his overall plans. We don't even know what will take place in the next five minutes or fifty years. So don't cringe or cower. Take the chance and entrust your dreams and desires in God's hands. He has an uncanny way of knowing everything needed for you to enjoy an unbelievably gratifying life.

Brownie Point:
In order to be purposefully effective,
you have to be wisely selective. #CB4C

There was a common phrase used in the '90s, which still packs an ample dose of wisdom: "You better check yourself, before you wreck yourself." In the realm of life purpose, make sure to analyze your motives before making certain moves in life. Ask yourself, "If this desire or dream is fulfilled, who benefits from it?" Purpose continually drives you toward selflessness not selfishness (which, by the way, is an excellent quality to have before Mr. Right). I'm not saying you have to totally neglect yourself and sacrifice foolishly in order to appease others. Purpose is not about stretching yourself so thin, you're no good to anyone. There's no sense in making so many unwise decisions that you are live in a constant state of fear and overwhelming anxiety. Living up to the real you involves listening to guidance so your dreams will put joy in your spirit AND provide breakthroughs for humanity.

Mirror Moment:

What dreams and desires have you been suppressing or abandoning because of fear of people, failure, unknowns, or success?

World Changer Born. Trailblazer Torn.

Right now you may be laser-focused on a specific goal, career path, or level of status you want to attain. You are behind the wheel and 110 percent convinced you are moving in the right direction. You've got your special playlist of "epic theme songs" blaring and catchy affirmations to get you pumped up for the journey. Your eyes are focused forward as you accelerate against the wind. You press the pedal to the metal and you got a trunk full of hope strapped down for the ride. But what if it's not meant to be? Life does not consists of an absolute straight, clear-cut, describable path.

If you keep running into brick walls, barricades, and blockades, you may be in a state of denial concerning your purpose. Now don't get it twisted. One repetitive theme I've seen with people living their purpose is not a life devoid of difficulty. They've had to endure long days and late nights to hone their skills, get necessary education, understand their strengths and weaknesses, and repeatedly practice the discipline of staying in their own lane. But eventually they get opportunities chasing them. Open doors are extended to them left and right. I believe when you live in purpose, your daily menu for years won't consist of begging for crumbs. You have the power to refuse exerting precious energy, time, and money toward a target you weren't created to hit. I know this may be a difficult pill to swallow. And discovering your purpose takes time, guidance, and a lot of answered prayers. But I don't want you to look back six years or even seventeen months from now and have a heart filled with resentment because you were moving in the wrong direction.

Before going to Tennessee State University, I had my mind made up. I was going to be a corporate lawyer. After my sophomore year, I was honored to intern with the deputy prosecutor of Howard County. After getting acclimated with the position, my demeanor changed. I started dragging into his office, in and out of court, and looking at countless case files. I would find myself counting down the minutes to my lunchbreak. I would yearn to get out and see life, people moving, breathe fresh air. I'd sit on a bench and soak in poetic verses from *For Those Who Ride the Night Winds* by Nikki Giovanni.

While at TSU, my college best friend and I formed the singing group Descendants of Reality. Little did Reecy and I know that we would sing together for more than ten years. As freshmen, our heads and hearts were filled with getting a big record deal and achieving world acclaim. As we got older, we learned more about the good, bad, and ugly sides of the music industry. We enjoyed some high times of traveling with our band around the United States performing at historical arenas, night clubs, expos, universities, churches, concerts, and festivals. But weathering the low times was very emotionally and financially trying. Throughout the years, I was blinded by a craving and steadily asking God *to ride along and bless our agenda*. All of our hands were on deck for one goal of music success and notoriety. And yes, both of us have musical propensity and a very strong passion for music.

But in 2009, my life perspective drastically changed when I listened intently to my pastor, Bishop Joseph Walker III, teach about the power of purpose. To this day, it still reigns as one of the most revolutionary, life-altering messages I've ever heard. For four weeks, he gave a lifetime of insight about knowing what you were born to do and what it yields. Deep inside my soul stirred. I was torn between the familiar (asking God to get on board and let me drive) and unchartered territory (surrendering the wheel and letting God determine my destination). After a thousand tears and facing a mountain of fears, I cried out, "I don't know what is going on, but I'm not satisfied in life. I'm setting free what I think is best for me. You're the only One who can truthfully answer this: Why did you place me here on earth? What do you want me to do?" I read books, took quizzes, and prayed relentlessly to find my life mission.

In 2010, our music group peacefully disbanded. Months passed. And then God spoke. Sometimes, your faith is tested and rewarded only when you're willing to let go of your plan A, B, and C. I had to become comfortable in being chauffeured and enjoy the scenic route. I was being shown my power, intuitions, instinct, tendencies, and ways I express myself best whether in solitude or among the multitude. Basically a breakdown of the reasons I was created the way I am. Now you and I are amazingly united via this book as evidence of God showing me what I was created to thrive in. By the way, I never dreamed of being a speaker or an author prior to this revelation. Yet fittingly, I've always been a talker who excelled at writing, and I absolutely love to encourage people. As for being an entrepreneur, well, it's multigenerational gene in my family. And even God's genius put that together.

Brownie Point:
Often from discomfort and difficulty we welcome our life mission, shake the hands of purpose, and allow it to have a governing seat in our hearts.
#CB4C

You may not know every step of the path ahead. Congrats. You've got something in common with me and the entire universe! Life is not about figuring it all out in one setting and then leaping into your calling. Life is about finding out more with a heart that's yielded to receive direction as you step out in faith. You may have to endure unplanned changes, releasing relationships, and alternate routes getting to where you need to be. But God won't leave you hanging and is able to make sense of it all. Like me, you may have insurance with Allstate and be in good hands. But I'm so glad we can have *blessed assurance* that our destinies are in God's hands. Whatever state you're in, his hands are still the greatest to be in.

In between our plans, life happens, but the reasons for a change will come full circle. If it's ordained for you to arrive at the destination you've been aiming for, you will get there. You'll lose your breath at times. You will stand in awe of the beauty and the challenges on a road you never dreamed of traveling.

You'll realize strengths you never thought you needed or could possess will surface.

I dare you to believe that what you've been focusing on is just a glimpse of the bigger picture. The bigger picture entails a spine-tingling view in which you can't presently see or attain. But steadily you will rise to that pinnacle or platform. And you will be completely amazed about how your purpose impacts lives (including yours) beyond imagination.

If no one has ever told you this, I'm telling you today:

You were born to be a *world-changer*.

You are a powerhouse of *activated potential*.

You are a deliberately *composed masterpiece*.

You are an *undeniable influencer*.

You are molded to be an *unshakable force of confidence*.

Mirror Moment:

Are you afraid of letting go of something or someone that's prohibiting you from moving forward in life?

What are you willing to sacrifice to shine as *the real you*?

Connecting with You Before Committing to Mr. Right

Too many people spend decades of their lives wandering aimlessly or nonchalantly floating in the breeze. They never come to realize a fourth of their potential. They never produce anything. Or they just rely on someone else's blood, sweat, and tears to keep rescuing them from succeeding on their own two feet. *Do you want this to be a lifelong description of you?*

As an entrepreneur and writer of *Interesting Things*, Steve Spalding suggests, "Eighty percent of people quietly despise their lives. Children typically like life a lot. Teenagers are a little wishy-washy on it, but for the most part they think it's the tops. The problem starts somewhere around the mid-twenties, when we get thrown out into the world to do 'whatever we want to' and we realize that the majority of that time will be spent surviving and helping others to survive. Kind of a bummer, especially when you spend the majority of your early days looking forward to the freedom of being an adult. This realization is enough to cripple most of us, and very few who survive it make it through unscarred."

In his book *Instinct*, T. D. Jakes wrote:

> Unfortunately, many of us often spend our lives living out of sync with this internal rhythm. We do what we're trained to do, what we're asked to do, or what others need us to do—all the while, feeling restless and unsatisfied, wondering why fulfillment eludes us. We know there's a bigger, elephant-sized life out there waiting for us, but uncertainty and fear keep us locked in our routines, contained in the cage of conformity. We watch others excel as they listen to their own instincts rather than please others. Yet we ignore the urgent message whispering within us, intrigued by its insistence but afraid to act on its information.

Now more than ever, single women need to connect with their purpose. We do more comparing of ourselves than conveying and communicating who we truly are. This has helped to convert a societal segment of women reliant upon anti-depressant prescriptions and unhealthy void fillers. When we could very well be finding joy in our purpose and rocking our confidence out loud!

Dr. Tony Evans once stated in his message *Becoming a Kingdom Single*:

> The successful single vs. the defeated single is the distinction between the called one and the one who does not know their calling. The one that does not know their calling thinks all of life is wrapped up in that man or woman they have not yet found and God has not yet supplied. The one who is not frustrated, still desiring, but not frustrated is [that way] because they have been called to something bigger that no other person can fix for them. They are into something so much bigger . . . God doesn't cancel out who you are [or your desire for companionship] to use you.

So what's to love about finding your purpose while single? Why should you care when your sole goal and aim has been finding a man and getting married? I believe the most fruitful, productive, and beautiful-beyond-belief marriages *begin while two secure individuals are apart*. Yet both are united to their unique life purpose. When Mr. Right comes in your life, you want to be able to introduce him to the real you. Singlehood is a groundbreaking time for you to fully grab hold of the advantages of seizing your purpose so no insecure, slick-tongued snake, or even Prince Charming who'll do more harming, derails you from reaching your destiny.

Brownie Point:
Being D.O.A. (delusional on arrival) should never be your intention in life or in love. #CB4C

5 Reasons to Know Purpose B4 Mr. Right

Reason #1: You Gain Direction

A constant need we have as humans is the sense of direction. Even with an array of phone apps, blogs, YouTube videos, and GPS systems, we still ask, *"Am I on the right track?" "Where is my life going?" "Is this really what I'm supposed to be doing?"* If you've been asking these questions lately, don't be discouraged. You are not alone. We all need guiding reassurance with the various twist and turns we experience.

At times, you can be on the right highway, but taking the wrong exit. There was once a football player who unexpectedly made it to the NFL. Upon graduating from high school, his heart was set on playing pro basketball. However, when he arrived at UNC—Chapel Hill, he realized he wasn't quite cut out to excel in the basketball program. Still being athletically skilled and impassioned, he eventually joined the football team as a walk-on. He excelled in balancing classes and the demanding obligations of football. After years of grit and dedication, he became a star athlete and an undeniable leader on his college team. So with his initial plans in the rearview mirror and God's path paved in front of him, he went on to the NFL.

Despite the average playing span of an NFL player ranging from three to six years and facing pressures on and off the field, he played in the league for more than ten years. Yes, it's true, his life story didn't turn out the way he had initially envisioned. Agendas were rearranged. The GPS destination was rerouted. But his story evolved in a way where his purpose flourished. Hard work, perseverance, and zeal got him to the field. However, his life's core value was beyond the score of the game. Beyond the summation of a sports analyst's critique and the litany of stats. God inevitably used this "unplanned" platform to entrust him with financially supporting less fortunate children, providing Thanksgiving dinners for needy families, and hosting faith-based summer camps for kids who aspire to be successful athletes. Now for the last several years, David Thornton has been serving as an exemplary example of leadership as the director of player engagement of my favorite NFL team, the Indianapolis Colts. One step forward kept leading him further toward living a purpose-filled and directed life.

Life isn't a straight line, there's lots of spins and bends. And the path is laced with plenty of attractions and distractions. When you need direction, pull to the side of the road and ask God for wisdom and listen for instructions. Stay in the present. Stay sensitive to what's happening around you and who you're connecting with. You don't want to continue taking the wrong exits in life or keep driving down the wrong highway altogether. Life is about having faith in your heart (to follow through) and flexibility in your back pocket (to take an alternate route if necessary).

You may hear some people identifying themselves as a "free spirit." Listen. In many cases, that's just an excuse to dabble in lots of things. Or they have no allegiance to complete an assignment or deal with their commitment phobia in order to excel in a particular area. *You've got to gain root to bear fruit.* And dabbling without devotion ain't going to cut it. Being selectively rooted allows you to be wonderfully effective as the real you. People's lives and breakthroughs are at stake when you possess an "scattered all over the place" approach to living. A confident woman knows she cannot boil the ocean, or better yet do everything in life. *New York Times* best-selling author and businessman Michael Hyatt has stated these three components regarding life direction and career fulfillment in what you do. Make sure you have each of the following:

- **Passion.** This is where it begins. What do you care about? What moves you? What problems do you want to solve or issues you want to address? If your heart is not in your work, you have a job, but not a calling.
- **Proficiency.** Passion alone is not enough. You have to be good at what you do. Being good enough will not give you the satisfaction you desire. You have to excel at your craft and be awesome. Mastery is the goal.
- **Profitability.** To enjoy a successful career, people must be willing to pay you for what you do. You don't have to get rich, but there must be a market for your product or service. Otherwise, your career is not sustainable.

For sustainability, growth, and significance these are important factors to cover. Being at the right exit means you can confidently possess a sense of peace and an assurance you're headed in the right direction. Purpose leads you to where the real you is in motion and growing for maximum effectiveness.

Brownie Point:
A confident woman understands selectivity before activity guides her to purposeful productivity.
#CB4C

Reason #2: You Understand Talent vs. Purpose

One of the most common misconceptions passed down through generations is mistaking talent for purpose. Talent often plays an imperative role in finding out more about ourselves and gaining self-confidence to share them with the world. Many times it provides enjoyment and income (for the possessor of the talent) and at the same time provides an escape from the worries and stress from life (for the recipients of the talent).

While watching Oprah's *Lifeclass,* I once heard T. D. Jakes wisely state: "You must understand that purpose is an underlying chemistry that makes you live your life. Many, many times we start working in an area where we have talent, but it's not our purpose. You may start out doing something that was not 'the thing' that you were created to do. It may only be the thing that leads to the thing you were created to do. So don't stop at where you are as if it were the *destination*, when in fact in reality it may be the *transportation* that brings you into that thing you were created to do."

Having a talent doesn't mean it's the end-all or the totality of the real you. This may not be the thing in which you'll invest all of your time, money, hopes, expectations, and resources. Talent may be the necessary vehicle to get you to a place. It may open the door to a scholarship at a university where you'll meet a renowned professor. Through his/her experience, a deep passion could stir within and you're awakened to another step leading to purpose.

Your talent may turn heads for an attendee at a networking event. After meeting, you could be offered a proposition which leads to realizing the vision you've had in your heart will become reality. Instead of it remaining as a buried treasure confined to the pages of a secret journal that's been tucked in a dresser drawer for years.

Talent may be the necessary vehicle to get you to a place. But purpose is the ongoing fuel that makes life worth living, giving, and remembering.

Reason #3: You See Your Greatness Unlocked

A Sony HD television. A Mac laptop. A BCBG rose-colored jacket. A bottle of perfume by Alfred Sung. A Rolls Royce car. Pick any product and one truth is universal. Each one is created to serve an intended purpose. And they carry out the mission of the creator. Have you ever heard of a product saying to the manufacturer, "When I get off this assembly line, I'm going to ignore the plans you had for me. And oh, by the way, forget about packaging me with a manual. It really doesn't apply to me any way." This sounds crazy and absurd right? Yet out of all of creation, we as humans are often the most reluctant, most rebellious, and most intimidated when it comes to life intent. As a result, we who are to possess the *most dominion* on earth, can in turn be the *most cowardly* without connecting to purpose.

Many single women choose to navigate through life by filling their hunger for purpose with materialism, relationships, entertainment, titles, and the look of financial prosperity. Sure, we all have a need for acceptance and assurance. But let me keep it real. These facets may add seasoning to your existence but can never trump the reasoning for your existence. All are vain outer impressions without authentic inner expressions. No one can solidify your life like God. Purpose offers you a seat in your divinely designated sweet spot. A place where you know deep inside: This is why I belong on earth and why I'm here during this time on earth.

Amanda Cook fittingly sings what God wants you to know when you wonder about your life direction: "I've made you beautiful, in my sight. The sound of war you're looking for is a lullaby. So come in close, lean on me. I'm saying (this) softly, but it will chase away the darkness. It'll chase away the fears, if you lean into me, cause I'm rewriting your history. I'm rewriting your history." Wow. After all, our future greatness is actually history in the eyes of God. I believe we are being introduced to our layers of greatness all the time. Some see the greatness rising and run toward it. Others hide, fearing the unknown. Some would rather be a spectator of greatness rather than a contributor of greatness. Some question it for so long, they allow fear instead of faith to answer. Do you know your greatness was never meant to be hidden like a forgotten chest in an old, cobweb-infested attic? *Your greatness is supposed to shine so bright forces of darkness are running for sunglasses. The armies of fear, insecurity, low self-esteem, discouragement and cluelessness are running for shade*. They're supposed to be running back to darkness for refuge. Why? Because you were born to shine with the power of purpose. You must diffuse your shine and not dilute your shine. So quit suppressing the questions swirling in your head or trying to figure you out all by yourself. Quit denying the thirst in your soul for more. Ask and listen to God so your greatness can be unlocked and the *real you* is revealed! Greatness is calling you out into the deep, will you answer?

Reason #4: You Distinguish between Mr. Wrong & Mr. Right

It is a widely known fact that one of the most imperative decisions a woman will make is deciding who she will marry. When a woman is assured of her purpose before Mr. Right, she sets herself and even their future in a much better position for a mutually beneficial marriage.

I remember talking to Sean, a guy who was head over heels in love with me. We met during college and he gradually but steadily expressed his desire for commitment. We lost contact after I graduated and moved back to Indiana. But several years later, we surprisingly picked up where we left off after seeing each other at our alma mater's homecoming. One thing I adored about him was how he was inquisitive and focused on me. Whether face to face or over the phone, he would gently pry open cans of conversation I wouldn't dare to share with other men in my past.

One day as I was driving on I-24 after work, I really started digging deep to find out his goals and ambitions. His response totally threw me for a loop. I could have literally slid over on the side of the road with skid marks in tow. My stomach became immediately nauseated. Sean informed me that he just wanted to "be easy," get married, have a little house, and just take care of his family. (No offense if this is your heart's desire.) But all I heard was "I. WANT. TO. BE. AVERAGE." It wasn't just what he said, but how he said it. A neon red flag was flashing far in the distance.

Sometimes a relationship which works for now, hints that it won't satisfy you in the future. Although I wasn't totally surefooted in my purpose, I knew in my heart that my happily ever after wouldn't include him. I could envision the tug-of-war strain and living under my potential by being with someone who just wanted to take life passively as is. Now I'm not saying he wasn't a good guy, he just wasn't good for me. This was truly confirmed when he ended our relationship and married another woman. To my disgust, a year or so later he tried to emotionally reconnect with me. He and his wife clashed on several levels, one being he was a Christian and she was a devout Muslim—slowly she was pulling him and their child into her belief system. Sean called and called me, he wanted to meet up. I could hear the angst in his voice, his regret for not choosing me. They deeply clashed, but they shared a covenant. So my response to making a U-turn back to him, a married man was: No way. No sir. No how.

The confidence, not cockiness, a woman exudes while living her purpose can help to weed out the Mr. Wrongs. She views her mission as a priority that must be carried out, not trampled over or belittled. Her purpose is not to be treated as a fleeting pastime. She understands relational balance, but knows that men who fuss about her *thinking too big, pushing forward too much* or *working toward something greater* from the onset of a relationship will not make a great marriage.

A man who is easily intimidated by your purposeful design and mission does not deserve your heart's focus. Purpose takes concentration and dedication. Initially, it may feel amazing to have the attention of a man. However, an insecure man will only have you backpedaling for affection and away from your purpose. He's like a pocket with a hole in it. No matter what you do, how long you stay, how much sex you have, how much money is spent, he'll never be satisfied. You can waste a lot of time and energy trying to make a man feel as secure as you are. You can try doing backward flips in efforts of trying to get him to flow in purpose. But guess what? Both of you will still come up short and more than likely looking outside of the relationship for fulfillment. Why? Because only God can reveal purpose to his I-need-to-be-deeply-filled soul.

When both man and woman are confident in their purpose, this decreases the tendency for competition (i.e. The "you better always choose me or there's no we" mentality or the "what I do is greater than what you're doing" attitude).

Not to discourage you, but let me let you in on what I wish someone would have told me a while ago. There can be some relational costs to living in purpose. Your confidence might repel some men, especially men who are in play mode or just wanting quick attention without lasting attachment. Don't be discouraged if your love story arrives later and differently than you hoped for. Your wait for Mr. Right might be a little longer than expected. (Believe me, I can attest. I just knew I would be married, have the dream house, and two adorable kids by thirty.) Your upward climb in your purpose may involve fewer men and fewer dates. Your journey may require you stepping away from your current zip code in order to be united with Mr. Right. I'm not trying to get you bummed out. I just want to be real with you. There's sacrifice with living in purpose.

After some failed relationships and run-ins with a few Mr. Magics (guys who just vanished with no explanation), I used to wonder what was wrong with me. Some days I wondered if I literally had a *"Do not even holla at this woman!"* sign on my forehead. But when I understood my purpose and the Y.A.S.O. vision, I knew God was setting me up for an even greater future by securing my focus away from a relationship. I now know that I'm supposed to be walking full throttle in my purpose without looking back or feeling shaky when a guy doesn't fit or challenges me about my life calling. Yes, at times the tears race down my face as I come home from another business trip and all I want is to share all the wonderful progress with my Mr. Right. Yes, there are days in which the wait feels like an unbearable weight. But I live to see another day and keep striding forward in purpose.

Dr. Stephaine Walker, the First Lady at my church Mt. Zion, once made this profound statement at a Women's Night Out event: "What you're looking for, is looking for you." So make sure you don't sacrifice your soul, your mission, and your calling just to have companionship. Mr. Right will honor and cheer you on as you thrive in purpose. In fact, you'll be each other's biggest cheerleaders moving forward hand in hand and side by side.

So have you been trying to appease friends and family with a relationship, just to say "I'm dating someone now?" But inside you know the connection is strictly for show. Daily you try to devise ways to lower the volume of the nagging voice of dismay. Maybe you've been settling for Mr. Right for Now, hoping he'll one day be Mr. Right, but deep inside you know he's wrong for you. Now is the time to LET. IT. GO. Girl, forget about hope deferred. Your hope needs to be redirected. Invest in a relationship where both of your life callings are being fulfilled and the real you shines brighter than ever.

Brownie Point:
Don't ever downplay your purpose just to upgrade someone who doesn't have a clue about theirs.
#CB4C

Reason #5: You Yield Confidence that's Courageous & Influence that's Contagious

I had the opportunity of speaking to hundreds of women at Lipscomb University on Valentine's Day eve. For weeks, I prepared and practiced to put my best foot forward. Secretly, I had been dreaming of a student receiving a revolutionary "Ah ha" moment. She would make a mad dash into my arms and tell me how her life would never be the same after listening to my speech. From the back of the balcony to the front row, I didn't see the illuminating glow I anticipated in the packed auditorium. Instead there were hundreds of beautiful faces who gave a mixed bag response of receptive smiles, stunned looks, and dull stares. As I got in my car to leave, I started criticizing myself and believing my topic was too blunt or "over the top." After all, it was on how a woman should handle a raging sex drive while dating, at a pretty conservative private university.

That same night I returned to host at a late-night event called, "Girl Talk with Brownie." The night was unforgettable! We openly talked about friendships. Dateless semesters. Expectations from men. Desires of men. Courageously speaking about abstinence and celibacy with a love prospect. Many women waited in line to speak with me about their fears of insignificance. Some privately admitted to never having a boyfriend yet were touched by the encouragement given by a single woman, for the single woman. Even married women admitted that they wished the speech with "straight up truth" was given to them during singlehood. Weeks later I came across this message from one of the students who sent me a mini-chapter of her life story that unfolded the day after I spoke:

> I just wanted to take the time to say how much what you said had an impact on me. I left with a whole new outlook on my worth and what I deserved. I've struggled all of my life with guys who have tricked me into thinking that they loved me in order to get physical affection from me. When he broke up with me and mentioned that [sex] as a reason, I automatically felt that I had to change to earn his love. We got back together on New Year's Eve. While we were together, he earned my trust and promised not to hurt me on multiple occasions. We even talked about marriage. I've continued to fight for him after the breakup, thinking that maybe I could earn him back. I talked with him yesterday (on Valentine's Day) and he basically revealed to me that he has a physical intimacy addiction and didn't want me to be the object of his fix. He's been dating for the wrong reason, just for physical intimacy. With the newfound courage that I got from your talks, I have finally accepted that I deserve so much better than what I was getting. I have finally accepted that I need to stop fighting. So that's what I'm going to do. Even though it will be hard, God has a much better plan for me than to be a piece of meat. I don't know why I'm telling you all of this, but I just wanted to let you know how much strength and

> courage you have given me. You have inspired me to walk closer with God and value myself more as his beloved daughter. I know I'm not the only one you will affect in this way.

Sometimes you may not see immediate results of working in purpose. I've been blessed to speak to numerous audiences composed of college students around the United States, married women, abused women, career women, elementary school children, and even needy children in Haiti. And there's still more for me to discover and share around the world. But I've learned immediate *outer reactions* of others don't determine the transformational response on their inner. So remain patient and humble. One of the sweetest facts of life is knowing purpose will clothe you in an intangible style that is uniquely yours and tailor-made to fit to a T. It gives you a "magnetic suit" which attracts those ready to receive a new perspective through your message or life story. It will tug on the hearts of those who need to benefit from your services. It will welcome those who need to buy your innovation that will revolutionize their life and future generations.

On the flip side, some people will reject you. Some will have an allergic reaction to your greatness and just aren't ready to receive the solution you present. But it's not your job to worry and be discouraged by their response. You will reach those you are supposed to reach . . . and repel those you aren't orchestrated to serve.

The Real You Emerges Now

Your beautifully sculpted purpose is worth your immediate pursuit and continual perseverance. No longer be a slave of fear, but be bold and face the real you. Some assignments are designed to be completed without your focus being derailed in a relationship (especially in one that's unhealthy and going nowhere) in this season. I sincerely hope and pray, your Mr. Right is getting firmly secure in his purpose before joining hand in hand with you. When neither of you know where you're going in life, you become walking billboards of devotion without direction which results in devastation.

To have something different, you have to do something different. To see your greatness change lives, you can't be afraid of change happening in your life first. Take the opportunity now to break the cycle of just going through the motions. Understand time isn't money. Time is simply time. And once it's spent there are no refunds. So wake up! Snap out of the stupor and be in the know about the real you. Realize your life purpose is a serious matter! Don't treat this season of singlehood vicariously. Seize your purpose so the real you can emerge and bring a remarkable brilliance to the world we live in. We desperately need *the real you*.

Chaos to Confidence

10 Questions to Guide You toward a Purposeful Life

1. **P** - What are three core values you *possess* and live by?
2. **U** - What are five things that *uniquely* bring you joy/fulfillment spiritually? Professionally? Personally?
3. **R** - If you could get a message across to a large group of people, who would be the *recipients*? What would your message be?
4. **P** - Throughout your life, what are some issues you always seem to identify and have a *passion* to solve?
5. **O** - What would you regret not *operating* in or doing at the end of your life?

6. **S** - What are your *spiritual* gifts?
7. **E** - If you were *economically* set and money wasn't an issue for the rest of your life, what would you do?
8. **F** - What do *family*, friends, even strangers consistently compliment you on?
9. **U** - What are you naturally good at doing that is also *useful* for others?
10. **L** - What activities make you *lose* track of time?

CHAPTER 5

I'D RATHER HANG OUT WITH THE GUYS

BFFS. GIRLS. ASSOCIATES. PALS. FRIENDS. NOWADAYS THE DEFINITION of friendships are constantly changing. They are especially different from our second grade school days. Remember having to look someone square in the face or pass a note during class to ask them to be your friend? Can you recall having play dates and birthday parties at each other's houses? Or being invited to stay for dinner after working on a science project? I recall sharing "BFF" earrings and charm bracelets with Linda. I used to make a mad dash to the phone (before Caller I.D. days) and shouting out, "Mom, I got it, it's for me!" whenever she called. As friends we would open up cans of conversation about homework. The cutest guys at school. Our secret crushes. The hottest celebs. And the latest music we would play away from our parents' eardrums. Our dreams of living outside of Kokomo. Wow, those days were priceless. Friendship and trust evolved from a "You like what I like, so let's hang out" grassroots kind of way.

But times have changed and how we connect has shifted. According to the Pew Research Center, "65 percent of adults now use social networking sites—a nearly tenfold jump in the past decade." Friendships are often defined as someone who likes, tags, follows, shares, or reposts via social media. Even online romance sparks fly due to an anonymous person cutting and pasting one-sized-fits-all compliments only to lure in those who are needy for attention and so thirsty for a boo/bae, they skip the necessary vetting process. One swipe on Tinder can be the defining line between hello and heck no.

I call this *cyber-affection dependency*. And I, too, have been sucked into the vacuum of technology's insatiable high from trying to do more and be in more places all at the same time. But it comes with a cost. Like it or not, we text more and call less. We email more and connect less. We trust in media more and test morals less. At times, I feel like it's a part of an underhanded plan to put more emphasis on *quantification vs. qualification* regarding friendship. You can be logged in on the trendiest social media platforms and have a fully charged battery on the fastest network and yet still be lonely. Feeling like no one really understands you or is fully invested and focused on getting to really know you. In spite of a plethora of cyber shared likes, tags, and comments, there still is a serious void if you have no one to sit down with, look into your eyes, and become a trusted audience of one. Literally, a person dedicated to hearing your thoughts and ambitions. Someone who picks up your quirky nonverbals. Detects your apprehensions. And tosses up pom-poms when you've conquered a challenge. *Honestly. We've got smart phones . . . but have they truly made us smarter?*

Right now, you may find yourself so focused on having companionship with Mr. Right ASAP. But it's equally critical for you to establish strong friendships with other females. The right friendships can bring a ton of wealth to your life. Treasures that accumulate more interest than Regions, Chase, or Bank of America can offer. Connections which would make even the New York Stock Exchange jealous of your gains. These relationships can even bring vitality and insight to your love life with Mr. Right.

Now don't be hasty and skip this chapter, thinking that I'm writing off men. I truly LOVE men and can't imagine God's green earth without them. But between you and me, we as women just bring something beautifully remarkable to each other in friendship. Values and qualities most men wouldn't bring even if they were planted in their back pocket.

Broken & Banking Hopes on Harry

Have you ever met a woman who doesn't have another woman to connect with and confide in? Do you know of someone who doesn't even respect or give a sister bond a second look? Maybe your mom, sister, roommate, or co-worker comes to mind. Maybe this describes you.

Take Lori for instance. When I met her, she hardly looked me in the eye and shook my hand as if I was holding a fistful of dirt. I was already conversing with a small group of women. She never said hello to anyone else after we were introduced. She "sized up" everyone and after quickly rationalizing we weren't worthy of her company, she fled the scene without a goodbye or a wave. Later on I found out a little more about Lori. She's known for being very judgmental and often views women strictly as competitors, especially when it comes to a man's attention. Flipping the "on" switch when surrounded or approached by a man is her lifestyle. Additionally, she only dates men with public status, fame, and fortune.

As time went on I wondered, "What in the world could bring a beautiful woman like this to be so distrustful of other women and even perfect strangers?" I eventually learned that

Lori had a tumultuous past. Her father abandoned her at a young age. He didn't claim Lori or her siblings and chose to commit to his *other* family. To top it off, he lived in the same city and served as a pastor of a church. Disappointments of yesterday still disservice her life today. Similar to old clothes stuffed in a suitcase and hidden in the back of a closet, Lori's issues display wear and tear, wrinkles, and blemishes of the past. So in efforts to not expose her hurts or trust other women, she hides and hangs out with the guys. Instead of investing in female friendships, her actions suggest this bond isn't worth it. She has become so magnetic to the outer look of success instead of recognizing the inner significance of friendship. Even when the cost is wanting a "When Harry Met Sally" experience so badly, the desire destroys the possibility to bond with incredibly supportive, life-upgrading women.

No Need to Beg, We Just Differ. And it's OK.

You see, many women feel justified with surrounding themselves with only male company. They use this as an excuse because they have not properly dealt with the hurt from a female in the past. Or to compensate for the attention they didn't receive from a man (i.e. father, father figure, or former boyfriend) whom they once admired and depended upon. Some believe hanging with the girls will decrease their chances of being in love one day. So off to the "male hunt for happiness" they go. All the while ignoring the moments to cherish with the chicas and banking all of their hopes on the "Harrys" of the world.

The result of *only* seeking and having guy friends is being relationally deprived, emotionally disappointed, and mentally frustrated. And rightfully so. You shouldn't start believing that men should and will bring the fulfillment only female friends are designed to give. No need to front, no one can take the place of a 100 percent genuine woman.

There's nothing wrong with having male friends. Hallelujah and woohoo for men! I have unbelievable platonic connections with a few guys and I wouldn't trade their insight and ways they've helped me evolve as a woman for anything. After all, the yin needs the yang. Lady Day needs the Noble Knight. Emotion needs logic. Push needs the pull. Freedom needs security. And yet and still, in the realm of friendship, a woman needs relatability and balance.

UCLA researchers Dr. Laura Cousin Klein and Shelley Taylor found through a study "that women, on the other hand [compared to men], are genetically hard-wired for friendship in large part due to the oxytocin released into their bloodstream, combined with the female reproductive hormones. When life becomes challenging, women seek out friendships with other women as a means of regulating stress levels. A common female stress response is to 'tend and befriend.' That is, when women become stressed, their inclination is to nurture those around them and reach out to others . . . friendships between women are special. They shape who we are and who we are yet to be. They soothe our tumultuous inner world, fill the emotional gaps in our marriage, and help us remember who we really are."

9 Differences of Men & Women in Friendships

Reader Alert: Men and women bring remarkable contributions to the table of friendship. The following information is not to promote or condone male bashing. Or to portray inferiority toward men. However, this section highlights the intrinsic attributes women possess and share in friendships.

1. Women are more apt to be open with their personal secrets, lessons learned, and fears in life. Men are typically more private and sparingly give out this information.

2. Women have a tendency to value emotional support in friendships more than men. (i.e. discussing obstacles and overcoming them vs. conversing mainly about similar interests, affiliations, and gloating about competitive instinct).
3. Women are invigorated by the "feeling" of doing things (fulfillment comes by how great it makes her feel). Men focus more on the "action" of doing things and how quickly they can move on to the next task to complete.
4. Women share life experiences and place them as priorities in friendship. Men usually make attainment, hierarchy, and power priority in their interactions.
5. Women are normally reared in childhood to connect. Men are more so raised and groomed to compete.
6. Women desire close connections to have continuity (through the highs, mids, and lows). Men usually focus on loyalty, especially during times of conflict.
7. Women are more apt to ask questions and build rapport. Men usually prefer to "show and tell" information to boost reputation before sharing a bond.
8. Women usually find solutions by sharing problems in a nurturing environment. Men generally approach problems by being direct and aggressively ready to take action without the use of many emotions.
9. Women are more apt to listen to the "unspoken word" (i.e. body language, facial expressions, and gestures). At times, men do not pick up on bodily hints and prefer emotions to be expressed in a verbal manner.

I Can Do Without Her, Right?

Just as sure as fall follows summer and the sky is blue, I have no doubt you've been offended by a female friendship at some point in your life. You may be so devastatingly scarred by these relationships; it seems only an act of God and maybe a law enacted by Congress could make you trust another woman. This is not a healthy state to remain in because whether you like it or not, we were created for more than rocking stilettos, starting businesses, elevating in careers, cooking, smiling through tears, establishing careers, marriage, birthing babies, spraying perfume, and looking fashionable. We are strategically aligned to enjoy and be further developed in friendships with each other.

Here are a few common reasons why some women do not have or even desire good relationships with other women:

- Lack of trust
- Loads of jealousy
- Lots of bitterness (callous heart due to past experiences)
- Lack of self-esteem (comparison game)
- Loss of competitive edge (vying for attention from men)
- Loads of grudges and judgmental attitudes
- Lack of seeing the importance of constructive criticism
- Lots of painful memories of losing a man to another woman

Brownie Point:
Harbored resentment can never lead to happy contentment, especially before commitment with Mr. Right. #CB4C

Victim (Before)	Victim (During)	Victim (After)
People pleasing	Losing identity and boundaries.	Experiencing burnout and being selfish.
Gullibility	Being deceived and manipulated.	Distrusting everyone.
Refusing guidance	Relying on wavering thoughts and emotions.	Inability to receive spiritual wisdom.
Ignoring red flags	Making unstable choices.	Being handcuffed to unhappiness.

Forgiveness: Breaking Out of Prison

Picture yourself willingly driving up to a maximum security prison. You go up to the gate, ask for admittance, and voluntarily decide to live in cell block #C-85354. (Crazy right? But stay with me.) Days, months, and years go by as you survive the dismal deprivation of imprisonment. Until one day you look out of a barred window that allows a limited amount of sunlight in and your breath is taken away. Your heart races. Your eyes tear up. Your throat lumps. Your anxiety rises. All because you see the person who hurt you, *the one you haven't forgiven*, is freer than a bird with two new wings. Thriving without handcuffs of shame or shackles of guilt. Not even thinking twice about the pain they caused you.

When you have an unforgiving heart, it's like being in solitary confinement. A woman who is limited by her own demise. It's downright chaotic to live as a victim while hoping your victimizer, too, is beating their head against the walls of a lonely prison. An unforgiving heart hinders you from friendships which can extraordinarily change the course of your life forever. Marianne Williamson once said, "Forgiveness is not always easy. At times, it feels more painful than the wound we suffered, to forgive the one that inflicted it. And yet, there is no peace without forgiveness." Forgiveness is an interstate, which shifts your inner state, and leads you to elevate beyond the prison of pain.

You may have gone through pain in the past due to some of these reasons. Honestly, I have been down the road of being taken advantage of and close friendships dissolving after my emotional and physical health were berated by one of my girls. There's been times when I put time, energy, and affection in a relationship with a guy only to wind up competing with another woman for his love, and losing. In fact, this tug-o-war match happened to me not once or twice, but three times. And each time ended with him marrying her. I've experienced being the brunt of cruel jokes and being called an array of derogatory names that are in no shape or form included on my birth certificate by a woman. I can also relate to feeling the pressure of not "fitting in" due to my race, size, age, and personality. And in essence, this rejection made me the target of standoffish attitudes which quickly reminded me that I was an official outsider of "the good old girls club." I can recall times when I've had strictly business or platonic relationships with a man, only later to find out that I received a *dishonorable mention* during an argument between him and his girlfriend. All due to her insecurities and perceiving me as a threat to their relationship.

So believe me, when it comes to experiencing pain from other women and regarding other women, I get it. Having your feelings trampled on and wanting to hold on to bitterness is real. I'm not saying you need to be in denial of this pain. But at some point, you have to cut off the stranglehold of distrust and quit allowing the hurt to dictate your destiny. How can you move from chaos to confidence unless forgiveness takes place?

Are You Living as a Victim?

There are various ways to be victimized. Yes by others. But even certain actions you take (like ones in the previous chart two pages back) can lead to victimizing yourself. One action leads to a chain reaction which connects the before, during, and after stages. You can be the main person sabotaging your confidence and delaying your progress toward a brighter future. It's time for you to take responsibility and get out of the prison. After all, you have an avid role to play in your freedom.

I remember the day I decided that I wasn't going to be locked up as a victim anymore. I was through with the hurt and tired of my heart being smothered by discouragement. It was officially time to break the chains of sadness and the desire for (but not getting) revenge after dealing with a hurtful female friendship. Verbally I had forgiven her, but honestly my heart sang a different tune. There's one thing I know about God. He pays close attention to lip service, but he avidly listens to the murmurs of the heart. So I did this exercise to break out of an emotional prison and reclaim my ability to live, laugh, and love again.

Mirror Moment: "Be a Forgive-Her" Exercise

1. Find a place where you're free from distractions and time restrictions. Take a notebook with you. Pick a place where you can think clearly, breathe deeply, and write freely.

2. Ask God for clarity and honesty concerning your deepest thoughts. It might take time to unpack the suitcases of sorrow because you've been suppressing them for so long. So be patient with yourself.

3. Make a list of all the ways she hurt or harmed you. Number each item. Label these the "Pain Points."

4. Read each item aloud.

5. On a separate sheet of paper, go down your list of Pain Points and write down how each pain has helped you be stronger or wiser. Or list the lessons you've learned from the pain. Label these the "Praise Points."

6. Read each item out load.

7. Now in efforts to remember this pain no longer has power over you, destroy the list of Pain Points, but keep the Praise Points. (Honestly, I tore out the Pain Points from my notebook, marched to the kitchen, and burned the piece of paper in the sink. I watched it disintegrate and took a picture of the ashes. Hey, I wanted a visual reminder that the pain was officially down the drain!)

Doing this won't eliminate the painful memories; after all, we are wired with a memory. And it doesn't mean you'll go back to being comfy, close, and cool with that person. However, the pain will no longer stagnate you behind bars.

I understand forgiveness is not the easiest thing to do in the world. However, forgiving someone is a necessary facet of life in order for you to confidently move from a chaotic state, no matter how good you put up a front to hide your emotions. Don't continue thinking that unresolved issues and suppressed hurt inside will never show up or affect you down the line. They will and can even have impacted your relationship with Mr. Right. Get in the groove of releasing and forgiving, because no one is perfect. Your feelings will get hurt in life. Disappointments will come. But having the power to forgive gives you an added boost of power to take authority over the painful baggage and to refuse to be a victim as your destiny lies in chains.

Brownie Point:
Victims give up trying. Victors keep flying. They can't board onto today's flight with yesterday's baggage. #CB4C

4 Key Connections You Need

Within the world of connections, there is a litany of relationships we share with each other as women. However, I want to highlight four kinds of connections you may currently enjoy, will soon establish, or be challenged to think about creating.

Connection #1: The Mentee

We sat next to each other at the stroke of noon on Wednesdays for months. The rise of music welcomed us from across the street into the red-carpeted sanctuary full of wooden pews and stained glass windows that stood the test of time. The intimate setting yielded a coziness similar to the church I grew up in. The creaky floors were reminiscent of my Nana's house on East Monroe Street. People from all walks of life scurry across historic Jefferson Street into Mt. Zion Baptist

Church just to get a midweek fuel-up, to be empowered, or to simply enjoy a break from their boss. During the meet and greet time, I would respectfully turn and give her a hug, and comment on how great she looked in yellow or pink. During the sermons, my mind would yearn to concentrate but often would shift into thinking of my ongoing to-do list and the items begging to be crossed off. Her focus was unwavering, she would take notes as a freshman in college determined to maintain a scholarship. (I later found out she took notes on behalf of her grown children who are at work. What an amazing mother.) Honestly, I don't know when Mrs. Stratton and I started digging deeper to know each other. Perhaps, it was when I told her about my business appointments within the Metro Nashville government and realized I've known two of her daughters for years. Or perhaps, it was when I missed several Wednesdays due to long distance trips for work and upon returning she shared with me how much my smile and energetic spirit always picked her up.

But one particular day, we started talking about marriage and relationships. Deep inside of me a chord was struck and I listened to her. Every syllable coming out of her mouth had me silenced. I was in awe of how gently yet respectfully she spoke about her husband, even though he passed away several years before. Long before e-Harmony, Match.com, chat lines, texting, swiping, and speed dating, she was privy to good old-fashioned pursuit. Her husband pursued, courted, married, cherished, and provided for her as well as their seven children.

After multiple conversations, I finally mustered up the courage and asked her to be my mentor. I realized what a treasure it would be to have an eighty-four-year-old woman to be a relationship mentor while I actively waited for my Mr. Right. Mrs. Stratton said yes and that she would try her best (it was a new venture for her). Yet ever since then my life has been remarkably enriched. Even to this day, I'll call her up to check on her and she'll freely impart knowledge and wisdom. We've celebrated birthdays regularly together and have officially declared the restaurant Rafferty's as "our spot." I love how she affectionately claims me as another daughter. I have claimed her as a woman whom I look up to as a love trailblazer. God willing, she's someone that my man will get a stamp of approval from (she's on my mandatory list for him to meet) before solidifying covenant. I can't imagine these last couple years of singlehood without seeing her strength and hearing her stories of challenges and triumphs up close and personal. She doesn't hide or flinch at questions I ask her. Her heart is an open book as she shares mistakes and missteps, all with the hope that I won't make the same ones. This vibrant woman is an amazing reminder of what rock steady commitment to God, husband, and family truly is. Mrs. Stratton has become an unexpected, yet necessary "fuel up" along my journey to Mr. Right. She's simply a woman whose love and faithfulness I long to emulate.

Mentors don't have to be confined to the area of romance and Mr. Right. There are a variety of areas you can be mentored in, such as education, community service, career development, talent/performance, spiritual guidance, physical health, emotional support, financial aptitude, marriage, motherhood, time management, and a plethora of other areas. There's a common myth of believing you can only have one mentor, and she must mentor you in every facet of life. Not true! No one woman has it all or knows it all. Plus this can be very overwhelming for a potential mentor. Proverbs 11:14 states, "Without wise leadership, a nation falls; there is safety in having many advisers."

Brownie Point:
Confident queens lead whether by personal choice or election. They help the next generation of royalty know they're top-shelf selection. #CB4C

I had the opportunity to meet and hear a powerfully influential woman speak. Her name is Connie Lindsey. As a former National Board President of Girls Scouts USA, she states this about mentoring: "I believe that each of them not only has something that I can work with them on, but I learn from them. And so one of my favorite sayings is the good deeds I do for others is the rent I pay for occupying space on the earth and every month I want to renew my lease."

Being mentored is a give-and-give relationship. You should never try to live life on your own! Every woman needs to hold the hand of someone who is several steps *ahead* of her, a mentor. At the same time she needs to hold the hand of someone else who is several steps *behind* her, a mentee. Receiving the time, love, attention, and wisdom from an excellent mentor should not only benefit you but also inspire you to share with another woman or girl who needs a helping hand as well.

Mirror Moment:

Identify a woman who is pouring wisdom, nourishment, and a listening ear during this season of your life.

Make an effort to connect or meet up with a woman who will do the same as you move into a new season of life.

Connection #2: The Mentor

Leadership is not always a position you jump out of your seat for, especially as you get older and analyze what leading entails. Many times others see leadership capabilities in you before you do. I used to shy away from titles and declared responsibilities. Back in my elementary and junior high days, the teacher would announce when nominations were open for class president, student council positions, and club elections. When it was time for the nominations to roll in, hands would shoot up, and I would scoot down in my chair and intentionally refuse to make any eye contact with anyone. But somehow, my name would end up on the chalkboard or on the ballot. Soon after I was selected to lead. At the young age of eleven, I was chosen to be the lead musician and director of the children's choir at church. A few years later, I started directing the youth choir and later playing for state convention choirs. Eventually I was president over school choirs and traveling out of state as a lead musician for theatrical choirs. Later as an adult, I was presented the Young Woman of the Year Award by Marilyn Quayle, the wife of former United States Vice President Dan Quayle.

No matter how hard I tried to dim my light and hide in the shadows, I kept getting called to center stage to lead. To make decisions. To give creative advice for a variety of causes and organizations doing national and international work. I had to finally accept being *singled out* to serve others through leadership.

Several years ago I co-founded a community initiative in which I spoke to an array of female students at colleges through She Power Rocks. Time passed and one day I heard individuals were needed for the Ladies of Virtue (L.O.V.) mentoring program at my church. Now it's one thing to speak to people using a mic on stage but it's quite different to feel worthy enough to speak into their personal lives as a mentor.

Honestly, some of my worst grades in school were receiving an "N" for talking too much. Lord knows, I've always had a knack for being "bossy, talkative, an advisor, or just a big sister to call up for raw truth." I've even had friends visit me and the next you know they are lying on a couch and I'm asking them questions while they unpack suitcases of secrets and vulnerabilities (as if I'm a practicing psychiatrist). But for some reason, I wrestled with the shameful thoughts of not being good enough to mentor someone else. What if I say the wrong thing? Am I really qualified to be a mentor? *How much do I have to sacrifice? What if I don't know an answer to a personal issue?*

Dr. Brene Brown once stated in her TED Talk: "That's what life is about. About daring greatly and being in the arena. When you walk up to that arena and you put your hand on the door and think, 'I'm going in and I'm going to try this,' shame is the gremlin that says, 'Uh huh. You're not good enough' . . . And if we can quiet it down and walk in and say, 'I'm going to do this,' we look up and the critic we see pointing and laughing, 99 percent of the time is who? Us. Shame drives two big tapes: Never good enough, and Who do you think you are?"

But moving past my fears with an overwhelming peace to go ahead and serve, I took the plunge and applied to be a mentor with L.O.V. For the several years, I witnessed a variety of young ladies learning from one-night stands, family challenges, fights over guys, depression, alcoholism, being indecisive about their future, and learning to find their voice. All because I was willing to be a mentor. Willing to listen and in return learn. I learned I didn't need to have all the answers, I just needed to be present and available. The answers of wisdom and advice came when needed. Nothing compares to the heart-to-heart talks I've shared with women during such a pivotal time of life, like college life. The late-night talk with Gina about her roommates working her last nerve and challenging her spiritual beliefs was unforgettable.

Encouraging Delisha when she was overwhelmed with leadership obligations and earning respect among peers was priceless. Getting to the root of why Angie kept getting drunk and having sex with guys for attention was powerful. Helping Brandy realize the value of standing up for herself and voicing her opinion was an honor. Telling Rana she is a diamond and worth a man getting his shovel out and digging beyond the surface to respect how she shines still blesses me.

Special moments like these remind a mentee *"You're not alone."* Mentoring is about personally looking into another woman's eyes. And being there to uplift especially when her mind is baffled, her heart is torn between two directions, or her overzealous outlook may need a serious dose of reality.

Brownie Point:
The best benefits aren't linked to an *insurance* policy, but an *assurance* policy you've helped someone attain their best in life. #CB4C

Connection #3: The Mutual

As you evolve as a woman, your expectations and fulfillment in friendships drastically change. You probably still have some core values you've carried from days of playing neighborhood tag, slumber parties, and enjoying pink cotton candy at the fair. Whether you're in college or progressing in your career, you probably still admire honesty, commonality, trust, and respect when sharing a bond with another woman.

On the journey of life we can have mentors (steps ahead of us) and mentees (steps behind us). But nothing can take the place of having a woman walking right beside you. A woman you know who is in the trenches with you. She shares some of those foundational qualities from back in the day yet she's evolving right along with you in your present state of life. Anyone that knows me or even sees me from afar can sense I'm a people person and typically don't meet a stranger. (I recently met a guy who asked me if I was from the country. I guess he thought I was a bright-eyed, back-woods bumpkin who was seeing the city for the first time due to my friendliness. Clearly he was mistaken. I'm just a city chick who likes to see new faces and new places.)

To say my life has been blessed with one of my closest friends on the planet, Tia, would be a gross understatement. Being on a college tour and receiving a scholarship to Tennessee State University brought me to Nashville. Tia arrived to the campus by way of Michigan a little after I did. We didn't become formally acquainted with each other until post-TSU days. I was in a musical group, Descendants of Reality, and Tia was a spoken word artist. We shared stages from B. B. King's to a variety of universities, churches, and festivals. We were both avid supporters of each other's artistic expression. I even produced a song on one of her past albums. Time went on and she got married and started having children. In retrospect, I see God effortlessly taking two pieces of fabric and gently sowing us together in sisterhood without us having a clue until 2009.

That was a pivotal year for both of us. She was transitioning into motherhood with her third child and I was on the brink of transitioning from my music group (which had been together for more than ten years). It was kind of like two people being in the same corporation, working under the same roof, but not until a specific project comes about do they get the opportunity to really meet. Tia and I don't have to talk on the phone every day. We don't hang out every weekend shopping and ogling over the latest MAC eyeshadows, Godiva chocolates, or studded stilettos. We don't have regular gab fests about the latest reality TV shows or the hottest celebrity hookups.

However, we have a sisterhood connection that is so unbeatable, I wouldn't trade it for the scarcest of riches in the world. When we get together it's typically for hours. With her, the pressure to persuade and prove myself is off. The "Don't let them see you sweat" mask isn't needed. I can be weak and she can be strong, and vice versa. I'm flabbergasted how we can talk about anything and everything in between. I suppose we've shared an enormous litany of conversations about physical insecurities, family changes, relationship mistakes, career apprehensions, personal vices, our resilient faith in God, and the visions we are working into reality. Honestly, I don't think You Are Singled Out would be in existence without her foundational encouragement and support as my trusted confidant. (After all, Tia was the first person I felt confident enough to share the vision with and how nervously excited I was about the "big picture.") I absolutely am grateful for the ability to worship God openly together (no restraint, no music, no pep talks, no premeditated itinerary). Talking about Jesus ushers us to the most wonderful front-row seat view of seeing his beauty and grace reflected in each other. The ebb and flow of our genuine sisterhood is not something you experience as a norm or with lots of people. No, it's a rare commodity, far more valuable than friendships based on handouts, hookups, and hidden agendas. I can't ever recall a time in the last several years where we've departed from each other and not come away being better, wiser, mightier, and brighter.

"Two people are better off than one, for they can help each other succeed. If one person falls, the other can reach out and help. But someone who falls alone is in real trouble." (Ecclesiastes 4:9-10) No matter what stage of life you may be in, you need to have at least one mutual friend. These relationships help to bring you down to earth when your head is in the clouds of fantasy. Sister-friends love you through your

good, bad, and ugly moods. They help you find solutions when you've made that bone-headed mistake, again. You can tell your innermost secrets and aspirations and bet your bottom dollar they won't be front-page news tomorrow. Sister-friends can serve as a getaway, when you're emotionally drained from the demands of other relationships.

Mutual relationships can even benefit your connection with Mr. Right by yielding balance. Sometimes you'll need to take a break from each other and enjoy QT with your girls while he's out with the guys. Don't get it misconstrued. A man can't fulfill every single void in your life, one primary role being your sister-friend. I highly suggest you don't become so engrossed in getting a man and isolate the need for a mutual sister-friend(s) out the window. Believe me, you need their support, care, trust, and love now. And you'll need them when you are united with Mr. Right.

Mirror Moment:

Who are at least two women in your life right now that sincerely love and support you to be your best?

How do you feel when you're around them (caged in or free)?

Connection #4: The Move Maker

This kind of relationship is one I respect increasingly more while being a woman on a mission to make a difference in the world. I often say, "A dream takes a team" and no matter what you desire to do in life, you can't do it alone. But there are pivotal people that come in certain seasons of your life and are strategically placed to push you to the next level.

Move makers are typically not your BF, your friend who's always ready to party, or someone who you consistently call just to chat. These connections exist because each of you are motivated to move forward. They stir up momentum in achieving goals you used to just sit on the sidelines and wish for. Move makers don't show up empty-handed and are not known for being plagued with the "I just need a hookup" syndrome. They are dedicated to working alongside people for mutual advancement in their respective fields, classes, careers, industries, etc. Their mindsets are focused on progressing and being a part of the solution. They're not consumed with living a dull life or complaining about what should be or could be. Proverbs 27:17 states: "As iron sharpens iron, so a friend sharpens a friend."

Move makers can show up unexpectedly, but when they do make sure you don't take it for granted. Seasons with move makers can last for fifteen minutes or fifteen years. Believe me, I've had numerous times when I met someone who was influential in their industry and clearly on their way to blazing trails as a world changer. But due to my insecurities about not being good enough, or afraid of them finding out I'm not "on their level yet," I let the connection convert into a lost opportunity. This led to dealing with the residue of regret. But. Not. Any. More. They're human and they bleed blood just like you and me.

So seize the opportunity to step out of your comfort zone and ask a move maker to meet up over coffee. Be willing to wait in line for an extra hour to get your business card or product in their hands. You never know, this could result in a life-changing connection. One thing I've learned about faith is this: *faith moves, faith is bold, faith is relentless, and faith believes in taking a breather later when you're around move makers.*

A few years ago I was at a chamber of commerce luncheon and I met a very special move maker friend, Megan. She is the founder of Doing Good, a nonprofit organization dedicated to promoting volunteerism. Their mission is to inspire, educate, and connect people and nonprofits throughout communities to do good. Megan and I conversed for a while, exchanged cards, and spoke of keeping in contact (the usual song and dance at networking events).

As time passed, Megan's vision expanded into bringing Nashville's Volunteer of the Month (NVOTM) on the radio. She remembered my experience with doing years of radio/TV voiceover work for the McDonald's Corporation. Months later she introduced me to a radio station host and I became dubbed as "the voice of NVOTM" and did live radio interviews of selected volunteers being honored. After a couple of months of seeing Megan's consistency with handling her business affairs, I asked for a meeting with her concerning Y.A.S.O. Within our various meetings, we've exchanged numerous business contacts acquired over the years. We have talked about business strategies for each entity. We've conversed about the struggles of motivating yourself when no one is looking over your shoulder.

Brownie Point:
Opportunity knocks. But you have to be ready to answer and sometimes open a window if necessary. #CB4C

It can be very challenging being a single woman who is a visionary. You often yearn to have a supportive sound board, someone to share the joy of finding a new business concept, and gain immediate feedback. Move makers can help to fill some voids because they can relate and empathize with compassion and action. Megan has shared books, ideas, and "dreamscape" moments with me. Having a move maker in my life like her has truly provided a rush of energy in completing my first book *Sane in a Sex Filled World* and an audio project on iTunes entitled, *10 of the Biggest Mistakes Single Women Make & How to Avoid Them.*

Make no mistake about it. All of us often need a push or a friendly nudge that says, "Girl, I see you're getting complacent." "C'mon this is your moment, seize it and run." When we're stuck in a rut or caught in a web of emotions, our goals can seem far-fetched and unattainable. But just like a marathon runner who is in last place pushing with all her might to finish the last two miles, a move maker can show up beside you with a burst of fresh energy. Just seeing them in action gets you moving faster toward the finish line and elevating higher in life.

Mirror Moment:

Who are you currently spending time with that motivates you to achieve your ambitions and turn plans into action?

Try to Trust . . . Again

Hopefully, you can see how significant female friendships are and ways they contribute to your destiny even before Mr. Right. Newfound confidence to lead, follow, share, and motivate other women is yours for the taking. Don't be afraid to forgive so you can gravitate toward wholeness and possess an optimistic perspective of sister-friends. Make a decision to quit trying to appease haters and naysayers who do nothing but downgrade you. Having trust in someone else isn't always built overnight. However, trust is a muscle that calls for intentional flexing day by day. So open your heart and connect! You still have mountains to climb and pinnacles to celebrate. You have miles to travel and unknown adventures to experience. Navigating through your life will be easier and even more fulfilling when you get beyond *just hanging out with the guys*.

Chaos to Confidence

7 Reminders about Establishing Friendships

1. **F**riendly people make friends. You often attract the energy you give off.
2. **R**elease pre-conceived notions. You can't always detect a friend at first sight.
3. **I**nitiate and invite others to meet up and converse about goals or hang out to have fun.
4. **E**ncourage her to keep going when she's weak and cheer her on when she's strong.
5. **N**ote her special interests, dislikes, and favorite ways to relax. Every woman needs someone to invest in her getting pampered and celebrated.
6. **D**on't be afraid of transparency. Openness about trials and triumphs bring people closer.
7. **S**eek to share solutions. Refrain from any friendship which constantly drains and discourages you.

CHAPTER 6

WALKING IN STILETTOS VS. HIGH HILLS

STILETTOS. THEY ARE THE CAPTIVATING SOURCE THAT GIVES US women an excuse to shop online for hours or stop by the store on the way home from a long day at work, come rain or shine. Their magnetic charm causes men to stop, stare, and admire our ability to flip the switch of sensual appeal on and simultaneously give our calves a workout. Favored as one of the most precious collections a woman owns, high-heeled shoes have actually been in existence since the 16th century.

Several years ago, Galeries Lafayette in Paris (which stocks 12,000 pairs of shoes) was massively outnumbered and outdone with Macy's Herald Square. Hailed as the largest shoe store in the world, it holds an impressive 300,000 pairs of shoes in a 63,000-square-foot facility. If that's not impressive enough, the store offers customers *champagne and a chocolate bar* to recoup after their shoe escapade. Wowzers. I'm sure some ladies have literally dreamed of ripping up their lease or mortgage and moving as a permanent live-in customer. After all shoes, bubbly, and chocolate galore might take some of the edge off of monthly cramps, Friday night loneliness, family and friend challenges, and nerve wrecking demands from work.

True, our heartbeats race. Our eyes sparkle with excitement. And the shoe boxes we stack by the nearest floor mirror makes decision making seem like a skill set beyond our grasp. Don't get me wrong, there's nothing wrong with being chic and fashionable from head to toe.

However, I think we long for a *deeper sense of elevation* even when we walk through the aisles of multi-colored and gravity-challenging stilettos. We want to reach a pinnacle beyond what a shoe boutique or department store can provide. Deep within our souls there's a yearning for greatness within leadership. To be on a pedestal of dignity and honor. We desire to be trailblazers worthy of acknowledgement and attained achievement.

So what seems to stop you from moving past the infatuation of high heels and being an influential leader on high hills?

5 Common Fears Women Have with High Hills

(Leadership)

1. These shoes are too big for me. (How can I handle this role? I'm afraid of falling, even more so failing.)
2. These are not my shoes. (Am I really cut out to be a leader? How can I compete with the person who used to do this?)
3. These shoes take more experience and credentials than what I have. (Am I qualified? Do I have the necessary training to be successful?)

4. This is the right shoe, but it's on the wrong foot. (Am I going to look foolish? What will others think of me?)
5. This seems like the wrong timing for these shoes. (Why did this opportunity have to come now? Am I really ready? I don't think I'm good enough yet.)

Leaving the Leader in You Behind

There's a fight within us. A bout I kept running into as a child. I was regularly perceived and called, "bossy, too talkative, and strong-willed or assertive." But as I grew older and went into middle school and junior high, my voice got suffocated under the fear of speaking up. I didn't want to seem foolish, so I didn't ask questions until after class. I shied away from being elected as a class official (although I typically was voted in). Speaking in front of the class was a bit agonizing, since I loathed the width of my hips, the thickness of my glasses, and even the color of my skin since I was the only African American in my class from preschool to ninth grade. But I kept being told I was different. I wasn't like the other girls. I was chosen to be *singled out*.

But being passionate about leadership, loving myself, and accepting my voice were layers of life that took me a long time to travel through. And I'm not the only one. When Rachel Simmons, co-founder of the Girls Leadership Institute, asked girls about leadership, there were varied answers. "Thirteen-year-old Julia played rambunctiously with friends, yet in class, her sentences trailed off. 'I feel like if I sound stupid or say the wrong thing, people won't like me,' she said. Another girl struggled to complete an exercise in which she was asked to list her talents and strengths to a group. 'I don't want people to think I'm conceited,' she said. Then, I asked the girls how they felt about leadership. As I ran through a list of skills—public speaking, debating an opinion, interviewing for a job—the girls' comments remained constant. 'Getting judged' was their worst fear."

According to Julie Zeilinger in *Why Millennial Women Do Not Want to Lead*, "We feel that we need to excel in our academic lives, maintain perfect romantic relationships and—above all else—maintain perfect bodies that match or rival those that are plastered in the media . . . Young women today are bred to doubt ourselves, question our worth and view ourselves as improvable projects rather than embrace the imperfection of our humanity. According to the *Dove Real Beauty Campaign*, 42 percent of first- to third-grade girls want to be thinner. Eighty percent of ten-year-old American girls say they have been on a diet. Fifty-three percent of 13-year-old girls are unhappy with their bodies—a number that increases to 78 percent by age 17. By the time we're old enough to seriously consider becoming leaders, the majority of us are crippled by insecurities about the way we look, which we internalize and equate with our sense of worth on all levels."

Wow. Not only are young girls struggling with the weight of perfection and fear of ridicule, but I see this in many adult women as well. This mindset of leaving the leader inside behind is certainly a devastating trend that robs the world of some of its finest jewels: women in leadership. It cripples societies and hinders nations.

Nowadays the fight that once was within, is outside of me. I now fight for young ladies who need confidence in using their voice in life and in love. Once finding my purpose, I realized my voice was the unmistakable audio print no one else has and it was given to me for leading others. And it's the necessary vehicle to shed the light of truth to persuade women to not lose their identity or integrity for the sake of a chaotic or toxic relationship. And guess what? I'm getting praised now for some of those qualities I once was punished for as a little girl. They are now some of my most valuable assets. I've had to use my mind and my mouth to win eight scholarships upon graduating from high school. My assertiveness has been useful while negotiating business contracts with state governments, private corporations, completing a proposal for NASA, and even getting the best deal for my SUV. The tone of my voice and my talkativeness is now admired in speeches, relationship panels, radio interviewing, and as a voiceover artist for the McDonald's Corporation.

You may be facing battles of inadequacy or inferiority right now. But I'm daring enough to believe you want to elevate in areas that even a pair of Manolo Blahniks won't be able to get you there. Sure, you may be stylishly stepping out and making every sidewalk you grace an instant runway. However, you can have shoes for days, *but your feet are absolutely going nowhere in life*. You can have a mountain of shoes in your closet, *yet be absolutely clueless about what's needed to climb high hills and lead in life*.

I love classic boxing and there's many life lessons you can learn from the sport. I once heard this on HBO Boxing special before the heavily anticipated Mayweather vs. Pacquiao fight coined as the *Battle for Greatness*: "You wouldn't want to ponder a world without fighters. You wouldn't want to ponder a world where everyone simply settled for the easy way out. There would be so much less to intrigue you. So much less to inspire you. There would be so many fewer great stories to tell. All legendary fighters have the same simple way of rising to the top. They do the same things over and over again. It's how they cultivate their gifts, it's how they tell everyone else who they are, and embrace a world where there's always something to fight for."

Don't abandon the fight inside of you to gain direction and be a leader. Don't allow past cynicism or present haterism to dampen your passion in reaching high hills. Or better yet the place of elevation that overshadows the hottest pair of high heels in sight.

Rising Up to Draw Battle Lines

There once was a woman named Deborah who lived high in the remote mountains of Ephraim. She was a leader whose office was under a palm tree. So you could say, "She had it made in the shade." People would climb the rugged terrain and weather the arduous journey for miles just to gain her advice on troubling matters of the heart. They would seek her counsel to be freed from frustration. Although she helped to settle disputes which produced mental and emotional troubles, the people were still physically held in bondage by an evil king named Jabin. One day she summoned Barak, an officer of the army, to come and receive battle tactics to take down Jabin's mighty army and his top commander, Sisera. He quickly obliged. She just had that kind of swag to make special requests along with a reputation to respect. Her insight was such a tremendous asset. For you see, Barak wouldn't set one foot into battle without her presence and wisdom. After hearing her reveal the strategy for victory he replied, *"If you go with me, I will go; but if you don't go with me, I won't go."*

Now let's hold it right there. As a leader who sat in a lofty mountainous area (free from the stains of blood, strains of war, and stench of death), Deborah could have easily told Barak, "Excuse me? Uh, sir, did you forget who I am and the position I hold? People come *up* to me instead of me going *down* to them. On top of that, what in the world do I look like joining troops on the battlefield?"

Deborah could have sat under her palm tree on a pillow of pride. She could have rolled her eyes, sucked her teeth, put her hands on hips, and got some serious neck rolling action in as well. But you know what? She decided to say, "I will go with you." On the battlefield, Deborah instinctively used her spiritual compass to inform Barak of a strategy that led to victory. She humbled herself to serve for the greater good. She aligned herself with divine timing to strike against the enemy. You see, a woman who submits to the Highest Authority, gets the support of allies, and the surrender of enemies.

When the official victory was declared, Deborah refused to strut with a sole of pride, but influentially took a stand on her *high hills*. In this sense, high hills don't symbolize a place geologically, but a place of leadership. This historic moment called for a decision to be made: be someone who will help others stay in bondage or secure a breakthrough. Deborah recognized she was placed on high hills to free her people. Her humility to join the troops ignited so much power, every single person on the enemy's side was defeated. And that led to another woman, Jael, rising up to personally eliminate Sisera. In the end, instead of being a leader who sang the blues of bondage, Deborah sang a beautiful song, which reflected the journey from trial to triumph.

Mirror Moment:

When has pride ruined a relationship or caused you to abandon an opportunity to lead?

What doors do you see opening when a leader is not consumed with just looking good but pursues the greater good?

Let me be real with you. There will be times when you are asked to engage in a battle or resolve an issue between two disagreeing parties. Sometimes you won't feel like stepping away from your title, office, or agenda to help the team. You might not always have the right answers, right away. But leadership is not just about looking the part, it's about playing your part. It's about giving deliberate support and not just stopping by when it's convenient for you. As a leader you'll realize many "inconveniences" were divinely mapped out to test the truest intent of your heart.

Deborah confided in God and counsel before drawing up a battle plan to lead an army and impact a nation. So remember to never accelerate without acumen. Also keep in mind, victories can't be attained by your team stepping up while you insist on not showing up. You want to possess a posture similar to Deborah. One void of panic and definitely without pride. You too are capable of standing up with poise and patience while seizing your leadership potential.

Learning the importance of balance now will help you endure far less blisters and decrease the amount of times you step on other people's toes! You're not called to allow others to abuse and stomp all over your toes either! My desire for you is to count more victories than calculating defeats. So make sure you regularly check the status of your soul, because it will inevitably guide the path of your sole.

Brownie Point:
High heels elevate and look stylishly cute, but humility walks on high hills with striking confidence. #CB4C

A Fairy Tale Fit for You

Do you remember reading or watching the whimsical fairy tale of Cinderella? As a little girl, I remember going to a tall brown bookcase located in the warmest room of the house. Out of all of the Little Golden Books, this story had me more so captivated by her elegant evening gown and dancing with a prince at the ball. In fact, it influenced me so much that when I was six and my mom was pregnant, I told people I wanted a little brother so I could have a dance partner. Subconsciously, I must have been prepping for Mr. Right even then. However, I was blessed with my incredible sister, Christina, who is a beautiful leader within Rite Quality, the company my father established over twenty-seven years ago. And I wouldn't trade her for all the riches, gowns, balls, and dances in the world.

Just like a salesperson goes back to the inventory to find our shoe size, let's go back through the inventory of this story to discover the shoes a leader has to able to fit. Seriously, the power is way beyond a lost glass slipper.

Cinderella wasn't elevated into position of publicized favor and admiration overnight. At the beginning of the story she is literally trying to survive around three drama queens who were highly jealous of her. Her stepmother and stepsisters were extremely abusive. They made her work overtime doing menial labor, which kept her bound to the house. In extended versions of this tale, she is given the name Cinderella because of her spending nights in front of the fireplace to keep warm. When she would awake, cinders (or ashes) would be all over her. And therefore prompting the tease-filled name, Cinderella.

Even when the Prince announced he was hosting a ball in efforts of finding a bride, she was not considered as a love prospect. She was left in everyday rags, a pile of tears, and a fresh list of household chores that should have been evenly divided among her stepsisters.

But then along comes her fairy godmother who answers her distressful cries and comes to her rescue with renewed hope. In the process, Cinderella is transformed to such a degree, not even those who live under the same roof recognize her at first glance. So how does this relate to you today? Your reality may have more in common with this fairy tale than you think. Here's a few takeaways for you to remember looking at *Cinderella before her fella.*

Your Worth is Valuable

Like Cinderella, you may have grown up in an abusive household, where physical scars still remind you of painful memories. Or you were called hurtful names as a child. And even though you're grown, you still haven't outgrown the verbal insults which echo in your head every day. Perhaps no one nurtured your confidence and helped you achieve your dreams. So mentally you struggle with the complexities of: *Am I good enough? Can this really come true for me?*

However, none of us get to have do overs with our childhood. We often rewind the past in our minds, but there's no reliving the past in real time. Like Cinderella, there are times when it seems people have left you in the ashes (or the dust). To be forgotten. To be abandoned. To be the recipient of abuse they tolerated and haven't healed from. To be a slave to their insecurities.

But you are not forgotten! You're not banished to a lifetime of emptiness and agony! You are a powerhouse packed with possibilities turning into realities. Dismiss the habit of believing your goals, self-esteem, and leadership capabilities are worthless. The lasting impact and appreciation of a leader is often birthed by one enduring hardships first. In essence, the tenacity is shown before the title is given.

All of the battles you overcame took an enormous amount of strength. Courage to love when hate wanted to lash out. Willpower to move forward alone when others kept company with misery. Generosity when you felt depleted and needed someone to pour into you. Dedication when everything in you wanted to walk away and take the easy way out. All of these are characteristics of a leader on the rise.

As a leader, value your worth even when others despise or miscomprehend it. You can alleviate a lot of stress, when you quit trying to cater to every single person's actions and reactions to your elevation. Cinderella had to first accept she was chosen by her godmother and worthy enough to be a participator, not just a spectator. She had to block out all the nasty words that were attempting to limit her from reaching her life path (which later included the prince pursuing her and choosing her to be princess). This is not an easy thing to do as a woman, because we're highly sensitive to what we hear. But one thing I've learned in life is this: *People are going to talk. Whether you do good or bad, people are going to talk about you.* Bottom line, you have to keep learning, leading, and living your life, because some people will just never be satisfied with anything you do. Don't let full time drama starters and dream snatchers allow your worth to dissipate into thin air. You've been through too much, not to be ALL you were created to be. Especially when you've been called to lead.

Brownie Point:
Working overtime to change someone's attitude about your altitude, makes you lose an opportunity to grow in fortitude. #CB4C

Your Cry for Help is Heard

There are days when it seems like you're last on the totem pole. Like the upward climb is as wide as the Atlantic Ocean and longer than the Nile River. Sometimes I feel like the walls are caving in due to surmounting responsibilities I have to take care of as a woman pushing to do more and be greater. Cinderella cried out and her godmother came to comfort her and changed her circumstance. Well, when the bottom is dropping out and the walls are caving in, you too can cry out for help. Instead of a fairy godmother, God the Father has ears that are always ready to listen. When people don't see the traces of your tears (behind the smile you publicly reveal), God does. No tear you cry is left unnoticed, my friend. No amount of anxiety about your love life, finances, working on that innovation or organization, or handling leadership is beyond his radar.

When family, friends, co-workers, boyfriends, or crushes don't zoom into the deepest part of your heart and pay you attention, cry out to God and you'll certainly have undivided attention. Supernaturally, he's the greatest refuge that will attend your every need. Why? Because he has the power to rescue you and prepare you for an amazing transformation. Like Cinderella, you'll go through a transformation that leaves you better than when you first cried out. I'm talking about tears of sorrow, turned into tears of elation.

I know firsthand about being overwhelmed when a project, an event, or vision assignment seems too hard to do from where you presently stand. Sometimes the picture is too broad. The to-do list is too long. Your mind is working overtime from the time you wake up to the time you lay down. In these times, you must reach out for advisors, mentors, and vision strategists that can provide insight. You might take a workshop, go to a conference, visit a business center, or invite someone who's experienced in what you're facing out to coffee. They often can look at the big picture and dissect it into bite-size pieces. Then you can feel more encouraged to elevate with direction instead of being lost in a jungle of demands you feel must be done by last week.

Pay Off is in Your Patience

Cinderella did what many women fail to do. She refused to rush and flaunt her transformation in a conceited way. She still had to exercise patience. Even though she attended the ball, left her slipper, and had to watch other women vie for her rightful place as princess. Her promotion as princess did not come about due to her running in the streets crying, "Step to the side and back up, ladies. Hey Mr. Prince, let me just cut to the chase. Remember, I was the one you were holding tight and grooving with the other night. So hand over the slipper, it's mine, and I'm the dream girl you're looking for."

Nope, she held on to her dignity with patience and allowed the prince to pursue her. Even when she reported back to work, she didn't allow a mouth full of pride to get the best of her. She knew her worth being publicly identified as the dream girl in due time. You have to give the girl props. Cinderella exhibited traits of a leader. Way before glass slippers entered the picture, she was already standing on her *high hills*. Having a heart of humility launched her higher and further than her stepmother and sisters could ever hope to be. Eventually her abusers adored her. Enemies became footstools. The last became the first, and the first became last. She went from rockin' rags to glass slippers. From sleeping in front of a fire to slipping into the arms of a prince who saw her rise above her circumstances as a strong woman. And on top of that he was Mr. Ready—ready to wholeheartedly commit to her!

The beauty of this story shouldn't only be centered on Cinderella getting a man and living happily ever after. But the big payoff was in how she evolved as a leading lady without the center of her heart becoming impatiently resentful. No, I dare to say her *happily ever after* altitude began with a *happily in spite of* attitude from the beginning.

Brownie Point:
Leadership should be accommodated with patience and wisdom, or it's bound to become a spectacle of glorified weakness. #CB4C

A Custom Fit for Your Soul

Now we've discussed stilettos and what it takes to be confident as a leader on high hills. But your ambitions to lead are not the highlight of this section. It's not about judging where the soles of your feet have gone or where they have led you. And if you choose to stride past this section, there's no pressure. It's okay. But I hope you'll read on.

Take it from me. My feelings have led my feet to look for love in all the wrong places. I've experienced blisters that no Good Feet store on earth could come close to relieving. I willingly signed up for pain by doing more footwork to appease a man who wouldn't even meet me halfway, much less be faithful to me. I have had sore feet as a result of going after guys that were never meant to be mine. Perhaps, you've been here, too. You may believe a fairy tale is the closest you'll ever come towards experiencing the elevation of real love.

Yes, Cinderella had glass slippers that were a custom fit for her sole. But you, my friend are entitled to have a *custom fit for your soul*. I wasted time and went through bouts of sadness due to frivolous chases and trying to force my foot into shoes (relationships) that were never meant for me to fill. Until I found a love willing to melt the pain away. His name is Jesus. He accepted me in spite of my bad decisions, prideful resistance, and bruised feet. He invited me to look at life beyond my high heels (the outward look of a woman who had it together, but was stumbling and falling inwardly). My eyes were opened to see how his love led the way when he died for us on the highest hill of all, Calvary.

Please do not get his love misconstrued. You can fit your soles into the world's finest shoes by Vince Camuto or Christian Louboutin. And God won't stop loving you because of your ongoing shoe collection. You could be addicted to Snapchat, had hookups, and had sex with men from here to Australia. God will amazingly tie a bow of love around you himself, restore you to wholeness, and still present you worthy of being loved by Mr. Right. Or you may have made costly mistakes as a leader. He'll lead you to a place where you can depend on him, forgive yourself, and regain trust from those you lead. God absolutely cares and wants to love your pain, shame, regret, and anxiety away. It doesn't matter. Blisters. Baggage. Buried secrets. Bruised feet. Blind eyes. Broken heart. His love is real. And it's a custom fit for your soul which far outweighs any fairy tale.

If the Shoe Fits, Should You Wear It?

In life, in leadership, and in love, you have the right to choose what shoe you'll wear or better yet how you'll handle the responsibility in that territory. You also will have to live with the consequences of your choice. The charts of Miss Hellavation and Miss Elevation describe two women who leave distinctly different footprints on the runway of life. Their footwear profiles indicate how they handle heights and leadership. One leaves the footprint of a "prideful path maker" and the other

Miss Hellavation	Sole Intention	Soul Issues
Stilettos	Stabs others in the back.	Tactics become dull and she's replaced.
Mules	Kicks backs, slides in, then takes credit.	Cover is blown and rapport is lost.
Slingbacks	Grips failure and is unforgiving of mistakes.	Loses control and intimacy with others.
Flats	Stays comfy and ignores other's hurt.	Doesn't realize she'll one day need help.
Pumps	Favors those who pump up her ego.	Can't see who truly loves her, not her title.
Wedges	Gradually opens herself to being ill-advised.	Leadership skin isn't weatherproof.
Platforms	Acts superficial to attain status and power.	Prestige is unstable and rep is ruined.
Boots	Disguises her true identity behind the position.	Withholds pain and has emotional blisters.

Miss Elevation	Sole Intention	Soul Impact
Stilettos	Rises to be a respected leader.	Has vision of solutions and brighter horizons.
Mules	Contributes by sharing past trials and triumphs.	Uses honesty to relate and empower.
Slingbacks	Gives and receives forgiveness.	Shows compassion to strengthen bonds.
Flats	Flattens the divide and welcomes inclusion.	Wisely uses teamwork for the dream work.
Pumps	Takes initiative to uplift others.	Encourages so lives are victorious.
Wedges	Receives advancements gradually in stride.	Exhibits patience with herself and others.
Platforms	Spreads love and leaves an admirable legacy.	Shares influence so others can bloom.
Boots	Provides a safe haven for others.	Emotionally healthy and is trustworthy.

leaves the footprint of a "powerful trailblazer." When it comes to life and leadership, their intentions and inner traits are on opposite ends of the spectrum. Which woman best describes you and where you want to be?

Leading Ladies Lead with Love

Unplanned to the T, I concluded writing this chapter while visiting the Love Circle Park in Nashville. It's a quaint little getaway nestled in the heart of a residential area. I accelerated enthusiastically while gradually climbing to the top. My upward climb of determination was rewarded with a beautiful evening display of Nashville's skyline. Being one of the highest peaks in the city, you can see for miles and miles. Strangely, I found it to be empty. In fact rather lonely, with no one in sight. I reflected on how this is similar to leadership.

Being a lady who leads is not for the faint of heart. No wonder eagles often symbolize leaders. They don't flock like robins, beg for crumbs like pigeons, or redundantly work in one place like the woodpecker. Accepting the challenges of a leader takes lots of perseverance. And yet there's nothing like being privy to a breathtaking pinnacle. But if love is not in the core of your mission, your arrival at the top won't be long or super sweet. You see love is not puffed up. And leadership is nestled inside of love. I believe while on earth, you must first lead with loving God and loving yourself before becoming a respected leader of others.

Brownie Point:
You can be surrounded *soles* that have prideful *souls*. But don't slip into a shoe that leads to the road of destruction. #CB4C

One day you may be a CEO of a corporation. In the future you may be married and taking on the COO role of your family and managing an ever-moving household. You may be a leading community advocate that rallies people together to take action for socio-economics and against social injustice. You may be a teacher educating future generations who will one day take the knowledge you impart today and use it to be a chemist, engineer, musician, tech programmer, or president. Or you may pursue life with the entrepreneurial spirit and develop your own business that thrives with your creating new innovations and solutions. However or wherever you lead, always remember pride is an accessory which will always clash with your inner fashion and outer influence. Leadership is not about perfection, but about dedication to value your worth and love those who are looking to you for guidance and teamwork. A healthy balance of humility and confidence will make your path more secure as you climb toward greater horizons. So shake up the world with your shine! Walk on your high hills and lead on!

Chaos to Confidence

9 Steps to Walking on High Hills with Confidence

1. **H**earing your distinctive voice is needed to change the world. Don't stifle it. You can lead with your voice in a variety of ways: speaking, singing, advocating, writing, inventing, voting, building, calculating, measuring, envisioning, etc.
2. **I**gnore the temptation to let a title or position go to your head. You may receive compliments and clout. But let your love speak volumes about your character.
3. **G**ain insight from other leaders. You don't have to be an expert in everything. Stop boiling the ocean in your

head, when you only have a bowl full of the sea to serve.

4. **H**and out your strengths instead of hyping on your faults. Avoid negative self-promotion like: "I'm not good at making decisions. I'm so dumb. I can never figure anything out. I wish I was like someone else."
5. **H**ave a humble, approachable spirit that is worthy of respect and honor from those you look up to and those looking up to you.
6. **I**nitiate a daily challenge. Do something that makes you nervous each day. So when a leadership opportunity arises and is aligned with your purpose, you've got a trained willpower and mindset to embrace the challenge.
7. **L**et go of the misconceptions of likability. Not everyone is going to like or agree with you. However, treat others with kindness and respect.
8. **L**ay aside your "she-go." Serve first, lead second.
9. **S**teer away from suppressing your capability to lead because Mr. Right hasn't arrived yet. Many leaders evolve, before blossoming in love.

CHAPTER 7

MASTER THE BAIT. MASTER THE WAIT.

It was a Sunday morning and I climbed out of bed ready to start a new day. Church at 7 A.M. followed by picking up groceries for the week. After that I would be ready for an NFL game or a movie, all before noon. (Yeah, I'm an early bird.) This particular morning I was groggy and blinking to clear my contacts, yet immediately noticed a slight dizziness. I proceeded to the shower and felt a little better as the day progressed. But when I woke up on Monday morning, I could hardly take baby steps without holding on to my bed posts and walls for dear life. *What is going on with my body? Did I do something wrong? Where did this come from?* Something inside jolted my equilibrium. After several trips to the doctor and trying multiple medications, nothing helped. My doctor finally referred me to an ENT specialist.

I was later diagnosed with Benign Paroxysmal Positional Vertigo (BPPV) of the occult. Simply stated, it's a condition where all you want to do is stay as stiff as a statue. Or risk feeling

BPPV	The Bait
Causes dizziness and the propensity to fall.	Causes unsteadiness and falling into obscurity.
Hidden from sight and hard to detect.	Provokes secrets you hope no one detects.
Tiny dislodged crystals disturb balance.	Tiny cravings hinder personal and relational balance.
In stillness you hope dizziness will disappear.	In stillness you hope sexual urges will leave.
Difficulty prohibits you from ordinary activities.	Distractions limit you from having extraordinary peace.
No quick fix, but possible to overcome.	No overnight remedy, but possible to conquer.

The Deep, Dark Secret

Brace yourself. Graphic content if you proceed reading. This subject isn't splashed across the front page news, a hot topic on Snapchat, included in textbooks, preached from pulpits, or readily addressed by parents. Consequently, as little girls we grow into adulthood and are often left to go and discover on our own.

This deep, dark secret creeps behind closed doors. And whether it's early A.M. or late P.M. it calls you to a hidden place of temporary pleasure. I'm talking about the one and only act we call masturbation or *the bait*. I recently realized how it has unique similarities to my bout with BPPV (as listed in the chart).

According to *Everything You Always Wanted to Know About Sex: But Were Afraid to Ask,* by Dr. David Reuben, masturbation is defined as: "sexual stimulation designed to produce an orgasm through any means except sexual intercourse. Interestingly, the term comes from the Latin word *masturbari,* which means 'to pollute one's self.'" Honestly, horniness is real. Raging hormones (beyond your teens) still rage on. At times your mind all the way down to your sacred valley just doesn't want to cool out and behave. Instead your hormones would rather march around with picket signs and relentlessly chant: "No pleasure, no peace!" "2-4-6-8 we just want to take the bait!" Sex drive is a part of our physiological makeup. And on some days, it just doesn't take much for our libido to want to let go!

like someone is constantly pulling the ground from underneath you. After doing a procedure, the specialist instructed me, at all cost, to refrain from titling my head to the side, forward, or backward. And to do this for the next seventy-two hours. Determined to not live like this forever, I had to get to the bottom of this. In spite of going home dizzy and nauseous, I whipped out my researcher instinct. I discovered that deep within the inner ear canal are tiny crystals that pack a lot of power in regard to our body's sense of balance. A crystal (or two) had become dislodged and caused my equilibrium to go haywire. The word "occult" had me upset as well (after all I all I could was think of a cult, of which I'm in no shape or form a member of). However, I found out occult is synonymous with "mysterious" and "hidden from view."

Dealing with BPPV caused an imbalance that was buried far beyond what the naked eye could see. But the specialist and I knew better. The symptoms were all too real. Every step I took was apprehensive and shaky. The simplest of daily activities were impossible to complete. And the inner struggle impacted my outer confidence.

Mastering the Bait

There's many people who think girls and women don't struggle with the temptations to masturbate and they can never be sex addicts. Flip the switch, ladies, this is a myth and so far from the truth! In 2014, *Women's Health Magazine* stated: "Most women report masturbating at least once a week, according to a new study in the *Journal of Sex Research*." According to the Introduction to Psychology Gateways to Mind and Behavior, "95 percent of men reported they masturbate at some point in time. While 89 percent of women reported the same." As you can see masturbation or "the bait" is an equal opportunity enticement that has the ability to enslave and its bait is gender neutral.

If this an ongoing struggle for you, I want to challenge you to be daring. Daring enough to care enough about your private integrity. Let's crack the lid on this dirty little secret. After all, what's done in the dark will be brought into the light. What you do behind closed doors weighs on your outer confidence. You may have wrestled with this issue and thrown in the towel. Well, heads up! Cause I'm throwing back the towel. If you've battled between "Is it right or wrong?", read on and make a decision for yourself. After all I can't live your life, but I can share implications you may not be thinking of. Knowledge is still half the battle. If you are tired of struggling with the bait, you are not alone and there's hope. You may be asking, *"What in the world does this have to do with me and Mr. Right?"* I'm glad you're wondering. Just keep reading.

Tight Like the Grip of a Snake

The bait can be compared to a tormenting master. It provokes doubts and fears in many single women. Fears that have you skeptical about your self-worth and pondering: "Am I worthy of being romantically loved and trusted? Do I have to settle for this because commitment with a man seems like a far off dream?" You can face doubts that leave you cynical about having sex with another human, much less your future husband. They long to be quieted ASAP. They keep pleading for a never satisfying fix. I too have been plagued by these fears which often shout, "This might be the only sexual pleasure you'll get, so go for it." "You might have to wait forever to have a date or even a mate, including sex, so do what you feel."

These fears, if uncontrolled, can dictate your life in alarming ways. Take for instance Dameco Lee who has publicly acknowledged her battles with masturbation addiction after years of struggle. Her first exposure to sexual acts surprisingly came through one of her close friends as a young child. This inevitably opened a huge gateway to lust. Like an unquenchable high, Dameco started doing acts to self-satisfy which escalated to her dependency on pornography for added sexual gratification. As years went by, she became addicted to masturbation even to the point of tearing tissue from her clitoris. Shockingly, she continued to masturbate in spite of the pain. Even to this day she doesn't know how she physically healed. There were seasons of her running to public places and having accountability partners around in efforts to abstain. But slowly but surely, she would come back and find refuge in the habit. She slipped in and out of severe bouts of depression. Dameco started believing she would be held captive with this secret struggle for the rest of her life.

She later stated, "During the days that followed, God was pressing me to bring it to the light, to confess it. Fear was also there with me. You see, I was afraid to expose myself. This fear wrapped around me like a boa constrictor in order to keep my mouth shut. I was so shamed and afraid of being condemned that I'd be scared to write my struggle with masturbation in my journal because I feared someone would find it. I was in torment."

But one day, her life changed. She was given a new lease on life laced with hope. God simply told her that she didn't have to be in those chains anymore. Dameco realized she had a choice. She didn't have to be an involuntary slave to this cruel master of bait and betrayal. Dameco overcame by taking authority over the bait. Over the porn. Over the torture. Over the agony. Over the disillusionment. She moved from chaos to confidence by exercising willpower to avoid traps which used to lure her daily for years.

The Bait: The Great Escape

I sympathize and empathize with you if feel like *the bait* is your only outlet to release. I know what it feels like when it's the equivalent of a glass of wine to soothe you. Your antidote to loneliness. Your pick me up when you had a bad day. Your private indulgence when you had a productive day. Your pacifier when no one danced with you or asked for your number that Friday night. Your entertainment when nothing on TV is worth watching. Your sleeping pill when you have a restless night. Your time passer when you're bored out of your mind. Your temporary happiness when you can't recall the last time you had a real, genuinely wonderful time with a man. Your spotter when you feel like you're carrying the world on your two shoulders. Your momentary bliss when you feel left out after another friend or family member announces their engagement. Your coping mechanism when you're tired of grieving over a breakup. Your outward display of "I'm mad at you" toward God when you don't understand his will. Your box of chocolates when you're -1 instead of +1 for yet another Valentine's Day. Your way of throwing a hissy fit when you're tired of crying, praying, and believing for companionship. Your commercial break when you don't like the episode playing on *your life time channel*. Your imaginative self-esteem booster when you feel you're not pretty enough to be loved in real life. I've been there, felt that. Been there, done that.

I know firsthand as a single woman, the wait for sexual gratification is no joke and can be absolutely frustrating. Especially when there's no suitor in sight. Or no compatible, commitment-ready knight in shining armor who will at least get you two steps closer to walking down the aisle. Yes, the struggle is real. The enticement of the bait is real. *But is it really an escape?*

No Happily Ever After

But even during the wait (for commitment and covenant), you carry lots of weight. No, not the kind which makes it hard to get in your favorite jeans or what you see when you step on a scale. I'm referring to emotional heaviness. Mental frustration. Physical abandonment. Spiritual confusion. Masturbation forces you to live under the weight of lust. Lust divvies out a variety of traps to make you live under its rule. Lust births a distorted view of intimacy and the beauty of sex between a man and woman. Simply put, it's a damaging web and masturbation is a temporary, tease-filled vacay. But the euphoria washes away quickly. You snap back into reality and realize it's superficial. However, this is not a weight that has to crush you. Instead it can be conquered by knowing your authority, cherishing your future, and understanding you deserve genuine love not lust. Even while you wait to be united with Mr. Right.

Have you ever watched a suspenseful movie or TV show that gradually gets you to lean in? You try to figure out the character's next move. You wonder if the villain is telling the truth or plotting a crafty setup. You anticipate the climax. You sit on the edge of your seat, almost tasting the resolve. You long for the clarity it promises to yield. You're in countdown mode and feel the end is near. And bam, boom, what?!!! Here comes the ever so cunningly served cliffhanger. Your curiosities are piqued, in fact you're a bit agitated because you were left in jaw drop mode. There's no happily ever after or closing. You took the bait . . . and still have to wait.

You may feel like you're flying to cloud nine alone as you seek to satisfy yourself through masturbation. The enticement to lean in, fantasize, and escape reality seem to scream your name. You accept the offer. And there you are. Dangling emotionally, physically, mentally, and spiritually from the cliff, about to climax to an abrupt end. And wham! Reality stares you right smack dab in the face. The aftermath is a sharp drop from la la land. You can't deny the fact, there's no hand to hold. A heartbeat to listen to. A loving embrace to cuddle in. A pair of eyes to share your gaze. A person who's fully invested in walking beside you the next morning or for the next chapter of your life. There's no covenant covering who's not just there for the sex, but for life. None of that is the aftermath.

Yes, biting the bait (letting the lustful thoughts multiply) and reeling in that sexual feeling (masturbation) feels good temporarily. No need to front. Plus there's a lot of books, reports, and opinions which will encourage you to masturbate whenever you want and as much as you want. However, one thing is for sure. It just doesn't and won't ever fully satisfy. Something that's based on fantasy won't wipe out the emptiness you have in reality. It won't ever be a comparable substitute for the companionship you adamantly desire and deserve.

Brownie Point:
Every woman wants a covering before, during, and after sex. But remember the master of cover-up, won't cover you up. #CB4C

5 Ways the Bait Hinders Intimacy

When it comes to marriage and sexual intimacy, *the bait* can put your connection in crisis mode. Here are five ways it drains your confidence and hinders true intimacy with Mr. Right.

1. Being Selfish vs. Selfless.

Dependency on masturbation makes you concentrate on how you can be fulfilled by yourself, for yourself. This form of selfishness can lead to you treating Mr. Right like a piece of side action, instead of the main attraction. Keep in mind his sexual needs have to be met as well. And I'm sure you'd prefer being the one who meets them. Plus, this "it's about my needs" or "me first" attitude can trickle into other areas of your relationship (i.e. finances, household responsibilities, communication, travel, recreation, children, etc.). Sacrifice now will help you be even more equipped when you have to sacrifice (put intimacy on hold) later. Not giving in now, will help you to be prepped and primed to give to each other in delectable ways later.

2. Being Unfaithful.

Biting the bait of sexual fantasy can drive you to be unfaithful to Mr. Right. Often when you masturbate, it's hard to control the mind. Mentally you dwell on various sexual positions, places, and people. This is a form of cheating and it doesn't just happen organically. You think and focus before you do. That's why "For as he thinks within himself, so he is . . . " is so true. Allowing a buildup of perverted thoughts of being with someone else sexually only draws you further away from your husband, who should be the man of your desire.

3. Being Unrealistic.

Being aroused without Mr. Right in the mix, can make it difficult for him to live up to your sexual expectations and imaginations when you do have sex with each other. Gratification steeped in fantasy will make him feel like he has to compete. Or that his performance is incapable of satisfying you. Men may like to compete in sports, business deals, and politics. But when it comes to sex, they want to be hailed as "the man who can."

4. Being Dependent on Other Stimuli.

Lust and masturbation are like a set of twins who can't live without food, fuel, and fantasy. They always need to be fed. They always yearn for something more. They need a realm of fabrication to stimulate the mind in order for the body to follow and thrive on what's imagined. If left to go haywire, lust can lead to being dependent on one of the top contributors to an unsteady, unfulfilling, divorce-ridden marriage: porn. This indirect stimuli can directly affect and even damage the intimacy you share with Mr. Right. Porn can make you feel like you need something more provocative, risqué, and reckless to be sexually satisfied.

5. Being an Unhealthy Rendezvous from Reality.

One of the prime benefits of being in a relationship is having someone to confide in and weather the changes of life alongside you. Stress needs to be dealt with, not suppressed. Fears needs to conveyed, not covered up. Anger, fatigue, and abandonment issues need to be addressed, not substituted with self-sexual arousal. Consistently finding comfort in the bait alone can lead to avoiding needed escapes you need to share with each other. The bait then serves as a "coping mechanism" which will only draw more distance between you and Mr. Right.

Vowing I Do, Means Vowing I Won't

Don't be confused or misled. I'm not saying you shouldn't or won't get horny. You're human and it comes with the combo. I'm not saying you won't face sexual temptations. Like me, you may face them every day. And if you haven't faced them, keep living. You will. However, indulging in masturbation can do serious damage to your inner confidence in being ready for Mr. Right. Don't fall into the trap of pride and start believing your *sexual gratification should come by any means necessary, no matter the cost or lost*. That's a very self-centered way to live and it will never transfer over well into a beautiful lasting relationship.

Right now you might think marriage will totally solve your issue with masturbation and quench your sex drive. However, you have to be realistic. Who spends 24/7 in bed having sex all the time? Do you want your marriage to be driven by lust or true love?

Even in marriage, there will be times when you want to have sex right at that moment, but won't be able to. You'll have to use self-control and aim to "save 'n share" your physical passion for your husband. Learning to wait on him now, is prepping you to wait for him then. Taking the easy route of satisfying yourself with a fantasy is not fair to you or your future husband. I'm sure you want your wedding vows to be faithfully upheld when you say, "I do," right? In many ways your "I do" also means saying "I won't" step outside or around you to secretly and sexually gratify myself. "I won't" let lust-filled bait master me. I want to share the best of me with the best of you. And that definitely includes exploring the wonderful world of sex together.

Brownie Point:
Your love story is worth being fulfilled with a real man, not a fleeting fantasy or faithless façade.
#CB4C

Mastering the Wait

Alright. Sexually gratifying yourself is one end of the spectrum. Having sex with someone else before Mr. Right is the other.

There are times when having sex feels straight up like a justifiable investment. You're worth it. He's worth it. The "we" is worth it. You may have used sex as a come-on when you're wanting to move from a "situationship" to an official relationship. All the while praying that giving him a *sneak preview* would convince him to stay for the *main feature* (i.e. commitment and eventually marriage). You may have had a one-night stand (or a few). Or perhaps you tried the infamous friends-with-benefits connection with a guy and afterward wondered why you started catching feelings quicker than a baseball in the ninth inning.

Maybe you didn't start off sexing, but eventually temptation surfaced. Another woman caught his eye. He threatened to leave. He made you feel like loving him absolutely required sex. So in order to keep his attention and more so his affection, you decided to have sex. Hoping to God your passion and performance would miraculously make him forever faithful to you. Believe me, throughout my travels and hearing lots of personal stories, numerous single women have shared how they've wrestled with issues stemming from sex whether in or outside of a relationship.

Hot Parties & Cold Pillows

There's an unquestionable amount of pressure living in a world where you're looking for a full-time companion, but a part-time lover keeps calling your name. I remember having a conversation with Danita about her sincere desire to stop having sex. She had set her sights on Nashville to attend college and pursue her dreams within the music industry. During her sophomore year she started wanting to meet more guys, so she readily accepted invitations to more parties. The parties somehow would transition into an after party at a guy's dorm room or apartment. In order to prove she could hang out and loosen up, she would drink. The more intoxicated she became, the more appealing sex seemed. And from the guy's view, the more liquor she consumed, the easier it was for him to win her consent.

But when the bottles were empty, the sex was over, and sobriety returned, Danita was faced with emptiness again. This cycle never ended with her being pursued for love or a lasting relationship. She would awake puzzled, yet knowing doses of alcohol and a guy's vicious appetite for sex only equated to a loveless connection. While confiding in me, I asked her a series of questions about her background. Often times, you react in ways that reflect your roots and how you were raised. I concluded that having sex was just a *response for attention, yet was never her premeditated intention*. Her response to a guy's invitation was an emotional longing she hoped he would fill with compassion.

Sex was just a suppressant and a temporary distraction from a deeper issue. The alcohol served as a momentary vacation to take her mind off of facing a pile of buried shame. Our conversation unpacked a variety of baggage. Danita started to recall being molested and sexually abused as a child. Scientific evidence shows us that enduring this type of trauma often causes a child to grow into adulthood still looking for security in the act that caused them pain years earlier.

Danita was inevitably trying her best to find security in what had been an ongoing thirst in her life. She finally realized sex was not the answer. Her emotional confidence deserved more than being left on a cold pillow, being given cold stares, and getting the cold shoulder the morning after.

Brownie Point:
Sex might make a man discharge, but it doesn't mean he'll take charge to commit. #CB4C

Giving Your All, but Not Getting Mr. Ready

After flying out of state for a business trip, I met Allison at a conference. Her eyes sparkled brightly and her smile was adorned with red lipstick that was poppin' for days. Excitement was in the air as I was one of the fellow business owners being officially awarded as a winner of the American Small Business Championship. After the workshops, presentations, ceremony, and dinner, a few of us decided to go out for Latin dancing. I jumped at the chance since most of my time has been dedicated to work, work, and more work. After doing a little salsa and meringue on the dance floor, we took a break and struck up a conversation. I had no idea a different rhythm was about to surface, a sustained song of pain and frustration.

While working on a play, Allison met Stephen. They were paired up as husband and wife for the production. Although their chemistry was prompted by theatrics, it spilled over to their off-stage life. Away from the spotlights, they started having sex. During this time they were still in the I'm-trying-to-figure-out-where-this-is-going phase. Four short months later, Allison found out she was pregnant. This was certainly an urgent, unexpected interruption in her life, her plans, and their relationship! This wasn't supposed to happen. Not now. Not without a ring. Without a dress. Without the security of prenuptials. But now she stood staring face forward at a predicament she had to make sense of. So Allison zoomed into "fix it" mode. (I was once told by a close friend that as soon as a woman conceives, she goes into a nesting phase, sometimes hurriedly but surely shifting into caring for the child's welfare in and outside the womb, by any means necessary.)

They moved into a house together and had the baby. Immediately, she started working overtime in her business endeavors to provide. After work, she would return to cook, clean, and try her best to make the house into a home. She wanted them to be a family. To love and support each other. However, Stephen never wanted to take responsibility or reciprocate the love Allison had in her heart for him. He didn't have a steady job. He wouldn't tell her she was beautiful. Wouldn't give her encouragement for finalizing a business deal. Wouldn't take her out on dates. Like many women in this situation, Allison kept working to cover the bills, diapers, and daycare. Hoping one day their connection would miraculously be healed and whole. But in time, Stephen moved out on his own.

Shortly after, Allison received word that Stephen was dating another woman. Since his departure, Allison hasn't been with anyone else. His moving out heavily weighed on her confidence. No dates. No serious relationships. No interest to trust again. He may have closed the door and left the house. However, the door of her heart has still been open for him, even two and half years after he left. As the Latin grooves were amplified in the night air, I could sense her inner struggle was intensifying. She was tired of crying. Tired of trying. Yet deep inside, she was still wanting his validation. She was oscillating between how to balance co-parenting and letting go of romantic hopes of being with him again. Or starting anew all over again.

Living with soul ties, caring for children, and facing unexpected responsibilities with a man who isn't ready or willing to commit is often an uphill battle many single women don't consider when having sex. These ties are always stronger and last longer than you think. So it's always wise to get to know a guy's intentions. *Investigate before you invest your heart.* Opening your legs is opening the entrance of your most sacred region and allows a man to connect with the deepest part of your soul. So take time to see his actions. Allow him to profess his love to you with a ring which tells the world that he's not afraid to vow his life to you. Unmistakably loving you is a worthwhile investment for him to make before giving him access to the most sacred part of you.

Mirror Moment:

Have you experienced giving 100 percent to a relationship and a guy not being on the same level of commitment with you?

What was the most valuable lesson you've learned after sex and heartache?

3 Dangers of Being FWB

Together they had weathered Band-Aids and Kool-Aid. Dugouts and dance recitals. Deaths and divorce. Prom nights and peer pressure. Their friendship was strictly platonic. Defined and settled.

Until one night Derrick came over to Rana's apartment to visit. They talked often but hadn't seen in each other in a while. He fell asleep on the couch but eventually woke up to use the bathroom. On his way back, he saw her lying wide-eyed on the bed. He went over to talk. Her talking, led to him kissing, touching, and hugging. Within seconds, clothes fell to the floor. And you guessed it. They had sex.

Initially it felt good being FWB (i.e. friends with benefits, sex buddies). But eventually, twenty years of a wonderful friendship was completely dismantled in five months. I once heard that having sex with a friend is kind of like leaving the birth canal. *Once you leave it, there's no going back.* So what are the costs when you dish out "benefits?" Here are three dangers. In actuality you'll see they're not really beneficial to you, your bum, or your chum.

1. You develop a resume with too many references.

Your mind can't help but process the post-sex divide. It causes the comfort levels in a friendship to be fickle and rapidly fade. Then comes the dreaded awkwardness when you reconnect. The anxiety. The attachments you weren't expecting to have. Each time you have sex, a sexual footprint is left in your memory. So many of your mental reference points made in bed can't be dismissed.

So while FWB may seem to be fun now, you may literally be building up a hefty rolodex of past partners. Which will be pretty darn impossible to delete when you arrive in the bed with Mr. Right (your future husband).

2. You're playing with glue, yet tearing apart.

Have you ever seen the movie *Friends with Benefits* starring Justin Timberlake and Mila Kunis? After sex, they tried moving on and seeing other people. Yet, the dividing lines of friendship and physicality began to blur. In the end, the bond of sex ties came-a-calling them right back to each other. Again and again.

Of course, Hollywood is not the purist reflection of reality. In life there's not always a warm fuzzy ending like the movie portrays. You can verbally declare, "I'm not going to be clingy." "I can handle just having sex." But you can't close the lips of your heart. Eventually you will start having feelings. You will wish you could dismiss the slight desire to have *something more*. Mmm. Like the beauty of a bona fide relationship.

Take two sheets of paper and glue them together. Let time pass and allow the glue to dry. Now try separating them. Each sheet will have rips and tears. There's only voids that long to be a whole sheet a paper again. Ditto with sex. And when you're FWB, there's no way on earth to separate your emotions and need for security from the physical act.

You can give many people your time. Money. Food. Opinions. A ride home. Or colorfully wrapped presents piled high and topped with a red bow. *But not everyone gets your body*. Not every guy gets to be physically inside of you and emotionally attached to you. So when feelings have grown and the sex stops, pieces of your heart will still long for him. Neither of you will ever be the same, including the friendship.

3. You work FT, but only get PT oneness

You may think, "We're not pulling an eight-hour shift in bed having sex." "We don't clock in and out; it's sporadic or when the mood hits." OK, true. Your finances might not take a dockin' just because your bed is rockin.' You may not be getting laid off for getting laid.

However, you are working full time, from a different angle. Sex involves *fully* giving yourself to someone during that time period. You are completely allowing him to penetrate and/or deposit inside the deepest part of you. You are *fully* invested in exchanging DNA, fluids, and creating soul ties over and over. And that my friend, is full-time work. FWB causes your cash out to be *part-time "cum"mitment instead of full-time commitment*.

Most FWB affairs gives those involved openness to explore relationships elsewhere, which may include sex. So who else's residue are you bringing to the bed when you reunite with your friend?

Think about it. You're selective about who views your social media posts (private accounts, selective group chats, and direct messages). Very few people get to drive your car. You don't just allow anyone in your house. So why would you allow a "friend" to dip in and dip out of the one private sanctum you have on earth? Forget about casual sex. Sex is way too spiritually potent to be shared in an apathetic, passive way. Your gates (entrance into your vagina, womb, and soul) aren't made for playmates, but a soulmate.

Brownie Point:
Soul ties are one of the most expensive exchanges a guy should earn through love, faithfulness, and covenant. #CB4C

Mirror Moment:

If you've tried being FWB, how did it impact your life and what happened to your friendship?

How many people will you have to mentally move past in order to be sexually present with Mr. Right, your soul mate, and the one you'll vow your heart to?

Getting Laid & How We're Made

Consider our anatomical nature as women and how it pertains to sex. We're physiologically made to receive, and men are created to penetrate. Of course I'm talking about in the buff, no sex toys, surgical changes, or added gadgets needed. We take in. We accept. We nurture. We nourish. We birth what is fertilized inside of us. This goes beyond cute and cuddly babies. Sexual residue and soul ties left within the fibers of a woman's body impacts her spiritual, emotional, mental, physical, and relational makeup.

According to *What Do Women Really Want?* by Noam Shpancer, PhD reports: "For women, possessing no seed to spread, sex with more people does not result in more potential genetic offspring. Moreover, women are at higher risk than men for sexual violence and sexually transmitted diseases, not to mention the unique risk of pregnancy. It pays for women to be careful in choosing their sexual partners.

"A woman who wants to increase her chances of [sexual] enjoyment and minimize her chances of harm is better off getting to know her partner well before she gets to sex. From this logic follows the claim that women are bio-programmed to want relationships, not sex; that they need a stable, intimate relationship to feel aroused and are therefore built for sexual monogamy and marriage."

Stats Don't Have to Be Your Facts

Take a look at these staggering and mind blowing stats reported by the Centers for Disease Control:

- Every year there are an estimated *20 million* new STD infections in the United States.
- Undiagnosed STIs (sexually transmitted infections) cause *24,000* women to become infertile each year.
- About *1 in 4* of all new HIV infections is among ages 13 to 24. About *4 in 5* of these infections occur in males.
- There are about *820,000* new gonorrhea infections each year in the United States (It's the second-most commonly reported infectious disease. Yet it is developing resistance to the antibiotics we use to treat it.)
- Human papillomavirus (HPV) is the most common sexually transmitted infection in the United States, with more than *40* distinct types. HPV types 16 and 18 account for approximately *70 percent* of cervical cancers worldwide.
- Consequences are particularly severe for young women as a result of insufficient screening, biological susceptibility, lack of access to healthcare, and multiple sex partners.

Now there are a plethora of sexually transmitted diseases that can be contracted, and some are curable. Yet there are other STDs not neatly listed in a pamphlet at your doctor's office. Ones not denoted at your campus or citywide health fair. Or even included in the birds-and-the-bees speech your Mom, Dad, or health teacher may have given you years ago.

I'm talking other STDs, *spiritually transmitted diseases*. True indeed you may be able to suppress gonorrhea, but fail to address "guilt-arrhea." You may be able to scathe from syphilis, but what about "shame-philis?" Face it. These and other inner warfare battles are REAL issues that neither OTC nor prescribed meds can cure. And they greatly impact your confidence. That's why it's imperative to understand the cost of having sex before Mr. Right. The dangers of having unprotected sex. The liability of adding more and more partners to your sexual resume. The risk for not getting tested for STDs. The wager you take whenever you don't ask your potential boyfriend, boo, bae, or Mr. Right about his sexual history and make it mandatory to get tested (and openly look at the test results together). Whether you decide to have sex or not. You don't have to contribute to these stats. By having the *hard talks*, making wise decisions, and taking necessary precautions, they don't have to interfere with or define your destiny.

Toys Are for Boys. Jewels Are for Gentlemen.

Imagine a king stopping by your house tomorrow to give you a rare luxurious necklace. Every inch of the jewelry is handcrafted with the finest technique and finesse. Although the jewels look flawlessly sturdy on the outside, the core is extremely fragile and worth millions. In essence, the necklace is a one of a kind treasure found nowhere else in the world. Would you place it on the edge of a counter? Would you leave it in anyone's hands? Would you allow a reckless child to play with it or a careless adult to take it home? No way, no ma'am, no how! You would treat this necklace as if it's the last collector's item on earth. Only someone who has proven they have maturity, sensitivity, and trust would have the honor of viewing, much less holding your jewel-encrusted necklace.

This is exactly how you should observe your body! Every inch of your body is a beautifully rare treasure found nowhere else in the world. It's capable of completing incredible feats and carrying out amazing pursuits during your lifetime on earth. God has given you the royal role to manage your jewels, your inner sanctuary, and your womb during this season of life. Don't ever downplay the significance in prayerfully selecting who gets to share the most intimate parts of your body. Philippians 4:6 says, "Do not be anxious about anything, but in every situation, by prayer and petition, with thanksgiving, present your requests to God." Don't rush! And ask for guidance before you get in the heat of the moment.

In nature, astonishing value is always hidden. It's not found on top soil, floating around the shoreline, easily found on market shelves, downloaded and delivered to your doorstep, or owned by the masses. Think about this. Gold, pearls, diamonds, sapphires, rubies all have something in common. They don't give free advertisement about their location . . . or their value. One must search, dig, work, focus, and be devoted in order to claim and collect these jewels. Commitment comes before seeing their intrinsic beauty in an up-close-and-intimate way. Although you can take a note from these, understand you are worth so much more than these! *So why are you going above and beyond showing off all of your assets?* Why are you advertising your body for free, when it ought to cost commitment to see? Why are you marketing yourself cheaply to get attention that won't ever convert to affection? C'mon girl, just stop. You can't just blame men. As a women, you too have a responsibility in knowing and showing your worth as a jewel.

Confidence before commitment is knowing your body was never created to be treated as a toy. Your body isn't to be bargained for lust. Intercourse shouldn't be prematurely entrusted to incapable hands. Don't be deceived! A guy can have a manly exterior and a childish interior. Guys with boyish mentalities won't mind how many "sex and on to the next" games have been played with you. In their eyes, you're just an object. Or better yet, a toy that can receive and react to *foreplay*, because you're viewed as a person just *for play*. They won't care about feelings or faithfulness, just as long as they get to have their fun when and where they desire.

But overlook the boys! Forget the jokers! Please understand a gentleman of standards will respect the fact you guard who and what goes in and out of your body. A gentleman is mature enough to handle your heart with care. He'll take on the responsibility of protecting you as a jewel. He is willing to avoid using sex as a substitute for commitment. So with that being said. Who do you want to be in love with, a boy or a gentlemen?

The Sex Aftermath: Live or Take Your Life

A friend of mine was once caught in a love triangle. Carla was in college and started having sex with a Brandon. Deep in her heart, she knew he was a player. He had other girls waiting in line for him. But it didn't matter, she was certain she could win him over. They agreed to have an "open" relationship, where nothing but sex strings were attached. Months went by. And one night at a party Carla found Brandon quite comfy close with another girl. Carla was fuming hotter than a four-alarm fire. This time it wasn't due to being hot 'n ready to hit the sheets. Yes, they exchanged an agreement verbally, but a bond deeper than meets the eye was shared sexually. She wanted revenge. So shortly after, Carla decided to hook up with Jeremy. They too had a sex-only relationship. But deep inside Carla longed to be the "player" instead of the one getting played to the left. She kept her sex life with Jeremy a secret from Brandon.

Eventually, Brandon called her out of the blue and she decided to give him another try. After all, he was the one she had grown to love. Well one day while having sex, Carla started acting totally out of the norm. Typically, she was sexually submissive with Brandon and aggressive with Jeremy. Her *bedroom identity* or sexual tendencies with one partner got criss-crossed with the other. Brandon immediately knew she was involved with another guy. He became irate and despondent (even though by now he was in a so-called monogamous relationship with another woman). But he just couldn't come to terms with Carla having sex with someone else. Shortly after, he broke off their sexual relationship.

Wow, how the tables turned. What Carla wanted to avoid the most (i.e. getting laid, then getting played) ended up staring her in the face. The phone calls ceased. The hookups came to a halt. The sex stopped. Neither Brandon nor Jeremy was in between her legs or in her life anymore.

Although these routines ended, the residue from sex ties was much too strong to dissipate with a said goodbye and the sound of a dial tone. The next few months of Carla's life were incredibly difficult. She went through severe bouts of depression. Her GPA declined as she missed many classes that semester. There were days of agonizing pain. Shame. Abandonment. Isolation. And not wanting to ever, ever love again. Her mother's comfort couldn't free her. Her roommate couldn't shake her out of the paralyzing stupor. The sex ties were sown deep and now only a knot remained. A knot which threatened her desire to pursue goals, graduate, and have a thriving career. Carla lost her will to live and started seeking ways to commit suicide. She couldn't even fathom loving anyone else again. Nothing but the feeling of obscurity resided in her heart. And even with that *filling of darkness*, she still felt empty.

But one day she asked God a bold question. After all she had spent a lot of time wrestling with pillow-filled tears and frustration. The depression had literally confined her to being in bed. *Will Brandon and I ever be together again?* The answer came in nothing short of an unforgettable way. As she drifted off to sleep, she had a dream. There were two scenes on one picture. On one side, she saw Brandon getting married. As she zoomed in closer, sadly, she was not the elegantly dressed bride. On the other side, she saw a funeral service. As she looked closer, Carla saw herself in the casket. She also realized Brandon was nowhere in sight, even at her own funeral! After seeing both sides of the picture, God told her, *"You can choose to live or take your life. But either way, you will not be with him."* In one of the darkest moments of her life, God's voice and vision gave her victory. Why? Because it revealed reality and truth. The dream awakened her and freed her from the corner of darkness which had held her back from living.

Maybe you believe sex will fill a void in your life beyond an orgasm. Perhaps, you may be like Danita, who discovered she was seeking temporary sexual pleasure to suppress the abusive incidents of childhood. Maybe you can relate to Allison, who found out that even a baby can't make a man convert into being Mr. Ready. Perhaps, you're like Carla who later found out she was looking to fill the void of her father's love through sex with different men. You may be engaging in a FWB connection, where it's impossible to separate feelings vs. getting freaky. Or maybe, you've been waiting to have sex for marriage and you're starting to feel like it's a waste of time and that you'll be the *lonely only* forever.

Mirror Moment:

Have you ever felt like you couldn't live without someone, especially after sex?

What present void are you trying to fill with sex?

The Surrender & the Superglue

Honestly, sex can feel good in the moment. And I believe it's one of the most powerfully beautiful forces in life. Yet it can't replace genuine companionship and having a man who seriously cares about your heart, prior to, during, and afterward. Danita, Allison, and Carla all experienced men who didn't mind them having an open-leg policy. As long as their hearts didn't open too wide, too long, and require too much.

Brownie Point:
Sexual intercourse involves *entering a course* that ties the finest fibers of two people into one. #CB4C

Having sex entails a multilayered form of surrendering that takes place. It's a huge deal for you to take off your clothes and be *naked and unashamed* in front of a man. You're giving him permission to see what the world isn't privy to: every dip, dimple, ounce of cellulite, birthmark, and blemish you possess. Then you take the biggest step of surrendering: you lay down, open yourself up, and allow him to come inside of you. And there's always a deposit.

Once a man is inside of you, there is an inexpressible euphoria that takes place. *Webster's Dictionary* fails to contain the words to translate the feeling. There's an exchange of kisses, which involves blowing breath into each other. There's a transaction of bodily fluids and fractions of each other's DNA being shared. Even if you're on the world's strongest birth control, double up on condoms, or he *pulls out*, a conception STILL takes place. A connection is conceived which penetrates your body and permeates your soul. These are known as soul ties. What's commonly overlooked or ignored is the spiritual exchange. Soul ties create oneness and are known as being "bonds that can tie you emotionally, mentally, and spiritually to someone."

Whether you like it or not, sex is a supernatural superglue that sustains stick-to-itiveness even after sex. Whether married or not, having sex with someone still creates the bond of two becoming one flesh. (Which is why it's originally intended for and a primary benefit of marriage.) However, when commitment and covenant aren't a part of the picture, there's always an opening for both individuals to relatively leave with ease on the physical tip. But not so much on the spiritual, mental, or emotional side.

Why? Because once a breakup occurs and/or the sexcapade ends, a tearing takes place. The more sex you share, the harsher the tearing can be when you split. The more people you have sex with, the more pieces of yourself are disbursed. Even if the words "I love you" never leave his or your lips, sex requires a deep piece of your soul to being given.

When He Doesn't Want to Wait

I understand the anxiety, the fears, and the doubts during the wait. I've dated guys who pushed my mental buttons and tested my sex boundaries. Some made fun of my standards while others saw me as a sport, daring to be the one who won sexual bragging rights before bouncing to the next woman. I remember going to Detroit and my friend's boyfriend being willing to bet money that his friend would convince me to have sex before the weekend was over (it didn't happen, my jewels ain't that cheap). Some men have asked for sex straight up with no chaser, or strings attached. And other guys felt that I was at least worth some work (i.e. dates, phone convo, and quality time until that night).

I can't put all the blame on the guys, though. There were times when I made some bad choices by having him over late at night. Sleeping over at his place. And letting him sleep over at mine. Putting myself in those precarious situations allowed temptation to simmer and spill over. After all, one sure way to get burned by the flames is to get super close to the heat. But I've wised up since then and those days are behind me. And thankfully, my heart's diary is not full of regret from my jewels being spread all over the world. The "situationships" *and* "recreationships" with the *challengers and the chasers* have disappeared. But thank God, my will to cherish my body's dignity and health is still intact.

Let's say you're dealing with a guy who doesn't want to wait. Here's an interesting view on pumping the sex brakes, according to *Boundaries in Dating* by Dr. Henry Cloud and Dr. John Townsend:

"Basically [self-control] is a sign to you that a person is capable of delay of gratification and self-control, which are prerequisites of the ability to love. If someone cannot delay gratification and control himself or herself in this area, what makes you think that they can delay their own gratification in other areas of sacrifice for you? What is going to curb the 'I want what I want now' mentality in the rest of life? If someone is able to respect the limits of hearing no for sex, then that is a character sign of someone who can say no to their own desires and hungers in order to serve a higher purpose, or to love another person."

Hear me well. The wait is not to deprive you. The wait helps to *protect* (you), *inspect* (Mr. Right vs. Mr. Wrong), *and respect* (your future marriage). I personally know of women *and* men who waited until they were married. They have been happily married for years and haven't lacked one iota of thrill in the sex department. Like me, I also know of a variety of women who are practicing celibacy or abstinence until saying "I do" to our husbands. There may be pressure, but there's no shame in waiting to have sex until marriage.

Waiting: Moving Beyond the When

Dating goes beyond sharing a cup of coffee, texting, holding hands while shopping, taking selfies, or cuddling with each other at a movie. Relationships will challenge your libido especially in private places, make-out sessions, and extended time together. As you get more emotionally invested and physically tested, the wait can start feeling like the impossible dream or delusional. But it's not.

A typical question that pops up in many single women's minds when they commit to abstinence or celibacy is: How long do I have to wait? Focusing on this unknown of when you will be married can be very intimidating. I wish I could give you the answer (even for myself, girl), but I can't. However, I highly recommend looking at the wait like eating an elephant. As the old saying goes, "How do you eat an elephant? One bite at a time." You have to take the wait one day at a time. None of us can live in tomorrow, next week, or next year. So be intentional and keep your no-sex boundaries and willpower intact for today. Then when tomorrow rolls around, just recycle those same efforts for that day. With each passing day, your strength to wait will grow and the integrity of your sexual stock value for your future marriage will increase. Believe me, the R.O.I. will be sweeter than you can imagine or expect.

Being a Masterpiece: Right & Ready

Hopefully, you can see the imperative reasons to *master the bait and master the wait* in the realm of sex as a single woman. I understand the battle with both facets of life is serious business. But, hey girl, I sincerely don't want you to miss your flight to the next level with Mr. Right! Will be you ready? Or will you be delayed due to messing with a man whose highest ambition is working ground control and playing "hit it and quit it" with any passenger he can catch? Will you have problems departing due to trying to fit the baggage of sex ties in an overhead compartment? Or will you be so caught up in fantasy land you fail to hear Mr. Right calling you onboard?

Confidence before commitment means understanding you're a masterpiece. A beautiful piece of art wonderfully sculpted by God, the Master. You may feel like you're a forgotten piece of art because a guy you slept with left you. Maybe you believe you're too tainted for admiration because you've been promiscuous. But no one is perfect! And so many people, including me, have fallen short and struggle with sexual matters. God views you as a piece of him. Remember you are forgiven. You are loved. You are adored. When it comes to mastering the bait and the wait, the Master is able to make what once seemed like the impossible dream, be the possible reality.

Love yourself enough to rock your crown of confidence and live as an honorable masterpiece. Your identity is not defined by past decisions, mistakes, and flat-out wrong choices. Don't allow lies, fears, and guilt make you miss this defining moment of renewed freedom. Embrace your power and defend your right to enjoy outrageously adventurous sex and a mind-blowing love life when you're married to a man who's committed to doing the same. You are capable of mastering the bait and mastering the wait . . . yes, even before Mr. Right.

Chaos to Confidence

6 Ways to Avoid the Bait & Endure the Wait

1. **M**ake sure you don't ingest pornography and linger over sexually graphic material. They will increase temptations and easily provoke regretful actions.
2. **A**sk for accountability. Choose someone who's truthful and has permission to *call you out* to help you keep goals of sexual boundaries.
3. **S**et your mind to focus on your stock value growing vs. what you feel you're lacking.
4. **T**ake it one day at a time. Avoid focusing on a month or year. Stay in today.
5. **E**xpress your "mastering" goals to a guy you're seriously considering having a relationship with before becoming an official couple.
6. **R**emind yourself daily your body, heart, mind, and legacy are jewels worth protecting before marrying Mr. Right.

CHAPTER 8
MIND GAMES: FACTS OR INFATUATION?

THE CURTAINS ARE DRAWN BACK. YOUR HEART IS THUMPING SO hard, it's almost deafening to your ears. Your friends are ridiculously clapping with excitement and jumping up and down in the audience. They've waited so long to celebrate this moment. Your lungs rapidly fill with more anxiety than air. You nervously gasp for more oxygen. And wha-la! Suddenly you hear an announcer say, "Congratulations, you're the winner of brand new attention, a new number to lock in, a new reason to nervously sit by the phone, wait for the next text, and hold your breath to see if your wishes will become reality . . . all courtesy from this guy! He comes with good looks, stylish clothes, charm to make your mother blush, and a serious dose of swag. In addition, he's got the warmest smile to make your heart melt like a popsicle on the Fourth of July!" (Dimples are included for grand prize winners . . . ooweee, I admit they're my weakness.)

Yep, sometimes a new guy in your life causes you to be filled with anticipation as if watching an episode of *The Price is Right*. (The theme song alone makes me bust out into my happy dance like a certified, bona fide, and glorified winner every time I hear it). The adrenalin rush compares to no other. The expectation of what you might share with him is magnetic.

But what if you're participating in a game that you were never designed to win? What if your connection to a guy makes you believe you're an authentic winner of his heart, but in actuality it's a façade? A false victory. After all, *the more you play, the easier it is to convince you to stay*. Just ask anyone who plays Candy Crush Saga, Angry Birds, or Diamond Dash on their phone. They're so addicting. Apple alone currently boasts 48.6 million downloads per day. Now just think about how many relationship mind games single women download per day. The number has to be astronomical.

Being infatuated with a guy who's playing mind games on you is one of the primary reasons why some single women get abused. Live like a loose cannon. Or totally give up on relationship promises and commitment altogether. When it comes to being a woman in a relationship, often times we invest more, risk more, and therefore have more at stake to lose.

Mirror Moment:

Have you ever been blinded by euphoria that you knowingly overlooked the wrongs of a guy you've dated? Why?

How do you feel when you or a friend gets tricked into thinking a man is fully committed only to find out he's not?

Fake It Until You Make It

Now more than ever, manipulative tactics and behaviors need to be exposed. It's time to stop sweeping them under the rug and turning a blind eye hoping they would disappear. You have to look them in the face and know they're wrong. I've been a victim of several mind games. The chain reaction was nothing less than painstaking. My life was jolted off course by staying in "fake it until you make it" relationships. I didn't want to face the deceit and how they were laced with unmet responsibilities. And boy did my heart pay for wanting to stay in denial. I was severely hurt. Bitter. Disillusioned.

Though I'm no longer in that season, I've got scars from when I didn't want to embrace my power and defend my worth. I've got stitched-up wounds from thinking I could outwit the game and change the guy I was dating. And come out with the upper hand by convincing him to love me. Nope. It didn't happen. (In retrospect, thank God it didn't happen!)

The Cruelest Kind of Love

I was watching the movie *The Holiday* a while ago. The opening lines gripped me to the core. All I could do was shake my head in agreement because they describe how you feel when you want someone who doesn't want you back:

> " . . . there's another kind of love: the cruelest kind. The one that almost kills its victims. It's called unrequited love. Of that I am an expert. Most love stories are about people who fall in love with each other. But what about the rest of us? What about our stories, those of us who fall in love alone? We are the victims of the one-sided affair. We are the cursed of the loved ones. We are the unloved ones, the walking wounded.

> The handicapped without the advantage of a great parking space! Yes, you are looking at one such individual. And I have willingly loved that man for over three miserable years! The absolute worst years of my life! The worst Christmases, the worst birthdays, New Year's Eve's brought in by tears and Valium. These years that I have been in love have been the darkest days of my life. All because I've been cursed by being in love with a man who does not and will not love me back. Oh God, just the sight of him! Heart pounding! Throat thickening! Absolutely can't swallow! All the usual symptoms."

Brownie Point:
Mind games only work when the manipulative mind gains the consent of the manipulated mind. Both have to be willing participants. The giver and the receiver. The player and the played. #CB4C

Personally, I get fed up with seeing amazing women being victimized and torn to pieces over someone who doesn't have the good sense to either love you or leave you alone. I'm determined to help you snap out of being doped up on dopamine and see foolishness for what it is, FOO.LISH.NESS. You may be thinking: "I can't ever see the guy I'm with treating me like that." "I'd know if I was getting played." "That could never happen to me." Drop the naivete. Think again. Open your eyes. This is not about making you apprehensive about commitment. Real love and a mutual willingness to be in a trustworthy relationship is beautiful and worth celebrating! But I want you to be empowered to look at facts so you won't be blinded by infatuation.

Mirror Moment:

What makes you stay in a relationship when you keep having an overwhelming suspicion that something is: Just. Not. Right?

Are you currently seeing someone that makes you feel uneasy about trusting him?

11 Mind Games Single Women Fall For

Mind Game #1: Mr. Smooth Talker Rugger Walker

Chaos: He communicates with you regularly via calls, texts, video chat, social media, and e-mails. You've met and may run into each other while out. But he never spends intentional face-to-face, quality time with you. When it's time to act on his promises, he pulls a no-show or piles on the excuses.

Infatuation: You absolutely love his attention. You adore how he compliments you, remembers details about previous conversations, and talks about "getting together soon." You believe he's telling you the truth and hang on to hope with every syllable.

Facts: Your heart *hears his words*, but you're not *listening to his actions*. "Getting together soon" is an excuse, a put-off mechanism. This guy is really saying, "I like you from afar, and that's far more than wanting you up close and personal." Being in person adds another layer of accountability and intentionality when two people connect.

More than likely he's passing time until he gets a woman he deems as worthy of getting his appearance not just his words. Or he's dipping outside of a current relationship already in motion. He may be cute, but he's cunning. He doesn't want to lose an ego-stroker and void filler like you. *But God forbid being seen out in public together*. Constantly refusing public appearances means he doesn't even want to look like he's in a relationship with you. He has no intent to commit. When he's ready, he'll walk away from your attentive ears and right out of your life.

Confidence: You deserve a man whose walk matches his talk. Mr. Right will show up to take the lead and love you. Not leading you on and leaving you hanging on a whim. Consistency in a man's character is very telling of his intentions. Accept that words without meaning eventually run out of mileage. Real love isn't fueled by syrupy syllables and blowing tons of hot air. Be assured Mr. Right will *say AND do* the right things to win your love and earn your trust, in private and public.

Mind Game #2: Mr. One Sweet Day

Chaos: You're in love with a married man or secretly dating a guy who's in a relationship. He's told you time after time that eventually it will be "just the two of us" in the future. He's told you that he'll eventually get a divorce or break up when the time is right. Then he'll be ready to commit full time.

Infatuation: You find it extremely hard seeing yourself living without him. You are totally smitten with his gifts, his touch, and his feel-good promises. You're readily accepting: "We'll see, but let's just enjoy what we have." "I'm still working through some things." "It's really complicated; you wouldn't understand what I'm going through just to be with you." "You know I don't want to hurt you, so let's just wait."

Facts: His mouth has made more promises dipped in the finest covered pile of manure this side of the Mississippi (said with a bit of country swag indeed). These excuses have done nothing but made an icky mess to mislead your emotions. And they've no doubt made your eyes tear up because your heart is torn. You battle between should I stay or should I go. You get tired of being the "other woman" he places on the backburner instead of being the one he's faithfully committing to and loving.

I admit I've indulged in ABC's highly rated show *Scandal*. However here's a few lines that absolutely responds to the "one sweet day" mind game and was surprisingly uttered from Olivia Pope's mouth:

> "*You have nothing. You have a pile of secrets and lies, and you're calling it love*. And in the meantime you're letting your whole life pass you by while they raise children, and celebrate anniversaries, and grow old together. You're frozen in time, you're holding your breath. You're a statue, waiting for something that's never going to happen. Living for stolen moments and hotel hallways and coat closets. You keep telling yourself they all add up to something really cause in your mind they have to, but they don't. They won't. They never will. Because stolen moments aren't a life. So you have nothing. You have no one. End it now."

A man who is married or in a relationship can never be fully capable of giving you his best. Sure you might have great sex, share dreams, and enjoy his wonderful sense of humor. But part-time attention doesn't qualify as full-time affection. If he's not completely over her, he's not entirely into you. If he hasn't totally let go, he can't possibly wrap his all around you. *You may love him, but you're not in love . . . with him.* Technically speaking, being in love takes two mutually consenting individuals who are willing to invest their all for each other. It takes two to tango. Since he's not officially divorced or broken up, this dance partner you desire gets to drag you along in the shadows. While his main squeeze gets the spotlight on the dance floor of his life (no matter how much complains about not loving her).

Confidence: He's a mathematical manipulator. He dishes out fragments of his love and expects you to be fulfilled. Are you cool with fractions of commitment? Don't you know you are entitled to have a man who wholeheartedly loves you (without treating you like a side chick)? It may be hard to break away, but you deserve better. You don't have to participate in enabling this man to cheat on his wife or girlfriend. You wouldn't want someone helping the love of your life cheat on you.

No matter how many times you ask, "Have we reached the land of us yet?" You're still a back-seat driver. And you have no *wheel power* to move him past his wife, girlfriend. Or to give him the *willpower* to stop promising, "One of these days." But you do have *real power* to vacate this ride of mind games so you can reach true love. Then you'll get to view your "sweet day" as a front-seat driver with Mr. Right. Rather than peeking out of back-seat windows and holding on to broken promises.

Mind Game #3: Mr. Spin Cycle

Chaos: You're in a relationship with a guy where you are together one minute and apart the next. He switches cycles more than a load of laundry in the washer. He disappears and reappears more often than your period. Both yield cramps. But at least your period's cramps are predictable, part of Mother Nature, and eventually fade away.

Infatuation: You become cool and complacent with instability. You give him permission to flip commitment on and off like a light switch.

Facts: This guy gets an applause for at least showing his true colors. When he disagrees with you, gets bored, or wants to hook up with somebody else, he bounces right on out of your life. He lacks loyalty, but somehow manages to keep you faithfully spinning around his world as you await his return. His puppy-dog-eyed apologies and excuses always come with a new spin. Wake up! This guy is not a helpless, lost puppy. He knows exactly what he's doing. Don't mistake his return as loyalty. If he was loyal he wouldn't have left in the first place. Every time you take him back, you empower him to perpetuate the spin cycle. In addition, he's probably taking another woman for a spin, too, during your breaks from each other. And guess who ends up with a stained heart, wrinkled rep, (and maybe even some extra loads of drama from another woman he's spinning around)? Yep, you do.

Confidence: True, you may not convince him to see what he's doing (having his cake, ice cream, and party, too). After all he doesn't want to disrupt his two ways of living and getting. But you darn sure have the right to bring the game to an end. He should be man enough to establish roots in a relationship and reciprocate love. Unwavering love is possible. You deserve a man who proves he'll solely be with you through thick and thin, good times and bad. Not in and out. Quit the spinning and start winning by leaving this unpredictable, insensitive relationship.

Mind Game #4: Mr. Out of Bounds

Chaos: You've been in a relationship for months (maybe years). Both of you have talked about getting married multiple times. You see the aisle. Taste the cake. Smell the flowers at the ceremony. However, there are key elements about him that leave you in limbo (i.e. his family, friends, house, job, childhood, or financial management, etc.). When asked about it, he brushes you off. Changes the subject. Tells you not to worry. Or somehow makes you feel that you're too demanding. You're secure as an individual, yet you're as clueless as a stranger when it comes to him being openly honest about his upbringing, support system, and influencers.

Infatuation: You've invested a lot of time, energy, and emotions. Most of all you've deposited a lot of hope in this relationship. But you've only been able to launch into full-court obscurity vs. knowledge and understanding. You're afraid to let go and show him that your requests are legitimate not ludicrous.

Facts: Patience is a virtue. But a woman waiting on this man is only settling for being in the *vicinity* of winning yet never declaring *victory*. He would rather stay out of bounds (selectively secretive) and keep you at arms distance vs. disclosing his innermost life facts to you.

He gets to do a double pump fake because you allow it. He plays you to the left because he can always count on your being a good bench warmer. Most men enthusiastically speak up about their money, cars, status, degrees, business contracts, and accolades. Truthfully, he's capable but unwilling to move mountains for your peace of mind. And that's just plain selfishness. Selective commitment doesn't benefit the "we," it caters to the "me."

When a man is serious about marriage, he does anything possible for his two worlds (you and other significant people in his life) to mix and mingle. He's either hiding something that would have you running away. Or he just wants to hold onto you until *the woman he really wants to marry* comes along.

Confidence: Honestly, it shouldn't take a man eons to know if you're the woman he wants to marry. Forever waiting on a man to get ready to have you as a dream team spouse, deprives you of enjoying a life with a man who's ready to show you off like a midcourt championship with you by his side. Your concerns and inquiries aren't stupid. Your peace of mind is important. Stop pacing the sidelines, hoping to get in the game and score more info. Move on, you deserve a man who will openly share about himself and value the trust you share as teammates in love.

Mind Game #5: Mr. Eco-Friendly

Chaos: You're in love with him and you want to move in together with the intentions of "trying to save" and "testing the waters" before marriage.

Infatuation: You believe moving in will get him two steps closer to popping out a ring with *carats* and getting on bended knee. But so far the only ones you see are the *carrots* you're picking up from the grocery store. Every day you pray this romantic roommate status will blossom into wedded bliss. You said "I do" to co-habitation. But you're failing to hear him say "I will (or won't) marry you."

Facts: Days turn into months and months into years. Until finally you decide to throw your hands up and settle for the next best thing: playing wifey. As time goes on, you steadily make withdrawals from your goals, hopes, and dreams of being officially married. Sure, it makes economic (eco) sense. Your bank accounts may have more money as you're consolidating bills, but what about the downsides of co-habitation?

Many guys believe if they can get hot savings, hot meals, hot lovin' (sex is even more probable when you share a living space), and a hot woman like you waiting at home without the ceremony and legal ramifications of marriage, they'll do it. After all, what's the use of buying the cow, if you can get the milk for free, right? Mmm. No wonder why he keeps pushing the conversation off the table and not lifting a hand to put a ring on your left fourth finger. The eco-savings are tremendous for him, while the eco-savings are costing your heart bundles beyond the bank.

According to *Seven Reasons Why Living Together Before Marriage Is Not a Good Idea*, compared with married couples, co-habitors report higher levels of:

- Alcohol problems
- Aggression (twice as common)
- Greater marital instability, lower marital satisfaction, and poorer communication
- Depression rates (more than three times higher)
- Women being assaulted (fifty-six times higher)

The Journal of Marriage and Family reported marriages that involve co-habitation before marriage have 50 percent higher disruption rates than marriage without premarital cohabitation. The National Institute for Healthcare Research reported that couples abstaining from sex before marriage are more sexually fulfilled than those who were involved sexually before marriage.

Confidence: First of all, if you're dating and pondering over making the move to move in, I highly recommend you reconsider. Look at what's taken place so far. Independently, you've both been able to pay your bills just fine and spend quality time. Why not enjoy the newness of graduating into the realm of romance, roommates, and revenue with sealed commitment? This way you'll have something to anticipate. To see the true intentions of his heart (being wifey) vs. a man who slides into a comfort zone and belittles marriage (playing wifey). Save yourself the time of premature U-hauling and potential U-turns if things don't work out. After all, married couples can't walk as easily as roommates. No doubt about it. You deserve Mr. Right showing you that vows are worth addressing before sharing an address with you.

Mind Game #6: Mr. Chameleon

Chaos: Wow, he's so engaged and demands to know more and more whenever you communicate. He asks you questions about work, what makes you tick, your friends, your favs, and what you want in a man. With each conversation, you do more sharing of your innermost secrets than he does. In turn, when you do flip the question, his answers line up with yours as if you're Siamese twins sharing the same brain. He conforms to or agrees with practically everything you say (with a "me too"). You can't believe how many commonalities you have.

Infatuation: You feel so lucky to have this rapid-fire connection. His sweet disposition seems to be caring and sensitive to what you've been through in the past. Sometimes you have to pinch yourself because you've never opened up like this before with a guy. You're starting to wonder if he's *the one*. The commonalities just seem to magically increase as you spend more time conversing.

Facts: Despite the myth, there are some men who are excellent listeners. However those who play this mind game don't listen with love in mind, but to learn about you. He'll ask a ton of (open-ended) questions about you because he's studying you. This is his master attempt to win you over and break your defenses down. With this mind game, you do most of the talking. When you try to ask about him, he modestly shies away and flips the convo back to you. Therefore, the "getting to know" process is more one-sided.

You candidly share your vulnerabilities, insecurities, and capabilities. Meanwhile, he's strategically *becoming* the man of your dreams according to your likes and dislikes. He's not *being* a man who is equipped with his own set of traits, preferences, experiences, and mindset. The character he displays feeds off of the woman of interest. So like a chameleon, he cleverly changes while posing to be Mr. Right. As he gains more of your trust, he'll ask (or convince) you to compromise some of your strictest relationship standards and boundaries for what he selfishly wanted from the start (i.e. sex, money, status, an arm charm, bragging rights etc.). This is calculated manipulation. A wolf in sheep's clothing. Don't fall for it!

Confidence: The only thing you need to have in common and share with this man is a swift dial tone and an erased profile from your phone, tablet, and memory. It may seem like the chameleon type is a rare jewel, but he's fool's gold. And you're nobody's fool. Telling your life story with an appendices within a few conversations is a strict no-no. Your prized secrets should not be given on a whim or out of emotional neediness. Get to know more about him first, before telling him layers of your life. A man shouldn't mind openly sharing who he is in conversation, so you can assess if he's commitment material. After all, what man downplays who he is unless he has something to hide, right? If a man truly wants to enjoy a bright future with you laced in love, he's going to keep a high (not low) profile with you. You've got the strength to woman up and give this "slick master of the switch up" game a classy goodbye and good riddance.

Mind Game #7: Mr. Online & Out of Line

Chaos: You've been building a bond over the Internet for quite some time. You've talked over the phone about taking your relationship to another level . . . even sharing a future together. But you haven't met. You haven't talked to any of his friends, family, or co-workers. And you certainly haven't verified his identity via background checks or a real good Google sweep. You've only taken in firsthand information, directly from him.

Infatuation: In your heart, you believe he loves you. You can't seem to think of anyone else. Meanwhile you've changed your online and real-life dating status to "I'm taken!" He's promised to come and visit, but keeps delaying the trip. Something always pops up. You keep telling yourself *he has to be worth the wait*. You've downplayed the importance of physical interaction and getting to meet the total package (i.e. his mannerisms, actions, and reactions).

Facts: How long will you keep saying maybe next week, maybe next month? How long will you keep ignoring the dilemma? You may have a strong Wi-Fi signal, but you've got a lost connection. Why should you hook up with someone who is so insecure about himself he would hide behind lies for months, even years? Bad choices, not mistakes, have been made here. He chooses to hide his identity. He chooses to give you honey-dipped lies (excuses) about why you can never meet. He chooses to refrain from video chatting and introducing you to other people who can confirm his identity.

And you . . . you choose to stay, wait, believe, and get suckered into this prolonged fiasco of a relationship. You're being played like a feature on MTV's *Catfish*. It's way too obvious, he's totally out of line. He has no plans to be honest and respectful of you. And you must have at least those two crucial elements in any relationship you engage in.

Confidence: No more covering up for him! This guy isn't worth anymore of your prime, time, effort, energy, data usage, phone space, or computer's battery. Letting it passively stew for months and then into years is leading to your demise. Don't you think you deserve Mr. Right giving you truth from the start vs. finding out about his fabricated identity later? Time is the most valuable resource you can no longer afford to take for granted. Lies aside, guys go for what they want. Your Mr. Right is not only going to pull his *weight* in the relationship, he's not going to make you *wait* forever to see him in person. Besides, a man who's serious is also curious. Mr. Right will want to see you in person. Why? Because he knows you're too much of a good thing for him to chance you getting away or looking elsewhere for love.

Mind Game #8: Mr. Ninth Inning

Chaos: He's been caught cheating and you've addressed it. He's had several chances to batter up and do better. Nevertheless he keeps blowing it.

Infatuation: You love him deeply and invested so much. There's a few fibers left in you that sincerely hope he'll change. Plus you're afraid of what life will be like without him.

Facts: He knows exactly what to say, who to blame, and knows how to be "good" for a certain amount of time. Until he gets caught up in another affair. Face it, he lacks the devotion for a monogamous relationship with you. He doesn't have the will to change. He couldn't care less about bringing added doses of drama, sleepless nights, mournful mornings, distrust, and maybe even STDs to your relationship.

He is capitalizing on your low self-esteem and lack of self-worth. Your vulnerability has become his claim to victory: having you when he wants, how he wants, and where he wants. Face it, this behavior proves *he's not yours for the keeping but yours for the cheating*. The temporary "keep him on a leash" tactics and micromanaging have failed over and over again. Please don't think for a second that marriage or kids are going to cure him. They won't. It's the ninth inning and he's struck out too many times. His consistency to cheat shows he has no goal of quitting the game.

Confidence: Refusing to let go and jump into the unknown (leaving him), prevents you from discovering what you could know. Like for instance, having a fascinating life with Faithful Frankie instead of Cheating Chauncey. A beautifully stable relationship is worth leaving this game even when the bases are loaded with his, "I'll never do it again" and "You're the only one I really love" pleading. Run. Run fast. And don't look back. Your Mr. Right is bound to one day come out of the dugout and score a home run by honoring you with fidelity, honesty, and love.

Mind Game #9: Mr. Jealous Jimmy

Chaos: You were in a relationship, but he broke up with you (and may have moved on to another woman). Now he's back on the scene all because a new man has entered your life.

Infatuation: You are caught between the two, stay with your ex or go with the next? It's hard to believe how much your ex has been saying that he misses you. Plus, he keeps mentioning the possibility of getting back together. You believe he's turned a new leaf and is ready to be sincerely in love with you.

Facts: Whenever you're standing at a crossroad, it's always wise to pump the brakes and analyze what's going on before proceeding. Your emotions are vying to lead you in the wrong hands for the wrong reasons. He broke up with you and only popped back into your life because someone else is there. Perhaps this has happened multiple times. Your ex's motive is pure jealousy. His aspiration is not to reunite with you, but to dismantle the chances of anyone else having a shot to win your heart. So before Mr. Next really gets too far, Mr. Ex is all of sudden piling on attention like it's about to go out of style. He might show even more enthusiasm and spunk than when you were in a committed relationship.

This reaction is nothing short of manipulation and control. Don't be fooled by this possessive behavior. Let me interpret it for you, what he's really saying via his actions is: "I don't really want you . . . more so, I really don't want someone else having you." With this game, you inevitably give your ex-man permission to mess up your potential with the next man, or better yet the next chapter of your incredible life.

Confidence: You are absolutely worthy of a man who's genuinely motivated to love you not because someone else has whisked you away. You're not meant to be objectified like a piece of property that a man can simply *compete for, then retreat from* when the game is over. Don't stroke this guy's jealous ego any more. Save your precious brain cells and beautiful heart strings for Mr. Right. He'll be magnetic to you whether you have a line of suitors or if it's simply you patiently waiting in line for his arrival. His motivation will be building a wonderful future with you, instead of aiming to break down another man's attempt of devotion to you.

Mind Game #10: Mr. Jack-in-the-Box

Chaos: Everything is going great, but one day out of the blue, he disappears without a logical reason, outburst, or explanation. Time passes by and you run into each other out in public. All of a sudden, he's initiating hooking back up and picking up where you left off. But his interest only reappears when running into you.

Infatuation: You start believing time has healed all wounds. His reappearance and aggressive zeal must mean it's destiny for you to be together.

Facts: Setting giddiness aside. Just think. Would he be showering you with calls and dates if the "run-ins" didn't occur? More than likely, your number hasn't changed. And even if it did, a man who really, really wants you, will find you. Mountain high, valley low. Wait a minute, *if he was truly interested, he wouldn't have disappeared without trace in the first place!* And since the last run-in, has he contacted you? Mmm. Mmm. Mmm.

As wonderful as you are, you're not that easy to leave and never contact again. Chances are you probably ran into him when he was in one of his dry spells, post-breakup periods, or hard up for some attention afternoons. You were wide-eyed and drawn in by his charm. Don't be fooled, his crank is in countdown mode. As soon as he sees another woman who piques his interest, his crank will turn and this jack will be out of your sight once again.

Confidence: Don't give this guy the chance to play you like a rebound girl. You can command that respect by picking up the next time he calls (if he calls) and playing Ray Charles's "Hit the Road Jack" until he gets the message. After all, you want your Mr. Right to see you as Miss Available to Love, and not hung up over a guy who's treating you like a leftover. You're too beautiful to forget that you not only can spark a guy's interest, you can keep the right man's interest!

Mind Game #11: Mr. Sampler

Chaos: Plain and simp, you are sex partners/buddies with him. You're wanting more commitment outside of bed, but haven't seen a sign of it yet.

Infatuation: You believe his constant returns for sex is getting you closer to a solidified relationship in the streets, not just the sheets.

Facts: He's playing you like a "browse-only and never buy" sampler at Sam's Club. For instance, shopping at Sam's Club often requires driving, parking, walking in, sampling, choosing, purchasing, bagging, and taking the item home and even caring for it (properly storing it) so it won't expire! Within this mind game, he's doing nothing but paying the minimal fee to gain entrance into the most sacred part of you. On top of that, he gets to sample all the other women in the world (if he wants) and walk away satisfied and full after sexing you. He doesn't have to commit anything that's nonsexually sacred to him for what he gets in exchange. And he won't. He flashes his sex membership card and the doors of your legs swing wide open. But do you even care about what dirt and filth he may be bringing into you? Sex doesn't make a man love a woman, but lust sure makes a man and woman love sexing each other. He enjoys the current convenience. After all you're the one paying his tab whenever he shows up to the checkout.

Confidence: Soul ties can't compare to all the riches of the world. Put him on a sex-free diet. Then you'll see exactly where his loyalty stands. Is it your life or what's in between your legs? Letting Mr. Sampler go means you can quit settling for being tricked into laying down the totality of your body, for a man who only sees you as an easy lay. Mr. Right will know there's a variety of women he can have sex with, but there's only a few who will ever have an unshakable place in his heart. You are deserving of knowing this by standing on your two feet instead of lying on your back . . . and handing out samples you'll never get back.

Sound the Alarm: Game Over

Settling to be under the spell of mind games will have you constantly converting your lifestyle and your way of existing. It also alters your perception of relationships. I believe to "co-mmit" is to "co-meet." This involves two individuals meeting and being in agreement to "co-move" forward together, not living planets apart with dishonesty at the helm of the relationship.

Mind games sabotage your greatness. If someone has manipulative authority over your mind, they can have reign over your life. This is a prime reason God wants us to be "*transformed not trans-tricked*" by the renewing of our minds. He's literally trying to save our hearts, bodies, and souls from engaging in mind games that lead us to agonizing defeat.

Yes, a man might look good, sound good, smell good, talk good, and have you feeling good. But being a confident woman means being realistic, alert, and astute. We don't live in a perfect world where every man has a righteous agenda. Or an "I'll treasure all women like I would my mother" badge of honor engrained in his heart. Having confidence also means not retreating back to a guy due to *Post Emotional Negotiation* (P.E.N., a term I made up). This often happens after dismissing a guy who's playing mind games. Feelings of guilt and questioning your judgment surface: "Was I too hard on him?" "Maybe he really didn't mean it." "Did I make a mistake?" Remember, if dismissing a drama king means availing yourself for your dream king, then tell the voice of doubt, "Shut up! I know my worth and I know real love upgrades, not degrades me!"

With mind games somebody's going to win, and somebody's going to lose. You weren't born to lose. And you weren't born to pass these mind games on to the next generation of beautiful, fantastically awesome women yet to come. Live in such way where even your life's legacy isn't categorized as a woman who was a sucker to mind games for most of her time on earth.

So ditch the baggage and embrace your power. Remember how you're extraordinarily equipped! You have a mind, *use it*. You have a heart, *guard it*. You have a body, *revere it*. You have a reputation, *protect it*. You have confidence, *keep it*. You have a future, *seize it*. And seize it with wisdom, not mindless abandon.

Chaos to Confidence

5 Ways to Stop Mind Games before They Start

1. **G**et gullibility out of your life. Don't be too hasty in letting him into your life. Allow a guy to earn your trust.
2. **A**ttentively listen vs. actively talking. Have ten to fifteen open-ended questions to randomly ask him and check for his character consistency.
3. **M**eet up in public places. Don't readily accept invitations over to his house or to your place. It's harder to manipulate in public.
4. **E**liminate justifying excuses for incompatibility and cheating. He's either in it to win your heart, or play with your heart.
5. **S**eek God, Google, and guidance before becoming his "one and only." Researching before releasing the doors of your heart can help expose manipulative behavior.

CHAPTER 9

CLOSURE: THE LACK. THE LOOK. THE LOVE.

NOT GETTING WHAT WE WANT IS NEVER A TOP GOAL WE RUSH toward in life. Nor, do we readily embrace the challenge of oncoming change or a closed door. For instance: your favorite clothing store shutting its doors and going out of business. The inability to find that tune you've declared as the official theme song of your life. The closest ATM you regularly go to being temporarily shut down for repair. Or that delectable meal you always order at a restaurant suddenly vanishing from the menu (and just when your taste buds wanted it the most). Yes, sometimes we absolutely hate change! But one thing that really gets under our skin as single women (more than a closed door) is not knowing the reason why a relationship with a guy ends. When it dissipates into thin air, it's easy to wind up hopelessly moping around wondering: Is it really, seriously, absolutely over?

I've suffered from the debilitating lack of closure after a guy broke my heart. It's too bad WebMD doesn't include this as an attack on the immune system. You know you're infected with a case of "closure-itis" when these symptoms appear:

- Heart palpitations at any slight indication he's contacting you
- Frequent crying spells day and night
- Mental cloudiness
- Emotional passiveness
- Repeatedly analyzing all of his messages
- Nervous itch to contact him or cyber stalk him
- Irritable mood swings with innocent bystanders (i.e. family, friends, co-workers)
- Avoiding other relationships and putting life on hold

How can you truly live when you carry a load of questions that leave you unsettled and untrusting? How do you react when a split leaves you peering out the window of your heart, wishing for someone's return? What do you do when you've got a pile of burning hope but tons of broken promises? How can you be free to love again when every guy afterward gets compared to him? Dealing with closure issues can be painfully frustrating and emotionally fatiguing.

A Man without Manners

The phone rang and my friend was hysterically explaining a mysterious disappearance. Kamia's voice was full of confusion masked by overwhelming fear, the fear of living life without him. "Girl, I can't believe this happened. Things were going so well with Tyler, at least I thought so. For the last ten months we've talked daily. We spent a lot of quality time, and discussed taking our relationship to the next level. He said he loved me over and over. Tyler even introduced me to his family! I really thought we were in love . . . that we had something special, until boom, he just stopped altogether!" By the time she and I conversed, two whole weeks had already passed. There were no calls, texts, emails, social media posts, or explanations. Nothing. Gone without a trace. Kamia had left at least twenty-two voicemails and 102 texts. Still no response.

She eventually called Sheila (a mutual friend of Kamia and Tyler) to see if she had talked to him. Surprisingly, Tyler had dinner with Sheila and her boyfriend a few days prior to her call. To add fuel to the fire, Tyler showed up at the restaurant with a new woman on his arm. Kamia was livid. "Sheila believes he's moved on, but I haven't! I want an explanation from him. He owes me that much. Why did he leave? Who is this chick? This is so unfair! Why did this happen to me? What did I do to deserve this? I'm so mad at him . . . I'm so mad at myself . . . I'm pissed about the whole jacked-up situation."

Have you ever experienced the baggage of closure issues before? The pain and humiliation cuts deep. You might literally want to run by his house or job and raise a lot of hell. You might want to even dial up his mother and demand, "Do you know what your son had the audacity to do to me? Now I know you taught him better than this!" But more than likely you won't. In fact, please don't. Go ahead, wipe the tears and save face. After all, you may have been dealt with dirty, but you're way too classy to be kickin' up any chaotic (and even crime-filled) dust.

The Unfinished Sentence . . .

Not receiving closure is like being the victim of dating's greatest grammatical errors. You start off writing a lovely *sentence* of attraction and affection together. You honestly believe the feeling is mutual. But before getting to the *period* of becoming an official couple, you're left with *question marks* galore. Or he leaves you with a *semicolon* where you're semi-stuck trying to figure out if it's a *comma* (a pause because maybe he just needs space). Or if it's a dreadful *period* (the relationship is finito).

Wow, if only we had been taught this type of grammatical lesson as little girls. Perhaps our hearts would be able to better brace the bruises when the sentence doesn't end with the guy being head over heels in love with us and topped off with an exclamation mark! (I think adding a subject like *Understanding the Foreign Language of Love* around fifth grade would save us a lot of issues and tissues, don't you?)

It's a pure bummer when a Mr. Right prospect turns into Mr. Magic and does a "poof pow I'm gone with a cloud of smoke" trick right in front of you. The aftermath is filled with questions not just about him, but about you, too. I've experienced how an unexpected disconnection made me feel unworthy. Undone. Unhappy. Unloved. It made what seemed crystal clear . . . blurry with so many "50 Shades of *Gray*." And yet somehow feeling as inquisitive and emotionally distant as Anastasia is to Christian in the top-selling novel.

Brownie Point:
Weeping may endure for a *knight*, but joy will come in spite of the *mourning*. #CB4C

But She's Not Me

I really had grown to love Jeremy. We talked about marriage, kids, laughing and loving while growing old together. We would talk all throughout the week and loved each other's company. With each passing conversation our feelings grew. Secrets were exchanged. Insecurities shared. My alarm clock would pale in comparison to his faithful morning calls. His massages felt amazing and were always on time. His prayers were powerful. His reminders of missing me whenever I was traveling kept us close. I knew I had passed the trust litmus test when he gave me the keys to his condo. We both felt as if we were pouring into a ginormous container of love . . . something much bigger than ourselves. We were steadily filling our love tanks. And in spite of what he brought to the table, he became the exception to my preference (he had been married, divorced, and had two kids).

It was a cold November day when Jeremy came to take me to the airport. I was going to celebrate Thanksgiving with my family in Florida. While getting ready that morning, I remember how a crazy thought entered my mind. Maybe we would share an amazingly juicy kiss. Right before the airport police started ordering him to quit holding up traffic. You know, one of those "only in the movies kind of kisses" where the world stands still for a few miraculous moments and nothing else seems to matter. Then breaking away for air meant the earth could officially start rotating again. The kind of kiss different from anything shared before . . . where both of you are left wondering, *What was THAT all about? I don't know, but we have got to talk... talk about us. Real soon.*

When he arrived and came in, he wasn't in the best of moods. So, I was forced to snap out of my daydream. His mood was contagious and put me on edge as well. By the time we pulled up to the curbside check-in, I shot out of the car. We quickly exchanged a distant embrace. No typical super hold 'n squeeze hugs. No kiss. No magic moment. No chance for time to stand still. I was a bit agitated, flustered really. However, all that melted away when I touched down to eighty-three-degree weather, held my brand new baby nephew, and started eating enough delicious food to make me think I had been transported to a Caribbean culinary heaven.

But as I returned home, the weather between me and Jeremy was nothing short of a gloomy forecast. During the weekend, he had met another girl. They quickly bridged a gap by talking for hours. He introduced her to his mother, and took her to a football game. (These last two steps usually were part of a slow, gradual process to achieve.) After all, his mother was next to God, and football was between the guys only. In our next conversation, he started going down a list of how much she was like me. *She talks like you. She's pretty like you. She's funny like you. She has strong faith in God like you. She's business-minded like you. She's so sweet like you.* I was shocked into silence. After the call, the bitter taste of reality lingered on my tongue and washed over my spirit. I wanted to scream, "But she's not me! I'm good enough to be your *almost* but not good enough to be your *absolute*? Seriously . . . just who am I to you?!"

Check Your I.Q.

After I hung up the phone, many fears coalesced in my mind and tears started falling down my face. They could have easily competed with the waterfall at Angel Falls. I never got a clear explanation on why he chose the other woman. When this happens, you may have a zillion questions . . . such as:

- What's wrong with me?
- Did I do something to deserve this?
- Do I need to change who I am?
- Did he ever really love me?
- Could I have done something different to make him stay?
- What can I do to prove "I'm good enough" for him?
- Will I ever be happy or in love again?

It's normal for these questions to surface. However, it's abnormal for you to allow these questions to fester too long and convert into baggage that does nothing but weigh you down as you seek to move on. It's imperative to "check your I.Q." I'm not talking about your intelligence quotient. Rather, when closure is lacking, I want you to analyze your *internal questioning*. Your self-worth and dignity is too incredible to stay down in the dumps forever.

Don't take it so personally that this added experience, subtracts your will to move on. The situation doesn't merit that kind of power over your livelihood! Oftentimes when a guy leaves, it doesn't ALWAYS mean there's something *wrong with you*. Look at it this way. Someone else is just *right* for him and another guy will be *better for you*. It doesn't mean you won't feel upset and disappointed. However, I guarantee you'll be happier with someone who is happy loving you. Don't allow one man's choice to move away, result in you having a knee-jerk reaction and start completely changing yourself. Someone else will adore the effort and energy you invest in a relationship. Besides, let's say there was something you could have done differently. A man (who truly wanted to stay) would have communicated that instead of doing a "Mr. Disappearing Acts" move.

My pastor, Bishop Joseph Walker III, once poignantly stated, "I cannot allow my yesterday to control me; that only retards the progress of my tomorrow." Spending a whole lot of time internally questioning yourself only shackles you to what has passed. Embrace your power and realize your time can be better spent on loving yourself and moving into prep mode for Mr. Right. With each passing relationship, you should see improvements in your selection of date potentials and relationships. It's a cycle of living, loving, and learning. I believe your Mr. Right will be an even better man knowing his Miss Right went through past travels to better appreciate her present journey. Don't give up. Eventually you will be ready to be with a man who's willing and working to love you more each day.

Brownie Point:
Don't allow your ex's action birth a lifelong dissatisfaction. He was willing to leave. Now will yourself to live. #CB4C

The Lack: 3 Key Stages to Overcome Closure Issues

OK. You've officially changed his name in your contacts. First name Magic, last name Disappearance. (And maybe a few other choice words to be honest.) However, let me share with you healthy ways to move on and regain power when you feel hopeless. These three critical stages are absolutely necessary for your healing and regaining confidence.

Stage #1: Admittance

Admit how you feel when you don't receive closure. Don't suppress your sadness, depression, anger, guilt, or apprehensions. You must grieve . . . in fact please grieve. Journal if you must. Vent to a trusted friend. Do a kickboxing workout. Get professional counseling if needed. However, this phase of self-pity parties ain't forever! Some people have a pity party so long they live in a perpetual pit. What's worse than having heavy bags under your eyes due to heavy baggage from a guy who didn't care enough to say goodbye? Genuine love will make you cry tears of joy not perpetual tears over a jerk.

You might think "Revenge is a dish best served cold." Maybe in a movie, but we're talking about real life. Unleashing revenge should never be a full- or part-time job you pick up. Let go and let God take care of those who have wronged you. Don't allow a breakup to rob you of your crown. Remain a queen! Think about your dignity while you're admitting your hurt. Even when you may be on the verge of saying or doing distasteful things you'll regret. Your rep is priceless and doesn't need to be dragged through the mud. So admit where you're at emotionally and confidently keep your rep sparkling like a diamond.

Brownie Point:
Your inner bling can't shine when you're holding onto tarnished memories and hidden heartache. Let it go. #CB4C

Stage #2: Acceptance

Accept what you had is no longer around. Face the facts. In the book *Real Men Don't Text*, Michael Dean states what he and a lot of men do when suddenly vacating a relationship: "Did I let her know kindly I wasn't interested and make a clean break? Unfortunately not. I continued to text her and respond to her text because, frankly, it felt good to be liked. I hoped that with each text my feelings for her would grow, but they didn't. I didn't want to hurt her or have a difficult conversation by telling her straight up I was not interested. I hoped that she would figure it out on her own . . . I finally stopped altogether (why didn't someone punch me in the face sooner?). I didn't know or even consider how my actions might affect her."

I don't mean to sound rude, but let me be honest. When a guy DOES NOT answer, *that is an answer*. You've consistently called, texted, driven by his place, and contacted him via all possible ways online. And still no response. Listen. He's no longer interested in you. I know, I know. You've been talking for months. Or you've been dating for a year or more. He said he wanted to be married, raise a family, and have a successful career with you by his side.

But where is he now? The smooth-sounding syllables have dissipated into thin air. And he has, too.

This is painstaking to compare, but I'll digress. You know how they say a divorce doesn't happen overnight? Well, I believe a guy's decision to leave while dating doesn't happen overnight either. He's known about having no intention to slip a ring on your finger and grow old together before vacating. Yes, it's not at all fair to have led you on and let your hopes be dashed. But he made his decision, and now it's time for you to make yours.

Chillaxing in denial (that it's over) robs you of life. *Plus, you waste a few precious commodities.* Little things like time, an appetite, brain cells, peace of mind, confidence, ambition, and even muscle mass. (Hey, it takes extra willpower or extra-strength meds to pull the weight of a dead relationship.)

You distance yourself from being ready for Mr. Right while holding out for Mr. No Longer Interested. Denial will have you allowing someone in their absence to dictate your present state of life. Quit giving the pain more power in your life! C'mon, does he really deserve that much post-disappearance credit?

Yes, he might have known what he was doing when he vanished. But get this. He has no idea what he's missing out on from being with an incredibly remarkable woman like you! *But I still love him.* I believe you love the man you *used* to know. What about the man who left you? Accept he was willing to leave. Accept that love sticks around through the terrific and tough times. Accept that love will communicate before deciding to vacate. Accept your best is truly yet to come. Accept the door he left open, will be the door Mr. Right will gladly come through. The choice is yours.

Stage #3: Alleviation

At some point, you have to pump the brakes and declare, "No mas!" By now, you've dedicated a lot of time wondering, weeping, worrying, and whining about not getting an explanation (rinse and repeat). Right now you might be in P.I. mode and could give CSI a run for their money in a trail of clues leading to his whereabouts. You've relentlessly reached out to him. His number hasn't changed. His voicemail box isn't full. His social media accounts haven't been deleted. He hasn't lost his phone. He hasn't broken his two thumbs. Enough with making excuses for him and going toward the flow of heartache! Take your foot off the gas. Now it's time to give yourself some relief.

A man will brave the harshest of calamities and climates, come hell and high water when he wholeheartedly wants to be with a woman. Do yourself a favor. Stop the lost-and-found chase. Alleviate the pressure to chase after someone who isn't pursuing you anymore.

Take a deep breath and ease up on yourself. Find relief in knowing you are NOT the only one in the world who has experienced lack of closure. You are NOT the creator, controller, or dictator of the guy who left. It's not right for you to blame yourself for someone you can't control. In life, we all go through challenges for which we didn't sign up. And not all of them are our fault. Recycling self-blame only distances you from forgiving those who've wronged you and embracing the next guy who will really love you. Pacify your mind by refusing to replay your "once was" like a never-ending TV show marathon. Embracing your power means taking back the remote control and changing the channel. *Subscribe to another network, so you won't lose sight of your net worth.* Turn to God and find comfort from confusion and bitterness. You're deserving of seeing a brighter future, not a blame-filled, baggage-toting one.

Last Girl Waiting in Line for Love

I used to compare myself to my incredible sister, Christina. No doubt about it, she is way more than meets the eye. She's a wonderfully wrapped essence of beauty on the inside and out. When I was in college, I invited her to spend spring break with me. During her stay, she received more double takes and attention from guys in one week than I did in the previous month. And she is six years younger than me. Talk about a blow to my *she-go*! Through the years I've witnessed how old, young, tall, short, thugs, and corporate-collared guys have turned their heads and mustered up the nerve to approach her. Honestly, sometimes envy would creep inside me. My self-esteem would tank. I'd instantly start making a list of why I couldn't garner a certain guy's initial interest. And I started listening to inner voices of lies telling me why a guy like that, would never pick a girl like me.

Have you ever secretly carried the baggage of comparing your love life? You might have a friend or family member who gets tons of male attention. And frankly you feel inadequate, inferior, and sometimes invisible. The sense of hopelessness occurs when you're hanging out. Or when you go home for the holidays and your relatives are trying their best to ask you every question in the book, beyond "Are you dating anyone . . . yet?"

Instead of due to a guy's disappearance, this lack of closure revolves around a guy's appearance in the first place. It's more so about not losing hope whenever doubt sneaks in and says, "Call it a wrap. It's never going to happen for you." Listen, you can't live life worrying about someone else's definition of your love life or a reality you can't change. Your job profile on earth shouldn't consist of working OT in comparing your love life.

Let me be straightforward with you. In life, some women get approached all day, every day. Some women could easily have every night of the week booked with dates if they wanted to, and sometimes they indulge the attention. But you might be like me, on the other end of the spectrum. Trying to decide between an incredibly vast collection of eligible guys vying for your affection is not a part of your daily routine. Right now you might be exhausted of hearing the excuses: *"You're just too intimidating. You're just in a league of your own. Guys know they can't step to you any kind of way. When it comes to you, they have to come correct."* Or you might be tired of being approached by guys you can tell from ten miles out that they're an absolute "Ohhhh, heck no!"

Now I'm not saying these things in a mean or envious manner. Seriously. You shouldn't hate on the skin someone is in or the attraction guys have for them. After all, they didn't create themselves or choose their body, skin tone, personality, or giftings. (So if you got a complaint, drop a note in God's suggestion box.) For real, be honest. You *are* happy about your third friend sharing her happiness over a new love interest. You *do* want the best for your roommate as you help her pick between the red, blue, or black dress for a first date with her campus crush. You *are* happy about your cousin getting engaged to her boyfriend of two years. You *do* look forward to being the best auntie ever after hearing your sister is having a baby.

But I just want to speak up for the souls who have started to believe singlehood is ultimately their fault and totally due to their "flaws." For you who internally battle with feeling like you're the last girl standing in line for love. You vacillate between keeping your cool and wanting to pout harder than "a born with a silver spoon in their mouth spoiled brat." Other days your tears scream, "I want to be in love, too!" Right now you may be longing for closure from God. You want him to close the chapter of uncertainty and just flat-out tell you when your love story will unfold. I've personally hit all these phases of singlehood over several years, so I understand.

In the real estate industry, there's a slogan that says it's all about location, location, location. Well, I want to remind you while you're standing at the intersection of Relationship

Avenue and Waiting for a Lover Lane, it's all about perspective, perspective, perspective.

Nowhere in 1 Corinthians 13 (the purest definition of love) does it state that love is about the *quantity of compliments, dates, number exchanges, invitations for sex, or boyfriends you can rack up before Mr. Right.* No matter how tempting it might be to compare yourself, don't do it. You are your mother's child, but you're not your mother. You might share the same last name and cravings for Grandma's pies, but you are not your brother or sister. You and your BF may have the same Michael Kors bag and share celebrity crushes, but you are not your best friend. Just as every inch of your DNA is uniquely woven, so is your love story. It's unprecedented. Unduplicatable. It is unlike anyone else's.

And you know what? You're not by yourself! You're not the last girl waiting in line for love. Neither am I. Life is comprised of some people just waiting a little longer. But there's a super sweet tradeoff. The wait may be arduous but not nearly as painful as putting up with countless run-ins with Mr. Wrongs and hellish drama from settling for a dozen "He'll-Do-For-Nows." And afterward still winding up miles away from true, lasting companionship.

Mirror Moment:

Are you easily offended or resiliently optimistic when someone tries to compare your love life to others?

Do you try forcing or hurrying relationships because of FOMO (fear of missing out) or comparisons? If so, why?

The Look: He's Just a Doorman

There is a new way of looking at ex-boyfriends and other guys known as the Kings of the Disappearing Act. Personally, I've come to understand their place as doormen in my life.

Have you ever been at a ritzy, five-star hotel? I've been blessed to stay at the Broadmoor, the Biltmore, and MGM Grand, to name a few. The treatment you receive while on the property is exquisite. You drive up, and immediately a valet comes rushing to your car door. He's ready to open it. A few words are communicated, keys are passed, trust is exchanged, and a commitment quickly evolves. Then you move on to the entrance doors. Another man or two anxiously awaits to open the door for you. A courteous, "Welcome and how are you doing, ma'am?" is tossed your way. Next up, bellhops ask to render assistance. They might look good, smell good, and sound good, but steadily you keep moving forward. Why? Because these men are strictly designated to keep opening doors, which ultimately lead to your actual destination. In the hotel sense, they lead you one step closer to a person who'll have the key to your hotel room.

Let me explain this in regards to a relationship. The purpose of some men in your life is to strictly lead you to the man who'll have the key to your heart. They'll lead you to a man who will have the courage, compassion, and capacity to commit. These "doormen" open doors, not their hearts. They don't open themselves to be depended upon, no matter what. There's no "I'm here for the long haul, through thick and thin" drive within them. Often, doormen will show you things you like or dislike in relationships. An experience with them can also shed light on who you are as a woman. And yet doormen (unbeknown to them) can mysteriously help make you an even more confident woman by the time you're face to face with Mr. Right.

So doormen have a place in your life. But you must never stay stuck believing they'll give you *closure or commitment.* Their job was just to push you toward the man you're destined to share your life with! So quit trying to make them into Mr. Right, when it's apparent he's Mr. Left-and-Gone. Quit trying to convert someone who no longer wants a connection with you. In fact, he left open a door that can usher you into greater. But you have to choose. It's a whole new way of looking at closure, right? Right.

Brownie Point:
Doormen welcome guests. A man of destiny welcomes companionship. #CB4C

This truth has helped me convert lemons to lemonade when I lacked closure about a relationship. A simple change of perspective can give you enough confidence to see facts and move forward.

Mirror Moment

Are you holding onto baggage while hoping a doorman will return and carry the load of hurt away?

How long will you continue putting life on pause for someone who's not willing to rewind back to you?

Sentenced to Life or Death?

Holding out for closure is similar to holding your breath under water. You're waiting for him to throw out a life preserver. Instead, he's a lifeguard gone AWOL. He's no longer investing in your life and sure as heck not interested in guarding your heart. Yet you're holding your breath, hoping he'll come back for your rescue. You're crumbling inside, and your confidence is dying alongside faded memories that are no longer reality.

Why are you allowing darkness and gloom to cause your dreams, determination, focus, and faith to die? Yes, you're still breathing and your heart is still beating. But refusing to close the lid on closure issues means you're not abundantly living. You're merely existing. *You're a survivor of today, a slave to yesterday, and a surrenderer of tomorrow.* Your feet might be facing forward, but if you're inwardly longing for the past, you won't be able to proceed. All of your heart, mind, and soul need to be astute and awakened to reality in order to overcome the lack of closure.

Brownie Point:
You might not get a period for every sentence. But eventually you've got to plant the punctuation. Move on to the next paragraph and the next chapter of your life. #CB4C

It doesn't matter how or why your boyfriend, boo, bae, or even fiancé left. By God's finest promise and penmanship, you've been sentenced to LIFE, not death. He's able to help you triumph over this unexpected caption and write a new headline that gives you victory over your struggles. The guy you once loved made his choice. Now it's time for you to embrace a new season. A new outlook. A new push to look up and see endless love surrounding you now. As I write this, I'm praying for abundant freedom to cover you now. And I sincerely hope you choose to live with power, passion, and positivity!

The Love: The Door that's Always Open

There comes a point in time where you have to embrace trust again. No successful relationship can survive without it. You might feel betrayed, bewildered, and bitter. But you can trust in love, again. I'm not condoning or excusing a guy who left the door of your heart wide open and bounced without a goodbye. But I sincerely hope through this challenging circumstance you realize you can trust God to love the hurt away. He's the ultimate door of love and to true love.

I sure needed that reassurance when Jeremy broke my heart. I would wake up with tears streaming and go to sleep sobbing. During those moments, God never left my side. God's love surrounded me when Jeremy moved on, fell in love, and got married. I prayed relentlessly for answers, cried for clarity, and begged for a breakthrough (i.e. for my love life to catch up with his so I could prove I moved on, too). I didn't receive answers immediately or a resolution overnight. And I'm still waiting on my Mr. Right to lovingly come into my life.

But during this hardship, God gave me something greater. He gave me a resilience to get up again. He gave me a peace that blew my mind and helped me to focus on the love I have. He renewed my hope so the mentality of "every man is a dog" would not consume me. He helped me process the good qualities I admired in Jeremy, which other men in my past hadn't possessed. God opened my eyes to view his negative qualities, which could have hindered his plan for me in the future. God showed me the importance of not putting a guy's attention before his affection for my life. Yes, through this heartache, God showed me that *not every man qualifies to be in my future no matter how much my heart gave him a passing vote in the present.*

Various times in our lives, we will stop in our tracks because it seems like God's love is insufficient. We feel it doesn't satisfy because it doesn't cater to our demands of today. But believe me, God's love is far beyond our logic. It looks out on our behalf and miraculously is never beyond our reach.

I don't know who left you. Or who caused your heart to bleed with a plethora of unanswered questions. I don't know specifically what you're contemplating right now. But I'm writing this to let you in on a fact. It was never God's desire to see you torn apart from the inside out. God is saddened by your thinking he's abandoned you. Don't allow a guy who willingly chose to walk out on you make you believe God has followed suit.

Some doors you are wishing to close are left open for a reason. Why? Because although a page has been written, this chapter of your life isn't over. It's just taking another direction than you planned. God is able to take what you see as a screwed-up situation and turn it into a powerful motivation where you arise in confidence.

Sure, you deserve an explanation, an apology, or an ounce (more so a gallon) of courtesy. But camping out at a crossroad waiting for these leaves you two options. Option A: Sitting around all day with a gloomy cloud over you. Sleeping the pain away. Going through boxes of Kleenex and cry spells over Mr. Yesterday while staying stuck in a *yesterdaze*. Tear-staining pillows. Deleting then restoring pictures of him on your phone. Rummaging through past belongings he left behind. Staring at his phone number. Replaying old voicemails. Stalking him on Snapchat, Facebook, and Instagram. Getting angry over his pictures with another woman. And wearing out your friends' ears about how he treated you like a joke and got the last laugh.

Or Option B: Snatching back your strength. Forgiving yourself for wallowing in worry. Squaring your shoulders. Smiling. Putting on a feel-good, look-good outfit. Pulling back the blinds. Playing a song to pump you up and letting the melody electrify you into a happy dance. Inhaling some fresh air.

Posting a new pic and #TeamMovedOn online. Meeting new people and adventuring to new places. And seizing the opportunity to live moment by moment for today.

For the sake of your destiny and all the wonder in store, I hope you pick Option B. Be encouraged, girl. I don't want you to get hung up on a "What happened?" I want you to flourish with a "What's next?" in your heart as you journey toward happiness, wholeness, renewed hope, and attracting Mr. Right.

Chaos to Confidence

7 Steps for Moving on After He Disappears

1. **C**ome to a solid conclusion that you deserve a guy who will be faithfully next to you and in love with you.
2. **L**et go of the resentment, forgive the guy who left, and forgive yourself.
3. **O**pen your heart to trust God and believe in love again.
4. **S**eparate yourself from things, places, social media, numbers, and people that will tempt you to start digging for clues on him while you recover.
5. **U**nderstand this is challenging, but not impossible. You will overcome and be a stronger woman.
6. **R**efrain from starting a new relationship right away and give yourself time to emotionally and mentally grieve, detox, and heal.
7. **E**xpect an even greater, fulfilling, and faithful relationship with Mr. Right.

CHAPTER 10

WHEN SUPERMAN PURSUES WONDER WOMAN

WONDER WOMAN, SIMPLY AN UNFORGETTABLE ANIMATED VERSION of prettiness and prowess. I would often try my best to have her similar appeal while dating. *Magic lasso, check*. I had to be ready to reel a man in close. *Bullet-proof bracelets, got it*. I had to protect myself from guys I knew were a "Heck no!" from fifty feet away. *Fierce bustier, oh yes*. Every woman knows what just enough cleavage can do to a man. *Polished gold headband, had to have it*. I still had hope of a king spotting me as his queen, even in not-so royal places. *Tights to accentuate legs, on it*. Well the tighter the jeans, the longer the stares. *Chic boots, indeed*. They always seemed to feel good until I had to face the long grueling, walk back to the car from a night out. *Invisible plane, double check*. After all I was trying to land a man, then recruit him to fly with me.

Prior to heading out the door, I would base many of my decisions on one main goal: being singled out by a man and eventually falling in love. It wasn't a requirement for this to take place all in one night. A gradual crescendo to publicly walking hand in hand, enjoying family barbecues, and dancing at our elegant wedding reception were perfectly fine for me. But in my mind I had to put my best foot forward. I had to go the extra mile, even if that meant going overboard to capture a man's attention.

If you pull back the curtains of my past and look close enough, you'll find the one and only, *Wander Woman.* That's no typo or grammatical error. The real error was my perspective of pursuit. The mental, physical, and emotional strain of chasing a man for love is so complicated and unnerving. *Merriam-Webster's Dictionary* defines "wander" as "to move around or go to different places, usually without having a particular purpose or direction" and "to follow a path with many turns."

I would often ask myself: Am I worthy of being pursued? Will I ever qualify to be the admired focus of a man's eye, even more so his heart? Do I even have what it takes to be considered wifey material? Reluctantly, I carried these disheartening thoughts for years as a Wander Woman. They sure were a far cry from the confidence exuded from the sultry, sexy, animated superheroine, *Wonder Woman*, whose debut in the 1940s forever changed the world of comics.

This proves that a single woman can have *accessories* for days and yet not have a clue about what really *accentuates* love.

Exhale. You're Made to Yearn for a Man

Even as I write this, I'm praying to see my Mr. Right appear on the horizon and head my way any day now. Yet, I know how it is to get so intensely fixated on having a relationship, you react out of anxiety. Or start having crippled thoughts and lame self-worth. All the while the world seems to cheer, "Be aggressive! Go get yours! Get what and who you want by any means necessary!" So we wander. Experimenting. Entering and exiting from dating apps, phone swipes, misunderstood texts, coffee dates, late nights, and revolving-door relationships.

But deep inside we want a caped crusader to cover us with kisses and attention, and to bravely come to our rescue. To be a dream team with him. To have an "It's us against the world while feeling your heartbeat next to mine" kind of love. We desire to be the object of his pursuit. And we can't really help it. As women, we were created to be relational. To literally thrive off of interconnections with others. God deliberately put a hunger inside of Eve and a magnetic pull in Adam toward Eve. So take a deep breath and relax. You don't have to fight the yearning for your Superman.

But you might be tempted to skip past the *God stuff* and get to the *good stuff* like Superman being in sight and in love with you. You're tired of watching clocks (via walls and wombs). You're ready for a speedy crash course on how-to-get-a-man schemes. However, impatience often results in mind games and mayhem in trying to make a man fall in love with you. I've learned firsthand that pulling, tugging, and pursuing a relationship that is void of reciprocity, leads to mental and emotional residue that's hard to overcome and forget.

However, something special took place way before you had your first crush. Or met the boy next door. Or went on your first date. Or got the latest flirty comment you got on social media. Or even before you were conceived in your mother's womb. You were on God's love radar. Ready. Aim. Fire. The core of your heart became the perfect target for a heavenly bull's-eye. It's like God manufactured a premiere Valentine's Day so exceptional for you, Cupid could only dream of having such accurate aim like he does.

Area of Life	The WANDER Woman
Void Fillers	Believes a man is the quick fix to live and be loved.
Positioning	Goes where men look for quickness vs. quality.
Personal Time	Stays on standby. Rarely says "no" to him.
Trust	Micromanages the relationship. He's first, she's second.
Assessment	Always asks for reassurance about the relationship.
Priorities	Abandons family and friends. Reneges on obligations for him.
Standards	Has too insignificant or too impossible ones to reach.
Treatment	Sweeps disrespect, abuse, and hurt under the rug.
Breakups	Clings to chaos due to fearing loneliness.
Marriage	Rushes past the process to get to the promise ASAP.

Area of Life	The WONDER Woman
Void Fillers	Knows Superman will add love, not a reason to live.
Positioning	Examines character and men who honor commitment.
Personal Time	Respects her schedule and knows when to indulge spontaneity.
Trust	Earns and gives trust over time. Spends QT but also gives space.
Assessment	Considers actions to determine sincerity and relational growth.
Priorities	Bonds with her support system and sticks to promises.
Standards	Standards are attainable with effort and devotion.
Treatment	Speaks up when disrespected and knows what's intolerable.
Breakups	Realizes when he's not Superman. Can say hello AND goodbye.
Marriage	Has patience. Lets him conclude she's worth wedded bliss.

Brownie Point:
You may want a Superman now, but remember God's love is always Superior. #CB4C

Simply, you and I were made to give love and be loved. Nevertheless, there's nothing like accepting heavenly love first. The Heavenly Father's love literally sets the tone for you to receive love from the *right* man, in the *right* way, and on the *right* terms. By that I mean a man who is willing to take notes from God so he knows how to pursue, connect, respect, and protect a marvelous woman such as you.

Mirror Moment:

Why do you doubt that you're worth being lovingly pursued, flaws and all?

Are you changing yourself and abandoning values to speed up a relationship you want?

"One night as I lay in bed, I yearned for my lover. I yearned for him, but he did not come. So I said to myself, 'I will get up and roam the city, searching in all its streets and squares. I will search for the one I love.' So I searched everywhere but did not find him. The watchmen stopped me as they made their rounds, and I asked, 'Have you seen the one I love?'" (Song of Solomon 3:1-3)

The P-P-Pow Factor

You might be rolling your eyes right now. But I'm trying to save you the grief so you can shine in your rightful glory. It's time to open your eyes instead of ignoring some of the bruises you've acquired from being in the *rush-n-run-after-him* kind of relationships. If you're a woman who is desperately parading around and pursuing a man, you're actually losing power, passion, and potential. Read on and let me show you.

Power

Do you know the strongest muscle you possess as a woman? It has nothing to do with cranking out two-a-days or how many sit-ups are needed to get your abs tight. But it does impact the core of a relationship and even the center of the universe. A woman's power comes from her influence. With your influence, you can inspire curiosity and open the door for a man's pursuit. Or you can conspire and rob him of a chase he was intended to begin and complete. The latter decreases his intrigue toward you. Even with your power, you can't fight the natural makeup of a man's instinct. You can't contend with the facts. A man needs to flex his muscle of pursuit. I believe it's healthy not just for his spirit, but even down to the marrow of his bones. When Adam saw Eve, he said, "Bone of my bone and flesh of my flesh." There was penetrating touch that awakened him all the way down to his bones. There was a deep inner and outer magnetism toward Eve. She didn't have to forcefully use her influence to get Adam's pursuit engine revved up so he would recognize his soul mate. When a man has a laser focus on commitment and is seriously devoted to pursue, he proves that he's ready to be trusted with a treasure as yourself. Plus that's one surefire way to test and see if his intentions are just lip service or his actions align with his words.

Passion

You lose passion when you play tug-of-war for a man's attention and pursuit. You get tired of bending over backward and rearranging your entire schedule to accommodate his. Being on standby 24/7 is so unfair especially when all of your efforts can't seem to get him to even lean toward you. Force feeding your love agenda to a man is never a sign of confidence. Actually, it's a sign of cowardice. It portrays that you want this relationship so bad, you don't care if it makes you feel bad, look foolish, or live beneath what you fittingly deserve. Devaluing his pursuit of your heart, will leave your love tank on E. And that should never be the reality of a confident woman who knows she can't afford to lose her passion. Passion helps fuel you up to fulfill your destiny and be charged up for your love story in the long run.

Potential

Trivializing a man's pursuit can seriously diminish your chances for a mutually beneficial relationship. Demanding attention and begging for affection only makes you seem like an easy give. An easy lay. An easy target for him to capture and have wrapped around his finger.

You might love feeling like you're in control by aggressively chasing. It may seem like you have the upper hand when you decide to use the "Pick Me, Pick Me Please!" sort of advertising. And sure these tactics might fly for a guy who's lazy, expects hookups, handouts, will later treat you as a handoff, and lacks the predator and protector instinct. But do you really want a guy like this for a date, much less a mate? I sure hope not!

Understand that you're worthy of a man who has enough backbone to step up to the plate. A man who has potential and is willing to go to bat for your commitment. A man who is willing to run from base to base until he scores a home run by winning your hand in marriage. It might be a board game, but in regard to a man . . . *his pursuit ain't trivial.* His pursuit is necessary for the livelihood and longevity of your commitment to each other.

Mirror Moment

Have you ever made a semi-permanent dent in your couch with tissues, sweets, and back-to-back WEtv or Lifetime movies because he didn't return ANY of your five thousand calls? (Been there, done that. But I was probably watching "Martin"!)

Are you going out of your way for him without hardly getting anything in return? (i.e. initiating calls, texts, dates, house visits, running errands, cooking, sex, playing mommy to his kids, etc.)

Note: Take the "Chasers Test" under the free resource section on my website: www.youaresingledout.com

You. The 7th Wonder (Woman) of the World

Seven is the number that symbolizes completion. When you know you're a Wonder Woman, you exude a powerful aura of confidence. No need for your she-ego (or female ego) to be constantly inflated, because your identity is already intact and built up by the highest, God.

And by persistently kicking doubts to the curb, you understand that you are a complete woman. No additives or preservatives needed.

Look beyond the bathroom mirror and the mirror of a man's eyes. Gaze past the sweet taste of a mocha latte, social media likes, Jimmy Choo bags, the latest makeup vids, and Juicy Couture boots. You are so exceptional, no other version has been or ever will be made of you. So when your Superman pursues, he'll pick up on what you already know about your awesomeness. As a Wonder Woman, you don't have to reduce yourself and vie for validation. You never have to work for worth.

Descriptions of You

(Post these in a visible area)

- "A Heart Worth Pursuing"
- "Keeper of God's 24/7 Attention"
- "Made Whole & Comforted Soul"
- "Restored Hope Walking"
- "A Jewel Worth Loving"
- "Liberated Lady"
- "A Brand of Unduplicated Beauty"
- "A Life Worth Dying For"
- "Classy, Cute, & Commitment Worthy"
- "Claimed Daughter, Crowned Queen"

Don't Put that "S" on My Chest!

Now brace yourself. I'm inviting you to swim out to the deep end of the pool, because if you want a Wonder Woman and Superman dream team, you have to understand a few transitions needed for a winning relationship. In order to get, you have to give. Being pursued by Superman involves yielding to a process. I'm about to say the "S" word. No, it's not the synonym for worthlessness or feces. Or what you may scream out when someone cuts you off in traffic. The word can cause sensations of nervousness and nausea all over a woman's body. It's a word which can send messages of "I ain't," "I can't," and "I won't" rapidly to her psyche. I'm talking about . . . submission. (Dum, dum, dum, dummm.)

I know, I know. This topic is tough, and it's not for the faint hearts hooked on "Miss Total Dependence on a Man" (or my world will cave in). It's not gift wrapped for the stubborn hearts bent on "Miss Independence" (my rules and my shots). We're talking about relationships, which are heavily predicated on interdependence. If either one of these *Misses* describe you, that might be a primary reason why you keep *missing* out on a healthy relationship.

Dating back to the first century, this subject relates to how we interact with men in romantic-attraction relationships. The fact of the matter is submission even impacts you before getting your "MRS." degree. It's a delicate issue. But before you skip to the next chapter or close the book, hear me out. You'll probably see we're not many miles apart.

When I was younger, I remember listening to the Sunday morning message at church on wives and submission. Ooooweee, it was quite distressing for me. Apparently, I wasn't the only one uncomfortable because the preacher would practically bleed sweat as he summoned all of his courage in delivering this *hard pill to swallow* kind of message. The overwhelming amount of "Amens" from women he received from other sermons now dwindled down to a sporadic few. You would have thought most women in the congregation went from sipping lemonade in the shade to sucking on ripe lemons.

I didn't want to understand submission much less hear about it. I could literally feel my insides start to boil. I became restless in the pew similar to having an inescapable nightmare. My pulse would increase and my blood pressure would start to involuntarily rise. There were times when I would fan myself with the church bulletin because I began feeling a bit light-headed. Inside my heart would yell, "Will you please get off the women? *Move on to the men and teach them how they need to treat us women!*" I'm so glad those words didn't get past the tollbooth operator of my throat and out of mouth's gates. Imagine the shock on the preacher's face or the astonishment in my mother's eyes. It would have been pure, unabashed grief. A moment in time absolutely guaranteed to outlive my time on earth.

The word "submission" used to bring a displeasing picture to my mind. On some days it reflected the barefoot and pregnant look. On other days, it was more of a "sentenced to living life only for and through a man" viewpoint. Sometimes I thought about scenes from the movie *The Stepford Wives,* in which women seemed to be happily programmed androids under the complete control of their husbands. Then at times, I felt the spirit of the Women's Suffrage movement rise within . . . except I wanted to vote and abolish the "S" word. As a Wonder Woman, I didn't want it on my chest. I felt like it would limit me, and I wouldn't be able to soar.

Living with a dazed, *do whatever you tell me dear* look in my eyes, just wasn't how I pictured me and my Superman. I wanted to be a super wifey, cape and all. I desired to enjoy a love-intoxicated relationship with my husband, thrive in my career, and be a doting mother shouting the loudest cheers for our children (and still will one day!). But needless to say, if submission was part of the package, I didn't want this "S" placed on my chest.

The Spirit of Wonder Woman

You might be wondering, "How in the world does submission relate to single women? "Isn't that something only wives have to deal with?" Take a deep breath. I've even had to have a change of heart over time as I learned more about the dynamics in relationships and eventually in marriage.

Brownie Point:
Submission doesn't mean you're subservient or subpar.
S.U.B.Mission is being on a mission to Seek to Understand Balance. #CB4C

I've learned that a woman who wants to partner with a man who selflessly loves her and mutually seeks the greater good, should have a heart open toward balance. Or better yet, letting him be who he's called to be as a man. Contrary to popular beliefs and attitudes, you don't have to be the man *and* the woman within companionship. Releasing this dualistic strain frees you up to be the most incredible woman you can be. And be ready to lead with respect and unbelievable support. The result of Wonder Woman and Superman being confident in their identities and what they uniquely bring to the table results in a balanced relationship. One that is poised for significance and ripe for success.

I believe a single woman needs to possess the spirit of submission or support. I'm not saying you should go straight into playing wifey. After all, you are deserving of being crowned wifey (settling for playing the role is for a Wander Woman). But even in a relationship, a man needs to see that you at least have the capacity or willingness to support someone beyond yourself. And when it comes to marriage, something bigger than yourself. For instance, a future where you're both building up each other instead of tearing down each other.

Yes, being an independent woman is wonderful. It means you can do things on your own and handle your business. But being too self-sufficient and standoffish will drive most men away. Seriously, who doesn't want to be wanted in a relationship? Steve Harvey, once stated on *Oprah*, "We profess, we provide and we protect. A man has got to see where he fits into the providing and protecting role. If you've got everything, you can do everything, you've got your own car . . . you've got a guard dog and a handgun. The guy is thinking, 'Where do I fit in here?' You've got to make a space for him to fit in so he can come in and do what men do."

Brownie Point:
A Wonder Woman is capable of doing a lot as one, but purposely leaves room for two to get the job done. #CB4C

Exercise interdependence and allow a man to exert his masculinity as a leader, provider, and a defender of your heart. Your sense of balance in the relationship will make you a *woman of mass distinction* vs. a *woman of mass division*. Think about it. Which one do you aim to be?

When Superman Takes a Knee

Did you know even men submit in a plethora of ways every day? Take for instance an NFL team. Each has offensive, defensive, and special teams' coaches. All of them exercise their authority in calling plays and gathering the best strategies for the players. However, there's only one head coach. All of the players and specialty coaches collaborate in order to submit to his vision.

Through blood, sweat, and tears, they work in unity as one team. Each individual plays his part with one pursuit in mind. He embraces submission for the sake of winning. This support helps the team succeed from game to game and especially on their journey to the Super Bowl. Even the head coach has to hold up his commitment as an effective leader or else he'll have to answer to the general manager. And don't even mention the fans!

Both men and women have to submit in life and in love. So you don't have to think of submission as chauvinistic and demeaning. If you're moving toward a long-term, committed relationship (and before you claim him as your husband), make sure he is willing to surrender to an authority higher than himself. I believe a true Superman submits to God and invests in learning how to replicate God's love toward you. He's not afraid of taking a knee to seek insight on how to care, connect, and communicate with you. He'll be willing to submit to counseling when your relationship is in jeopardy. He'll respect his boss, listen to elders, and even stop for directions when his inner or outer GPS isn't working. And in marriage, he'll be willing to surrender his ego by saying, "God, not my will, but yours be done."

However, a man who won't submit to God will not fully commit to cherishing you and honoring sacrifice. He doesn't view God as the 100 percent accurate professor from which to learn. It's critical for a man to exhibit unselfishness and understand the world doesn't revolve around him. If he possesses the "my way or the highway" mentality, you're definitely headed for the danger zone. No matter if he's flashing an "S" on his chest, make sure there's an "S" that stands for submission in his heart.

Superman's Word Power & Will Power

When a Wonder Woman is already in flight (with her identity secured on board), she thinks twice about landing for a man who doesn't know his value or disrespects hers. She's also less likely to nosedive in a relationship that's not going to take her to a higher level in life.

When Superman pursues a Wonder Woman, he puts in work. Yes, having an occupation or career is crucial, but, ladies, I'm talking about his mind working. I'm talking about a man who is alert, inquisitive, and determined. He's capable of asking questions to get to know your innermost secrets and desires you've been wanting to share. He's willing to make moves and take risks (within context) for your affection. Why? Because a Wonder Woman is already in motion . . . and to catch her means a man can't be complacently posted up on the sideline expecting her to chase him. Or to put her life on complete hold until he's ready to commit. You see a man on a mission to win your heart won't be lazy. Superman is willing to take out a shovel and dig to get closer to the treasures inside you. I believe there should be a lot of "inquisitivity before intimacy." After all, your dreams, vulnerabilities, insecurities, and companionship desires are not front-page news. He has to do more than just memorize a few cliché phrases or ask the typical topsoil questions to convince you of his sincerity. (i.e. What are you up to? How are you doing? What do you want to do tonight?) He won't try handing you played out pick-up lines with a one-size-fits-all mentality.

On the flipside, make sure you note his use of words with other women, too. If he's really into you, you will be regarded as the special target of his compliments. You aren't applying for ear candy (sweet nothings) and to just be toted around as his arm charm. You have to differentiate between Superman and men disguised as silver-tongued snakes.

Now don't get me wrong. There are some amazing men out in the world who will give you props based on his genuine feelings. They mean what they say and say what they mean. Superman knows his words have high value and won't spend them carelessly to look good, because deep down . . . he is good. "A good man brings good things out of the good stored up in his heart, and an evil man brings evil things out of the evil stored up in his heart. *For the mouth speaks what the heart is full of.*" (Luke 6:45) He knows capturing your ears and heart has immeasurable benefits. After all, the beautiful significance Wonder Woman brings to his life is far above rubies and far beyond any adventure he's ever experienced before.

Every Guy Doesn't Qualify

Interdependence doesn't happen in rapid-fire fashion (i.e. after the first date or in the "getting to know" phase). Your intertwined support does not apply to just any and every man. A Wonder Woman works side by side with a guy who exhibits wholeness, direction, compassion, discipline, honesty, and faithfulness. Why? She possesses these qualities, too. And being drawn to a clueless, misguided, immature relationship is not on her to-do list!

A man has to be willing to be glued (mind, body, and soul connected) to you as a woman. You may have heard, "Therefore what God has joined together, let no one separate" (Mark 10:9). This is true and yet we as humans have free will. If a man is not willing to be glued to you, don't get your heart stuck on him. You'll just be treated as a Post-It note. *Close enough to be near and adhere, yet still removable . . . and replaceable.* If a man is not ready to be glued to the committed relationship you desire, don't wake him up. Honestly, some guys are relationally "sleep walking." God is pressing snooze on them for a reason.

Before Adam was united with Eve, he had to submit to a process of readiness. A man has to come to the realization and say, "I'm through with the games and trying to run this on my own. I need God's help in getting a Wonder Woman who is compatible with me." When God wakes him up, he'll show the man what a wonder you are and how wonderful you'll be by his side.

Respect is earned. Trust is grown. Knowledge is acquired. Understanding is intellect working overtime. But love is different. Many believe love is like "pulling teeth" in order to win his commitment. But love is a gift. Love is a deliberate choice. In fact, it's intentionally given and strategically shared. When it comes to pursuing you, your Mr. Right is going to be Mr. Ready to Commit and Submit. He's going to be willing to lay down a "me agenda" for the "we lifestyle."

Mirror Moment:

Have you ever been with a guy who didn't submit to authority or heed wisdom? How did his attitude affect your relationship?

What makes you feel comfortable enough to trust a man?

Is he sincere about being faithful or does he joke about it even through his actions?

No Roles Reversed Here

Envision a skyscraper that stands tall in the heart of a city. The shiny glass exterior of the building can be adored by millions. The lobby and conference rooms can be filled with the finest contemporary décor. The executive suites might have lavish furniture shipped in from Italy and ancient relics from South Africa. However, if that building does not contain a strong infrastructure, it will collapse. The architectural design or blueprint means nothing without the willing support of structural beams.

This is similar to what a Wonder Woman brings to a committed relationship and covenant. A man might look up to par on the exterior and have a lot of snazzy things to collect and brag about. He might seem to fly through the air with the greatest of ease. Or be counted on to prevent a massive breakdown at work. Whatever the case might be, he absolutely knows that life wouldn't be the same without a Wonder Woman's incomparable nourishment.

A Wonder Woman is his ace in the hole. She's a foundational element to his sanity. In fact, the "S" on his chest serves as a constant reminder of the superior support he receives from her in order to succeed in a cold, cruel world. Leading with support doesn't make you less of a woman. You've got undeniable power and influence! It's kind of like what the mother said in the movie *My Big Fat Greek Wedding*, "Let me tell you something, Toula. The man is the head, but the woman is the neck. And she can turn the head any way she wants."

I've been blessed to know several beautiful Wonder Women who powerfully lead with support in their marriages. Even through trials, they've reaped personal benefits that have helped them evolve more. My amazing godmother Mama Sharon's capacity for showing compassion to her husband's parents states that the "in sickness and in health" marriage vows go beyond just the two of us. Annette's flexibility and financial fortitude during her husband's temporary layoff shows that support truly means through "thick and thin." Jocelyn's joyful countenance while being right by her husband's side through health changes teaches that love must grow in spite of shifts in well-being. Tiara's continual dedication to pray for and speak highly of her husband during his career transitions reiterates that a woman's words can be a protective covering from discouragement men face every day.

Men are more sensitive than what they care to admit. A man often wants and needs his ego to be stroked. This kind of love reaches them down to the core. There's nothing sadder than seeing a man who's been beaten down by life and walks around with an "I'm a loser and my lady confirms it" stance while in a relationship. You should never underestimate the life-changing influence you have on a man when you woman up to support him.

Look at how strong you are and the duties you take care of as a single woman: paying bills, car maintenance, home upkeep, community service, church involvement, planning schedules, decision making, mapping out logistics, continuing education, working a job/career, pushing toward dreams, and possibly providing for children. That is A LOT of power! So remember interdependence and support is not about stifling your strength. It's about ingeniously balancing that power for the advantage of two people.

At the right time and season, a Wonder Woman doesn't fear taking the leading role in supporting her Superman. And Superman yields by acknowledging the instrumental value her support brings to his existence. Neither role is less valuable than the other, so there's no need to exchange roles. Superman and Wonder Woman work together as a team, striving for one goal. A goal for love to be mutually wanted and given.

Brownie Point:
The art of pursuit is like a painting. A man yields a canvas while the woman adds brushstrokes of color. Together they portray the irreplaceable call and response of love. #CB4C

Shifting Gear, Shifting Hearts

Knowing how a man pursues is one thing. Allowing him space to do so is totally different. For example, consider the gears of a car. Gears are needed in order to properly operate the vehicle. However, switching gears helps you get to your destination. The parking gear is needed to keep your insurance premium from skyrocketing due to costly crashes and injuries. You can talk about, dream of, and wish for your destination but unless drive is utilized, you're not going to get there.

This is similar to relationships. A Wonder Woman understands she can't always be in drive and steamroll mode. I know this personally can be a challenge. Throughout a career in sales, being a marketing VP, and having my own business, I'm so used to making the first move with prospective clients. Whether it's via email, phone, or meeting face-to-face, I have been taught to "initiate so they will participate," "stay persistent, so they won't forget," "set up another appointment and seal the deal." These tactics might work for business success; they don't necessarily transfer well in the love department. I even had a guy tell me once, "You know it's after five, it's no longer business hours. Your man is going to want to know that you can switch gears."

Ooowee, it's easier said than done. However, shifting gears for a man to chase after your heart is possible! According to best-selling author Rori Raye, "To create that all-important space, you'll need to shift from a mindset of 'doing' to one of simply 'being.' You're going to go against your usual impulse to make something happen with a man and instead allow things to unfold—which will naturally shift him into the doing role. When you're on a date, if you can allow yourself to simply "be" and resist the urge to take charge—even if it means dealing with some awkward lulls in the conversation—a man will actually feel more comfortable in your presence and will naturally feel compelled to come closer to you."

Greg Behrendt, author of the *New York Times* best seller *He's Just Not That Into You*, writes, "Men, for the most part, like to pursue women. We like not knowing if we can catch you. We feel rewarded when we do. Especially when the chase is a long one. We know there was a sexual revolution. (We loved it.) We know women are capable of running governments, heading multinational corporations, and raising loving children—sometimes all at the same time. That, however, doesn't make men different. — *When it comes to men, deal with us as we are, not how you'd like us to be*."

Brownie Point:
Regarding men: No chase means no challenge. And without a challenge, there's nothing for him to cherish. #CB4C

Crowned & Ready for Pursuit

So step back and take off your inner Nikes. Quit chasing a man like there's no hope for tomorrow. Take a step back from demanding conversations, giving ultimatums, stopwatch gazing, and paranoid tendencies. These are simply reactions to the fear of loneliness, being the odd one out, and believing this guy is the last train to leave the station.

However, rocking your crown of confidence as a Wonder Woman doesn't mean sit on the sidelines and do nothing. Your focus shouldn't be on perfection. But avidly taking care of your responsibilities while in prep mode. (i.e. becoming stronger in reaching career goals, finishing your education, prayer life, finances, health, household tasks, nurturing skills). A batter doesn't start getting ready to swing when he's standing at the plate. He's in the dugout warming up. A football placekicker doesn't wait until he hits the field to practice right before getting called to score a game-winning field goal. He's on the sidelines warming up.

Girl, listen. *You say you want a Superman, but are you ready?* Readiness is a responsibility. Readiness is a specialty. Readiness is a quality. One that distinguishes the whiners vs. the winners. And separates the chaotic chicks from the confident queens. It's literally the difference of being Miss Hold-Up-Wait-a-Minute vs. Miss Ready. It's a part of life that you have to be intentional about. Know that you are a queen. And if you claim to be one, quit banking on tomorrow and saying "when Mr. Right comes I'll . . . " or "when I get married I'll start . . . " or "when Superman comes to my rescue." You have the permission to rock the crown and have your mind made up to be ready. Ready for commitment. Ready to think of more than yourself. Ready to give. Ready to effectively communicate (speaking and listening). Ready to encourage. Ready to decorate a home with love. Ready to work hard and grow together. Ready for the next chapter of life. Ready for the pursuit of Mr. Right.

But overall remember if he is your Superman, he will do anything to wholeheartedly pursue you. Just look at the things men brag about the most? Championships. Money. Business contracts. Cars. Having fame. Hunting. Winning arguments, video games, votes, marathons, and breaking records. Even climbing to the top of a mountain. These are just a few things which make men proud. What do they all have in common? All of them take pursuit. But what typically supersedes all of these quests is winning the heart of a remarkable Wonder Woman. A woman you are very capable of being.

Chaos to Confidence

7 Questions to See if He's the Superman You Want Pursuing You

1. **P** - Does he possess *personal* maturity (direction, focus, and goals)?
2. **U** - Does he *undervalue* your strengths, abilities, and support?
3. **R** - How does he *regard* you compared to other females in his life?
4. **S** - Does he display *sexual* integrity by respecting abstinence/celibacy goals before marriage?
5. **U** - Does he seek to emotionally *understand* your needs and listen to your desires?
6. **I** - Is he *inquisitive* about your dreams, secrets, beliefs, and opinions?
7. **T** - Does he lack or have *tenacity* in initiating communication, quality time, and introducing you to others close to him?

CONCLUSION

I REMEMBER WHEN I WAS EIGHT YEARS OLD. IN MY FAMILY, WE HAD a typical morning routine on school days which usually consisted of me hiding under the covers and wanting to press snooze. The only problem I had was that my alarm clock couldn't be unplugged or pressed for an additional ten minutes. You see my alarm clock was basically Mom flipping the light and declaring, "Wake up, time to get up sleepy heads!" And as a woman on a mission, there was just no way on earth of pressing snooze on her.

But as I proceeded to get dressed and primp in the mirror for one last time I moved on to the dining room table. And out of the 2,920 mornings that I had previously lived through, this morning was different. You see a unique conversation ensued between me and my Dad. I finally got the courage to ask a question that had been burning in my mind for quite some time.

"Daddy? I got a question." He responded, "OK, shoot." "Well, I was wondering, how old were you and Mom when you got married?" He quickly gave me a look as if to say, *Just what are you up to little girl?* He replied without too much or too little excitement, "Twenty-five." Now as an eight-year-old, twenty-five seems like an eternity away right? But since I was bold enough to ask, I felt bold enough to take it a little further. "Well, Daddy, can I get married when I'm twenty-five?" He bit his lip, looked down at his oatmeal, and slowly said, "Yes." Well, that got my adrenalin pumping and I'm thinking it's time to seriously negotiate. "Well, OK, Daddy how about when I'm twenty-four?" "Yes." "What about when I'm twenty-three?" At twenty-three, he pumped the brakes and said, "If you make good grades, graduate, go to college, get a good job, find a good man, then maybe yes."

Well fast forward several years, and along comes twenty-three. I'm waiting. Twenty-four arrives and still there's no sight of a ring. Twenty-five knocks and still there's no sight of an aisle. In fact the only "I do" I'm committing to is another business trip, music gig, or a quick tease that I knew deep down in my heart did not qualify as a potential husband. Well now that I'm in my thirties, I've been through some relationships, heartaches, and headaches. And I'm still desiring and will one day be united with my husband.

So believe me I understand what you may be going through before commitment. You may getting lonelier by the day, in fact by the minute. You're tired of waiting. You may feel like life is tap-dancing on your last nerves. Some days you want to yell, "So help me God in heaven above if I hear about somebody else getting married next year, I'm about to blow!" One more time. Perhaps you're extremely frustrated because your feelings and emotions have been played with more than a brand new Tonka truck on Christmas morning. You are tired of waiting. Still you may be trying to detox and break away from your last relationship. You're literally stuck at a crossroad wondering if you should hold out for what was or move forward to what's to come. You are tired of waiting. You may be discouraged because it seems like your family and friends have just given up on you ever being in a rock-steady relationship or married. I'm talking about no more honorable mentions or questions about your love life. Listen, I get it. You are tired of waiting.

But now is not the time to dwell on what you're *tired of*, instead I want to remind you what you're *tied to*. You see, you are tied to greatness. Gift wrapped to hope. Bound to blessings which are surfacing in this season of love that will work for your good in the next season of relational love.

I remember recently wrestling with the "when" of my love story. God tenderly invited me to look through a larger lens and see how love stories impact many lives and travels miles beyond the right now. He lovingly reminded me about the power of divine, right timing. This is what I heard: Your trust in the right timing is necessary because someone you have yet to meet, will need to see both of you as walking billboards of hope after they've experienced a *breakup*, after a *breakdown*, just so they can get their *breakthrough*. Your trust in the right timing is necessary because the visions you work on together will need to be birthed and change the world at an appointed time. Your trust in the right timing is necessary because the children birthed through your union will need to connect with specific people, at a certain time, and create solutions when the world has a void only they can fill during their lifetime. Not too soon and not too late. Your trust in the right timing is necessary because a friend or family member will need to see your commitment with Mr. Right on display. And as a result, their heart will change. They'll leave an unhealthy or toxic relationship and depend on me to be their matchmaker. Your trust in the right timing is necessary because a young lady or young man is going to one day admire your love story and ask, "How did you meet your husband?" "What did you do while you were single?" "How did you endure the wait?"

As a little girl I really thought the timing of my love story would happen like my parents, high school and college friends, and even some colleagues throughout my career. No ma'am, no way, no how. But one thing I've realized is that each of our journeys in life and love is miraculously yet beautifully different.

No duplicates needed. So before Mr. Right, don't get caught up in comparing your relationship status to someone else's. Anticipate and celebrate what is and what will take place on your path to companionship. Flow in your purpose and be productive in your lane. Don't wait for romance with Mr. Right to give you permission to live, give, laugh, smile, and savor moments. It's time for you to look like what you're *expecting*, not what you are experiencing. Refuse to look tired, hurt, frustrated, unloved, lonely, and bitter. Quit giving these feeling first priority in your mind! Remember you've got the power to rise up and not blend into the chaos. You are specially selected, chosen, and called forward into greater. *You are singled out* to rock a crown of confidence.

So the next time you feel discouraged, frustrated, or unhappy about who you are and where you are in life, read this declaration. It will renew your mind and rejuvenate your spirit *before commitment* shows up on the horizon. Hold your head up, pull your shoulders back, and shout it out loud with determination!

Declaration of Confidence

I am a woman
and I'm making the choice
To fully embrace who I am
and use my voice.
I am absolutely, positively, definitely,
worth being respected
Before my heart is invested.
I don't have to be anyone else or perfect
I'm already beautiful, and know that I'm worth it.
I will not settle for a "situationship"
Because I am deserving of a loving relationship.
Starting today, I'll be living this
Cause I'm moving from chaos to CONFIDENCE!

RESOURCES

Chapter 1: God Specializes in Guidance, Not Guydance

1. Piper, John, "Manhood and Womanhood: Conflict and Confusion After the Fall," *Desiring God*, May 21, 1989. www.desiringgod.org/messages/manhood-and-womanhood-conflict-and-confusion-after-the-fall
2. *Everyday Matters Bible for Women*. The New Living Translation, 2nd ed., Tyndale House Publishers, Inc., 2012. Print.
3. Blige, Mary J., *Real Love*. Uptown Records/MCA, 1992. CD.
4. "Mary J. Blige's VH1 Behind the Music Special [Full Episode] Hip-Hop Wired." *Hip-Hop Wired*, Randy Roper, July 28, 2011. Web: October 27, 2016.
5. Guy, Raz, and Leslie Morgan Steiner. "Why Don't Domestic Violence Victims Leave?" *TED Radio Hour.* March 28, 2013.

www.npr.org/templates/transcript/transcript.php?storyId=175617775

6. Steiner, Leslie, "Why Domestic Violence Victims Don't Leave." *TED Talks*. January, 2013. www.ted.com/talks/leslie_morgan_steiner_why_domestic_violence_victims_don_t_leave/transcript?language=en
7. Vagianos, Alanna, "30 Shocking Domestic Violence Statistics That Remind Us It's an Epidemic." Huffington Post, October 23, 2014. www.huffingtonpost.com/2014/10/23/domestic-violence-statistics_n_5959776.html
8. Musk, Justine, "The Art of Being Different: Why You Shouldn't Compare and Compete, but Seek to Change the Game." Justine Musk, June 29, 2011. justinemusk.com/2011/06/29/the-art-of-being-different-why-you-shouldnt-compare-and-compete-but-seek-to-change-the-game/
9. Congreve, William, *The Mourning Bride a Tragedy: As It Is Acted at the Theatre in Lincoln's-Inn-Fields by His Majesty's Servants*. London: Printed for Jacob Tonson, 1697. Print.

Chapter 2: Dealing with the Silent Treatment

1. Burns, Marsha, "Small Straws in a Soft Wind." *His Kingdom Prophecy*, September 12, 2013. www.hiskingdomprophecy.com/spirit-of-prophecy-bulletin-september-2013/
2. *The Holy Bible*. English Standard Version, Crossway, Good News Publishers. 2001. Print.
3. St. Amant, Betsy, "The Waiting Rooms of Life." iBelieve.com, September 5, 2013.

www.ibelieve.com/faith/the-waiting-rooms-of-life.html

4. Caldwell, Bobby "Open Your Eyes," *Cat in the Hat*,1980.
5. *God's Little Devotional Book for Women*. Honor Books, 1996. 10th printing. Print.
6. *Everyday Matters Bible for Women*. The New Living Translation, 2nd ed., Tyndale House Publishers, Inc., 2012. Print.
7. *Holy Bible*. The New King James Version, Thomas Nelson, Inc., 1992. Print.

Chapter 3: De-Mask Us Road Diva

1. Hawthorne, Nathaniel, *The Scarlett Letter*. Ticknor and Fields, 1850. Print.
2. Svoboda, Elizabeth, "Field Guide to the People-Pleaser: May I Serve as Your Doormat?" PsychologyToday.com, June 9, 2016. www.psychologytoday.com/articles/200805/field-guide-the-people-pleaser-may-i-serve-your-doormat

Chapter 4: Introducing . . . the Real Me!

1. Rees, Erik, *Only You Can Be You*. Howard Books, 2009. Print.
2. Turkel, Bruce, "Living a Life of Purpose; The Richly Working." Bruce Turkel, October 6, 2009. www.turkeltalks.com/living-a-life-of-purpose-the-richly-working
3. Jakes, T. D., *Instinct*. FaithWords, 2014. Print.
4. Evans, Dr. Tony. "Becoming a Kingdom Single." YouTube, November 28, 2015.
5. Winfrey, Oprah, "Oprah's Lifeclass: Transform Your Life with T. D. Jakes." Oprah.com.

www.oprah.com/oprahs-lifeclass/oprahs-lifeclass-transform-your-life-with-bishop-td-jakes

6. Cook, Amanda, "Spontaneous Worship." Bethel Music. www.bethelmusic.com/artists/amanda-cook/2014.
7. Hyatt, Michael, "The 3 Components of Job Satisfaction," Michael Hyatt.com. www.michaelhyatt.com/job-satisfaction.html

Chapter 5: I'd Rather Hang Out with the Guys

1. Kamen, Dr. Randy, "A Compelling Argument About Why Women Need Friendships," Huffington Post, January 29, 2013. www.huffingtonpost.com/randy-kamen-gredinger-edd/female-friendship_b_2193062.html
2. Perrin, Andrew, "Social Media Usage: 2005-2015." Pew Research Center, October 8, 2015. www.pewinternet.org/2015/10/08/social-networking-usage-2005-2015/
3. *Everyday Matters Bible for Women*. The New Living Translation, 2nd ed., Tyndale House Publishers, Inc., 2012. Print.

Chapter 6: Walking in Stilettos vs. High Hills

1. Simmons, Rachel, *The Curse of the Good Girl: Raising Authentic Girls with Courage and Confidence*. The Penguin Press, 2009. Print.
2. Zeilinger, Julie, "Why Millennial Women Do Not Want to Lead." Forbes.com., July 16, 2012. www.forbes.com/sites/deniserestauri/2012/07/16/why-millennial-women-do-not-want-to-lead/#3b69d7e5160a
3. "Floyd Mayweather vs. Manny Pacquiao." HBO. May 2, 2015. Television.
4. GRAPHICS: http://freevector.co/tag/heels/

Chapter 7: Master the Bait. Master the Wait.

1. Reuben, David R., M.D., *Everything You Always Wanted to Know About Sex: But Were Afraid to Ask.* Pan Books, 1971. Print.
2. Gueren, Casey, "7 Surprising Facts About Masturbation," *Women's Health Mag*, March 25, 2014. http://www.womenshealthmag.com/sex-and-love/masturbation-facts
3. Sinclair Intimacy Institute. Masturbation. Health—How Stuff Works. April 1, 2009. www.health.howstuffworks.com/sexual-health/sexuality/masturbation-dictionary.htm
4. Lee, Dameco, "Overcoming Masturbation." We Used 2BU.com, November 10, 2009. www.weusedtobeyou.com/dameco-lees-story-overcoming-masturbation/#.V_Ljv_ArKM8
5. *New American Standard Bible*. La Habra, CA: Foundation Publications, for the Lockman Foundation, 1971. Print.
6. Shpancer, Noam, Ph.D., "What Do Women Really Want?" *Psychology Today*, August 22, 2013. www.psychologytoday.com/blog/insight-therapy/201308/what-do-women-really-want
7. CDC. STD Prevention Infographics. Centers for Disease Control and Prevention. December 10, 2015. www.cdc.gov/std/products/infographics.htm
8. CDC. College Health and Safety. Centers for Disease Control and Prevention. August 9, 2016. www.cdc.gov/family/college/
9. CDC. Other Sexually Transmitted Diseases. October 18, 2016. www.cdc.gov/std/stats15/other.htm#hpv

10. Cloud, Henry, and John Sims Townsend, *Boundaries in Dating: Making Dating Work*. Grand Rapids, MI: Zondervan Publishing House, 2000. Print.

Chapter 8: Mind Games: Facts or Infatuation?

1. *The Holiday*. Nancy Meyers and Bruce A. Block, directors. Columbia Pictures. 2006. Film.
2. "Boom Goes the Dynamite." *Scandal*. ABC. February 21, 2013. Television.
3. Chambers, Arron, "Seven Reasons Why Living Together Before Marriage is Not a Good Idea." My Lord and My Blog. February 24, 2009. www.mylordandmyblog.wordpress.com/2009/02/24/seven-reasons-why-living-together-before-marriage-is-not-a-good-idea/
4. Bumpass, Sweet and Cherlin. "The Role of Cohabitation in Declining Rates Marriage." *Journal of Marriage and the Family*. 1991. Print.
5. Larson, David B. M.D. "The Costly Consequences of Divorce: Assessing the Clinical, Economic, and Public Health Impact of Marital Disruption in the United States." National Institute for Healthcare Research, Rockville, Maryland. 1994. Print.

Chapter 9: Closure: The Lack. The Look. The Love.

1. Dean, Michael and Ruthie, *Real Men Don't Text*. Tyndale House Publishers, 2013. Print.

Chapter 10: When Superman Pursues Wonder Woman

1. "wander." Merriam-Webster.com. Merriam-Webster, 2016. Web. 2016.
2. *Everyday Matters Bible for Women*, The New Living Translation, 2nd ed., Tyndale House Publishers, Inc., 2012. Print.

3. Harvey, Steve, "Love Expert Steve Harvey Analyzes the Male Mind," *Oprah*, June 12, 2009. www.cnn.com/2009/LIVING/personal/06/12/o.steve.harvey.male.minds/index.html?iref=nextin
4. *The Holy Bible*. New International Version, Biblica, Inc. 2011.
5. *My Big Fat Greek Wedding*, Joel Zwick, Nia Vardalos, and John Corbett, directors. Gold Circle Films. 2002. Film.
6. Raye, Rori, "Are You Stopping Him from Falling for You?" e-Harmony. www.eharmony.com/dating-advice/about-you/are-you-stopping-him-from-falling-for-you/#.WBJfJPkrKM8
7. Behrendt, Greg, and Liz Tuccillo. *He's Just Not That into You: The No-Excuses Truth to Understanding Guys*. New York: Simon Spotlight Entertainment, 2004. Print.

ABOUT THE AUTHOR

DECLARED AS BEING SWEET, YET BOLD AS A LIONESS, KIMBERLY "Brownie" Vaughn is an energetic woman who delivers power-packed messages to hit the bull's eye of the single woman's heart. Brownie is the CEO and founder of You Are Singled Out (Y.A.S.O.), which specializes in "moving women from chaos to confidence . . . before Mr. Right." She is a professional speaker who has presented at a variety of universities, colleges, churches, and conferences throughout the United States. In 2015 she was awarded the American Small Business Championship by SCORE and Sam's Club.

Originally from Kokomo, Indiana, Brownie arrived in Nashville by way of a scholarship to Tennessee State University. She graduated Magna Cum Laude with honors and holds a B.S. in Business Administration degree with a concentration in Marketing. She was awarded the "Young Woman of the Year" award by Marilyn Quayle, the wife of former Vice President Dan Quayle. Her gifted voice has also enabled her to be a recurring voiceover artist for the McDonald's Corporation. She has also served in the Ladies of Virtue ministry at her church as a mentor to female college students. She has also made numerous mission trips to distribute supplies and teach children in Haiti. She currently resides and stays in preparation for her future Mr. Right in Nashville, Tennessee. At her heart's core, Brownie yearns to bring hope to women around the globe who long to make wise decisions in dating and relationships and overall excel in life!

For additional information and to join the Y.A.S.O. movement visit:
www.youaresingledout.com

For Brownie's speaking page:
www.browniespeaks.youaresingledout.com

For booking or speaking inquiries:
booking@youaresingledout.com

Follow on Instagram, Facebook, Twitter, and YouTube:
@URSingledOut